Roland ⅃

A Missionaɪ y Life

Roland Allen
A Missionary Life

Steven Richard Rutt

The Lutterworth Press

This book is lovingly dedicated
To my wife and best friend
Sue

The Lutterworth Press
P.O. Box 60
Cambridge
CB1 2NT
United Kingdom

www.lutterworth.com
publishing@lutterworth.com

ISBN: 978 0 7188 9475 7

British Library Cataloguing in Publication Data
A record is available from the British Library

Contents

List of Illustrations

Acknowledgements

There are many to whom I am indebted for their encouragement, support, assistance and guidance during my research for and writing of this thesis, which has now developed into two volumes; *Roland Allen: A Missionary Life* and *Roland Allen: A Theology of Mission.* I am grateful to my doctoral supervisor at the University of Lancaster, England, Professor Christopher Partridge, who graciously guided me and, at every turn, demonstrated patient analysis and critique of the numerous versions that this dissertation process produced. Professor Partridge always offered wise counsel and helpful advice for the refinement of the thesis' content and style, in order to enhance skillful doctoral work, which also included the publication of a few of my articles during the thesis' development. I count it a privilege to have been supervised and mentored by such a wonderful British scholar. I am also grateful to both Dr Gavin Hyman and Dr Ngai-Ling Sum, who, during the early stages, consistently shaped my thinking; Hyman steered me towards a clear rationale of argumentation and Sum, the thesis' methodology. An immense debt of gratitude is owed to my doctoral examiners – Professor Linda Woodhead (University of Lancaster) and the Rev. Dr Robert Pope (University of Wales, Trinity St David) – who carefully read and critically evaluated my thesis. I truly benefited by the questions they presented when I defended my thesis and I owe them much for sharpening my thinking, as well as encouraging me to seek publication of this research.

During the first year of my research, I made contact with Hubert J.B. Allen, the grandson of Roland Allen. From his wise counsel, generous hospitality and immeasurable assistance, I benefitted greatly. I am deeply grateful for the time he took to tell my wife and me stories about his grandfather, share family memorabilia, connect me with significant friends of the family and answer my frequent questions. Upon every visit to his village home outside Oxford, we were greeted with kindness, and, of course, he always surprised me with interesting items from 'Grannie's boxes' (Roland's wife, Beatrice) or some letters of importance. His ongoing communication still enhances my work significantly and serves to present a more accurate analysis of Roland Allen's life and thought. I am also genuinely appreciative that he has contributed a reflection of his grandfather's life within the context of this first volume.

In 2008, I met certain bishops who advised me to begin the process of analyzing the missiology of Roland Allen. Therefore, I would like to thank the Rt Rev. Ray Sutton, PhD (Presiding Bishop of the Reformed Episcopal Church), the Rt Rev. Royal U. Grote, Jr (deceased), the Rt Rev. Robert Duncan, the Rt Rev. Winfield Mott – bishops within the Anglican Church of North America – as well as the Rt Rev. Dr John Fenwick (Bishop Primus, the Free Church of England), for their initial encouragement to pursue research in the United Kingdom. Special thanks is given to the Rt Rev. Michael Nazir-Ali, PhD (former Bishop of Rochester, England), who, due to his familiarity with the missiology of Roland Allen, generously agreed to writing the Foreword for this volume.

I must give special thanks to the staff of Rhodes House and the Weston Library (Bodleian Libraries, Oxford) for their willingness to provide access to Roland Allen's archives. I am particularly indebted to the Senior Archivist of Weston Library – Lucy McCann – as she has helped me immensely to focus attention on various aspects of the missionary work within the United Society for the Propagation of the Gospel (USPG) and she was always helpful to locate specific archival documents for me. I want to especially thank Dr David Emmanuel Singh (Research Tutor/Editor), who graciously invited me to lecture on a few occasions at the Oxford Centre for Mission Studies and then kindly published two of my articles in *Transformation: An International Journal of Holistic Mission Studies* (SAGE Publications). I am also grateful to my valued friends who serve on the board of Covenant Renewal Ministries – Jeff Gordon, Bill O'Brien, and, former board member Grant Sardachuk – because of their financial commitment and encouragement along the way. In fact, this missiological research stemmed from an ongoing dialogue with Jeff Gordon (lasting for the past 35 years) concerning the importance of Roland Allen's thought for indigenous Church growth today.

I am eternally grateful for my 'missionary' parents – Richard and Kathleen Rutt – who nurtured me and my sister, Faith, in the Christian faith and significantly shaped my belief that 'every Christian is a missionary'. And, it was my father who, some years ago, while we were doing ministry in Lithuania, first encouraged me to pursue doctoral studies.

Lastly, this thesis is an extension of many years of missionary service that my family – my wife, Sue, and our four wonderful children, Shannon, Sherri, Steven and Seth – experienced in various countries. I am continually thankful that our children continue in the Christian faith, married Christian spouses and have given us eleven delightful grandchildren. Therefore, I want to thank the caring support of my family – Shannon and Ron Wills (Ella, Wyatt, Juliet and Luke); Sherri and Bram Wouters (Bram, Colbie and Kale); Steven and Joanne Rutt (Annie, Ginger and Holly); Seth and Katilyn Rutt (Bryson) – for patiently supporting our transatlantic move to England from 2009 to 2013. Finally, I can never envisage the process of writing these two volumes without having had the loving support and persevering confidence of my wife and best friend, Sue, to whom this book is dedicated. She was approved by the University to function as my 'research assistant' and given official status within the Bodleian Libraries of Oxford, to do archival research with me. She spent endless hours assisting by analyzing Roland Allen's archival letters, sermons and teaching notes. The words from the Book of Proverbs best describe Sue:

her children rise up and call her blessed; her husband also, and he praises her. (Proverbs 31:28).

Foreword

by Hubert J.B. Allen

It is remarkable that fresh books examining my grandfather and his ideas are still being considered worthy of publication seventy years after his death. Dr Rutt's magisterial study is an important and wide-ranging contribution, so I am happy to have been invited to express some introductory thoughts. For more than that, however, I must simply refer to the brief biography which I composed over twenty years' ago, largely to edify his descendants[1].

I need, however, to emphasize that I myself and the only other three persons known to me who can remember him in his lifetime, were, in those War-time days, mere schoolchildren. My contemporary accurately described Roland as *'a fine-looking man who was both kind and also rather stern and austere'*.[2] I only recall one example of the impatience some people attributed to him, at a time when he flung a book on the floor, expostulating: *'Calls himself a scholar – and his book doesn't even have an Index!'*

But in those declining years in Nairobi, his health was not good, so his wife Beatrice became formidably protective. Consequently, just as one of us three grandchildren had begun some truly fascinating conversation with him – not, of course, at our age discussing his controversial adult ideas about missionary methods, the established Church, or the Apostolic succession, but rather such topics as poetry, or cathedral architecture, or maps, or public speaking – then only too often Grannie would intervene and tell us to *'run along now, and stop tiring your grandfather'*. Nobody ever argued with Grannie, so all of

---

1. Roland Allen, *Pioneer, Priest & Prophet*, Eerdmans/Forward Movement, 1995.
2. This third living witness is Valerie, the daughter of Mr Hermann Fliess, a German Jew, who early in the war acted as spokesman for all his fellow Germans in Kenya's internment camp at Kabete. Roland and Beatrice removed her and her brother from a feckless landlady, and took care of her until the end of the war.

us – including our equally disappointed 'Granfer' – would dutifully disperse: he probably to working on classical Swahili poetry at his desk, we children to read on the verandah or to play in the *banda* – the circle of eucalyptus poles supporting a thatched roof, which served as a simple gazebo, protecting us from the tropical rain or sun. My two sisters remember Granfer using that *banda* to teach them how to project their voices, so that a whisper could be heard right across it, notwithstanding the lack of walls.

In 1945, after spending almost the whole of World War II in East Africa, we three children set out for England with our parents by train, bus and river steamer down the Nile to Cairo. On the final morning, Granfer, knowing that it was extremely unlikely that we should ever all be together again, celebrated full Holy Communion for the whole family, assuring my doubtful mother: '*Of* course, *Nell shall receive both the Bread and the Wine!*' – although she was only seven years' old, and none of us three were yet confirmed.

In spite of my emphasizing this background, Dr Rutt is not alone in attributing to me a very much more profound knowledge and understanding of my grandfather's life, ideas and literary legacy than I, in fact, possess. It is true that in my own declining years I sought to provide – especially for his direct descendants – an outline of his eventful life-story, together with an ignorant layman's understanding of some reasons for his continuing notoriety. But I have spent very much less time than many scholars studying his published works – and indeed some of his books I have never read at all. On the other hand, I have been privileged to live close to Oxford University's Bodleian Library, where I have been able to read much of his private correspondence and a few of his unpublished (or incomplete) writings, which the librarians have carefully preserved.

Furthermore, our children and grandchildren are able to share the family's pride in such memorabilia as the little brass gong, which Granfer made use of instead of a church bell to summon people to prayer in Peking (*Beijing*) during the summer of 1900, when the Boxer movement was besieging the greatly hated foreign Legations. From that same episode, we also possess a small brass tray, on which he was carrying refreshments to a patient in the makeshift hospital, when a sniper's bullet knocked a chip off its rim, instead of hitting his heart. His medals, unmounted on their ribbons and never worn, we found in an old tobacco tin long after his death. He had great admiration for courage, so he respected any award for brave deeds; but he had no patience with medals '*simply for* being *there*', like his China Medal or his

1914 War Medal.[1] Such medals, he considered, if awarded at all, should have been awarded to *everyone* – to all people in any way adversely affected by the war (even – or perhaps especially – to non-combatants and conscientious objectors).

Most of what I learned about my grandfather's character, and idiosyncracies, was derived at second hand, from my father and other older friends and relatives; and in this book and its anticipated companion volume Dr Rutt alludes to nearly all the incidents and episodes, by which I sought in my monograph to illustrate such aspects of my 'Granfer'. So I think it only remains for me to express admiration and gratitude for such a very learned and painstaking tribute to the Rev. Roland Allen.

Hubert J.B. Allen

---

1. This was awarded for his wartime chaplaincy in the hospital ship 'Rohilla', from which he succeeded in swimming ashore when she was wrecked off the coast of Yorkshire on her way to Belgium in October 1914.

Foreword

by Bishop Michael Nazir-Ali

Roland Allen has Still Much to Teach us

Most people have diverse experiences in life and are formed by different influences. The media likes to group us and stereotype us as 'conservative' or 'radical', 'evangelical' or 'catholic', etc. In fact, we are often the result of myriad influences during the course of our lives. Roland Allen was no different. His mother's Evangelical faith was formative for him and remained with him for the rest of his life. His interest in evangelism and mission stemmed from it, as did his reverence for biblical authority. At Oxford, he encountered some of the finest minds of the burgeoning Anglo-Catholic movement. His concern for a proper ecclesiology and his emphasis on the sacramental life arose from such exposure.

It is, of course, well known that Allen's interpretive approach to Church, mission and faith was based on his reading of St Paul's missionary methods as set out in the Acts of the Apostles and in Paul's Letters to churches and individuals. Thus, he is not only Pauline but Lucan in the way he reads history as a history of mission. From the *Didachē*, he acquired a view of how the primitive church would organise itself, taught new converts and administered the sacraments, as well as his ideas about local and 'trans-local' ministries. His beliefs about the local church, the role of the laity, the relation between the Priesthood of all Believers and the Ministerial Priesthood all derive from what might be called 'primitive catholicity'. Although Allen is well aware of the dangers of 'African', 'Asian' or 'American' Christianity, he does not face issues arising from claims to radical autonomy. He is content with the Quadrilateral of Bible, Creeds, Sacraments and Ministry as the marks of catholicity but does not ask how such catholicity is to be maintained as a legitimate diversity in unity. What is the place of a proper teaching authority in the Church? How are decisions that affect everyone, to be made together and what are the proper instruments to do this? Perhaps such questions had to wait for a later age to be asked, if not answered.

Allen believed passionately in church-planting strategies which did not perpetuate mission structures. Following the educationalists of his day, he held that a good church-planter should first assess the social and spiritual situation, then, in the light of this, to share the good news of the Gospel with the people, to disciple converts, to train the leadership of the new church and then to move on. He rejects the possibility of church and mission continuing indefinitely to exist side by side but fulfilling different roles, rather, the church is to be the vehicle of its own missionary mandate. In his belief that such a church should be self-supporting, self-governing and self-propagating, he is thinking of every aspect of a church's life, not merely economic independence, but structures of governance, training of clergy and other leaders, organising for mission etc. Once again, however, as a man of his times, he does not discuss, in detail, the partnership and interdependence which these churches would also need.

The social and cultural context should alert the missionaries to the necessity of what today we would call inculturation or contextualisation. The Chinese love for order and propriety or the spiritual longings of East African Sufism should be reflected in the kind of Christian faith that emerges among a people. Equally, Christianity is also a world view and this would assist the people to develop a world view and a proper anthropology which aids all round development of all that is God-given in their culture. Allen was, like William Reed Huntington, wary of religious systems, whether administrative, hierarchical or even liturgical from becoming dominant over the fundamental principles of mission and church. He believed that a local church should possess everything it needs for its common life. His passion about the necessity of sacramental life in a church led him to the somewhat odd conclusion that, in the absence of a priest, lay leaders should be allowed to preside at celebrations of sacraments. It may have been that rigid ideas in his day about what constituted 'proper training' for ordained ministry, which led him to this startling conclusion. There is, however, no necessary conflict between the requirement that a duly ordained person should preside at celebrations of the sacraments and the belief that a local church should have all the ordinary ministry it needs for its common life. What is necessary is a process of discerning gifts and callings in the local church so that the wider Church can recognize them and so that, those whom Allen labels, 'trans-local' ministers, can then ordain, authorize and commission such people for appropriate ministries in their local church and beyond. Anything can happen in an emergency and this is never 'nothing' but it cannot be made a basis of church order. In the process of inculturation, a proper balance has to be maintained between what is

Apostolic and, therefore, required of every local church so that it may truly be in fellowship with the Church down the ages and across the world, and what is *cultural* in the way it orders its worship, discipleship and decision-making.

Allen did see the local church as having a mission beyond its own community. He was affected by the practice in China of a newly planted church in a village setting out to evangelize the next village, a practice which still continues. Such a view of mission could, of course, be extended across regional, cultural, linguistic and national boundaries, though there would need to be careful co-ordination and co-operation amongst the churches to avoid duplication, optimize resources, develop centres of training and so on.

Allen knew that the *Pax Britannica* had provided an opportunity for mission in many parts of the world but he knew also from personal experience, during the Boxer Rebellion, the ugly fruit colonialism can produce on every side. Indeed, much of Christian mission has been about withstanding the temporal rulers, colonial or communist, nationalist or fundamentalist, whether in his day or in ours.

The fact that books have continued to be written about Roland Allen since his death and that they are still being written alerts us to his significance for mission-minded thinking for today's Church – and tomorrow's. Steven Richard Rutt has put us all in his debt by bringing Allen's thought and practice, once again, to our attention.

Bishop Michael Nazir-Ali
Advent 2016

Introduction

An Analysis of the Context and Development of Roland Allen's Missiology

An Overview of *Roland Allen: A Missionary Life*

The focus of *Roland Allen: A Missionary Life* and *Roland Allen: A Theology of Mission* is the examination of the missionary ecclesiology within the ministry of Rev. Roland Allen (1868-1947). These works present an *intellectual biography* of Allen's missiology of indigenization. The theses explore the influences that shaped the development of his missionary ecclesiology (Church-centred mission) and the reasons why his writings tenaciously challenged the methodology of colonial missionary societies – established and independent – thus, disclosing the hegemonic causes that he believed hindered indigenous-led Church expansion. Allen believed that the Apostle Paul's precedent of 'Spirit and order' – which integrated perspectives both *pneumatological* (the doctrine of the Holy Spirit) and *ecclesiological* (the doctrine of the Church) – provided the basis for addressing the missionary situation with what he considered to be universal *apostolic principles*. These, he believed, would empower the indigenous Church to work independently of the prevailing colonial authorities. Both these volumes especially depict an overview of Allen's apostolic missiology, which contributed to a more comprehensive advancement of lay ministry and voluntary clergy practice associated with the mission of the Church.

In order to understand Roland Allen's missiology, it is essential to explore how these *apostolic principles* served as the central planks of his Church-centred approach to mission, along with an understanding of Allen's *apologia* for an improved missiology in his day. To explain why he thought Paul's missionary methods, as he understood them, trumped all other methodologies, the historical context of his early missionary experiences in China (1895-1903) and the end of his ministry in Africa (1947) requires examination. After careful analysis of the archival primary sources available,[1] this work discloses how Allen's missiology of

---

1. Deposited papers: Roland Allen; Boxes 1-8, Special Collections & Western MSS, Bodleian Library of Commonwealth and African Studies, Oxford,

indigenization provided farsighted clarity for the contemporary (and later) changing situation of mission within world Christianity. Thus, this work undertakes three important tasks, which have, until now, received little scholarly attention: (1) to provide an 'intellectual biography' to elucidate *why* Roland Allen thought the way he did; (2) to explore which people and ideas primarily influenced his thinking; and (3) to analyze in detail how his missionary ecclesiology developed throughout his life. These volumes required the first close analysis of his unpublished writings and neglected sermons. This, in turn, revealed, along with much else, the 'warm' pastoral nature of a parish priest and a 'perceptive' missionary theologian who served the Church for over five decades.

Methodology and Structure

To a large extent, this task is an exercise in *historical missiology*. As such, the methodology used for this study has consisted primarily of archival research. Together with Allen's published works, and that of select contemporary missiologists, special attention has been given to extensive analysis of primary archival sources – letters, articles, sermons, speeches, diaries, unpublished papers and books – preserved by the United Society for the Propagation of the Gospel (USPG; formerly called the SPG) and deposited at The Bodleian Library (Oxford). Interviews have also been conducted with those who still remembered Allen, particularly Hubert J.B. Allen, Roland Allen's grandson and biographer. Specific detailed information has been acquired from these interviews, especially critical information which has not previously been disclosed within missiological studies. Of course, special attention is given to Hubert Allen's biography which unveils firsthand knowledge of his grandfather's life and ministry. Finally, my research has included engagement with missiologists who were familiar with Allen's works. Much contemporary missiological discussion has focused on certain aspects of Allen's analysis of Western missionary organizations, thus making his work valuable again. However, most of this analysis examines only a *small portion* of his writings and missiologists have tended to ignore how his thinking developed over the five decades of his ministry, especially the last twenty years of his life.[1] To address

---

Bodleian Library, Roland Allen archives, USPG X622.

1. Missiologists *generally* cite Roland Allen's *Missionary Methods: St Paul's or Ours? A Study of the Church in the Four Provinces* (London: Robert Scott, February 1912; in the Library of Historic Theology. Repr., October 1913. Revised edition published by World Dominion Press, second edn, August 1927. Repr. 1930, 1949, 1956. Reset – with memoir by Alexander McLeish – Grand Rapids: Eerdmans, 1962. Repr. 1993. Repr. Cambridge: The

this enormous gap within scholarship, Allen's missionary ecclesiology is here articulated as an extension of my engagement with not only his most popular books, but through an extensive analysis of his archival deposited papers and other works usually unobserved. As indicated above, the present thesis consists of two principal parts: (1) a historical understanding of Allen's missionary ecclesiology; and (2) an analysis of the apostolic principles that formed his missionary theology.

Overview of Chapters in *Roland Allen: A Missionary Life*

Part I: Historical Milieu (1868-1947) analyzes the ecclesiastical background that pervaded Roland Allen's earlier theological development within Anglicanism. An assessment of the contributing scholars who assisted his formation of a *principled* approach rather than a *systems* approach to missiology is scrutinized in the context of nineteenth-century thought. As a former missionary to China with the Church of England Mission in North China, during his first year of mission (1895) and then with the Society for the Propagation of the Gospel (SPG until 1903), his preliminary surveillance of contemporary missionary practices motivated the formulation for his theology of the indigenous Church and has been articulated through what he believed was a proper hermeneutic (interpretation) for Pauline theology and practice.

The context of *Roland Allen: A Missionary Life* consists of eight chapters which analyze the development of Allen's ecclesiology and missiology. Chapter 1 presents the 'Formation of an Anglican Missionary (1868-1907)' by disclosing his heritage within the Church of England and provides the framework for his churchmanship, theology and missiology. A historical overview of how Allen's apostolic faith permeated his life, ministry, friendships and publications is taken into account within this chapter. Chapter 2 is introduced as 'Missionary Experiences in China' in which Allen's missionary experience in China is outlined, which is followed by an exploration of how this prompted his critique of the 'mission station system' and various paternalistic missionary practices. Initial evidence is proposed within this chapter (and unpacked in subsequent chapters) for a better understanding of his emerging missiology of indigenization. Chapter 3 'From Systems to Principles: How Allen's Missionary Experiences in China Shaped

---

Lutterworth Press, 2006); Roland Allen, *The Spontaneous Expansion of the Church: and the causes which hinder it* (London: World Dominion Press, 1927. Repr. Eugene: Wipf and Stock Publishers, 1997); and David M. Paton, (ed.) *The Ministry of the Spirit: Selected Writings of Roland Allen* (London: World Dominion Press, 1965).

his Missiology (1895-1947)' examines how his missionary experience
in China motivated him to evaluate missionary methods in its historical
setting and how these events occasioned his propensity for becoming a
missionary methods analyst.

Chapter 4 introduces 'Allen's Analysis of St Paul's Missionary
Principles' by examining how his missionary experience in China inspired
him to evaluate the missiological situation of his day and documents how
this contribution to the study of indigenous church-planting provides
a continuing relevance for theories of Church growth, as we see today
in the Majority World (Africa, Asia and Latin America). My analysis of
his *Missionary Methods: St Paul's or Ours?* (1912) attempts to reveal and
articulate an *indigenous* missionary ecclesiology. The chapter discloses
his philosophy of ministry that extended from deep theological and
missiological reflection. That said, the chapter further explains how
Allen's missiology within a colonial context caused him to articulate an
indigenous 'missiology from below' which sought to empower Chinese
Christians to manage their own churches.

Chapter 5 is entitled 'The World Dominion Movement and Its
Evangelical Mission' because it describes Allen's association with the
World Dominion Press (London) as their representative theologian
for its publications on foreign missions, especially for their cutting-
edge missionary journal entitled *World Dominion*. The primary leaders
of what has been called the World Dominion Movement were S.J.W.
Clark, 1862-1930 (Congregationalist), Thomas Cochrane, 1856-1953
(Presbyterian), and Roland Allen (Anglican). This chapter discloses that
from the onset of their missionary publication's existence, the editors
made sure that all of their publications maintained a 'belief in the Deity
and Atoning Death of the Lord Jesus Christ, the World's Only Saviour,
and in the Final Authority of Holy Scripture'.[1] This evangelical emphasis
provides the backdrop for Allen's (and the others') missiological writings
and the missionary survey analysis which they conducted. Chapter 6
is described as 'Field Work in Various Countries' because it outlines
Allen's missionary journeys to India, Canada, South Africa and Southern
Rhodesia (Zimbabwe). This field work began in 1910, when both Roland
and his wife, Beatrice, visited Delhi, Calcutta and Madras, India. The
chapter discusses the emergent friendship that began with Vedanayagam
Samuel Azariah (later consecrated bishop in 1912) and Bishop Henry
Whitehead (Madras). Details on Azariah and Whitehead are described in
the next chapter, as well as in *Roland Allen: A Theology of Mission*, which

1. 'Mission Statement, 'Table of Contents', *World Dominion*, XVII, no.4 (London:
   World Dominion Press, October 1939).

specifically unpacks Allen's visit to India, years later when he conducted leadership training with the clergy of Azariah's diocese (Dornakal). Also, the chapter describes his mission trips to South Africa and Southern Rhodesia (Zimbabwe) in 1926.

Chapter 7 is entitled 'Friends, Family and African Ministry' as it highlights significant relationships with friends of the Allen family, especially the Christian friends who had missional influence in Africa. This chapter also sets the framework for understanding the various ways in which his family began to settle down within African culture. Attention is given to Roland's willingness to learn Swahili during his *mid-60s* and the inclination to improve his linguistic skills through the help of his son John (a Swahili scholar) is evidenced through the translation work of Muslim epics that he translated from Swahili into English. Chapter 8 is defined as 'Select Sermons and Teachings on the Old Testament' and advances an introductory disclosure of the archival collection of Allen's sermons. After extensive archival research, a wealth of *unexamined* information concerning these sermons and teachings has been uncovered. The purpose of this chapter is to introduce the reader to this collection and to reveal his thinking on the relevance of the Old Testament, particularly, the Ten Commandments and the relevance of the Commandments for Christians. For those familiar with Allen's most famous books – *Missionary Methods: St Paul's or Ours?* and *The Spontaneous Expansion of the Church* – one might assume that his theology was shaped *only* by the New Testament.[2] That would be a misunderstanding of what shaped his theology. With that in view, this chapter sheds light on his engagement with the law of God as the prophetic proclamation that speaks directly to Church and society.

This research essentially analyzes the context and development of Roland Allen's missiology. In particular, the first volume introduces what he believed was an ideal example of apostolic ministry as disclosed through the missionary work of the Apostle Paul. Based on this analysis of St Paul's missionary methods, Allen proposed various apostolic principles, which, he believed, provided the central planks for a missionary ecclesiology; that is, a church-centred approach to mission for the expansion of the indigenous Church. Special attention is given to his interpretive approach of Pauline practice through the plethoric writings located within the archives of Allen's journal contributions, articles, letters, unpublished works, as well as his books, sermons and speeches. While these items are discussed more extensively in the second volume, the focus now turns to the background of the early life and missionary calling of Roland Allen.

---

2. The Scripture Index at the end of both of these books disclose biblical passages only from the New Testament.

1. Formation of an Anglican Missionary
Familial Legacy: Evangelical Anglicanism

When Hubert John Brooke Allen, the grandson and biographer of Roland Allen (1868-1947), was 'about twelve years old', he asked his grandfather ('Granfer') when he would be allowed to read the books that his grandfather had written.[1] His grandfather told young Hubert: 'Oh, yes, you can read them by all means – but you won't understand them; I don't think anyone is going to understand them until I've been dead ten years. . . . "[2] Later in life, Hubert decided to honour his grandfather's legacy by writing a biography of his life entitled *Roland Allen: Pioneer, Priest, and Prophet* (1995). Interestingly, shortly after Roland Allen's death, various missionaries and missiologists began to engage with his ideas through their publications on mission work, as well as to apply his methods on the mission field. However, Hubert indicated that, of these writers, 'almost all of them have been well-intentioned and fairly accurate' yet the biographer argued that: 'many of them have portrayed a rather dry theologian, rather than a warm and kindly – if rather austere and argumentative – human being.'[3] These characterizations of Roland prompted a familial response to clarify the narrative. Hubert's informative biography tells the rest of the story from his own personal interaction with his grandfather while living in East Africa, his 'inquisitive' analysis of Roland's books and archives, and further disclosure through 'family memorabilia preserved by Grannie, which came to light . . . [Hubert says] after my wife and I took over my parents' home in Marston Village, near Oxford'.[4] Missiologists are indebted to Hubert Allen for providing clarity about his grandfather's life. In 2010, after referring to Hubert as the foremost authority on Roland Allen he quickly responded to my comment in an unassuming manner by assuring me of his [Hubert's]

---

1. Hubert Allen, *Roland Allen: Pioneer, Priest, and Prophet* (Grand Rapids: Eerdmans and Cincinnati: Forward Movement Publications, 1995) vii.
2. Ibid., vii.
3. Ibid., viii.
4. Ibid., x.

Figure 1. Hubert J.B. Allen, grandson of Roland Allen,
and the author outside his home near Oxford.

missiological ineptness. 'I am neither a theologian nor a missiologist, so am unlikely to have anything useful to say',[1] he modestly replied after enquiring about Roland's thought. And yet, despite Hubert's self-effacing disposition, I always come away with significant insight into what familial and cultural influences shaped Roland's life, due to the ongoing communication with Hubert Allen.

Roland Allen's missiological writings have inspired missionaries from Roman Catholic, Orthodox, mainline Protestant and Evangelical denominations and especially those from the newer Pentecostal and independent Charismatic branches within global Christianity. The former African secretary for the Church Missionary Society, John V. Taylor, referred to him as 'that great prophet of missionary method'.[2] Missiologist William J. Danker (Lutheran) in 1960 argued:

> It is time that Roland Allen had his day. A prophet with little honor, rather nearly everywhere spoken against in his own time and especially in his own Anglican Communion, this quiet Oxford graduate and sometime missionary to China . . . systematically planted ecclesiological time bombs whose delayed action fuses are going off right on schedule today . . . Certainly Allen is one of the most seminal missiological and ecclesiological minds of this century . . . .[3]

Who were the instrumental people that influenced his character development? How did the historical context of missionary theology shape his thinking? Roland's formative years are addressed in a concise manner, in order to advance the primary focus of this work, which analyzes the historical context and theological development of his missiology.

Background

On 29 December 1868, Priscilla Allen gave birth to Roland and one month later he was baptized at St Werburgh's Church (diocese of Derby), England.[4] Roland was the sixth of seven children born to the

where? Derby?

not in 1868

---

1. Email correspondence from Hubert Allen (27 October 2010) and other conversations with him in Oxford.
2. John V. Taylor, *The Primal Vision: Christian Presence Amid African Religion* (London: SCM Press, 1963) 33.
3. William J. Danker in David Paton (ed.) *The Ministry of the Spirit: Selected Writings of Roland Allen* (London: World Dominion Press, 1960. Repr. Grand Rapids: Eerdmans, 1970) comment on back cover.
4. Hubert Allen, *Roland Allen*, 10.

Charles Fletcher Allen family. Roland's father, Charles, a priest in the Church of England and sometime headmaster in Derby, left his post, and, when Roland was only five years of age, 'travelled out to the colony of British Honduras, without his family . . . conducted several services in St John's Anglican Church in Belize . . . [and] a week later he died there, at the early age of thirty-eight.'[5] Priscilla (Malpas) Allen and her children moved in with her parents – her father being the vicar of Awre for approximately 50 years – until her parents died, when Roland was ten years old.[6] Roland's early years were shaped within an Anglican ethos that was undergirded from the 'principal formative influence' of his mother, who, rooted his spiritual formation from her 'evangelical persuasion', which, according to Roland's nephew, was understood as 'the tradition of the old Evangelical Movement'.[7] This child rearing accounts for his continuous high view of Scripture as an Anglican churchman.[8]

As a widow, Priscilla, during the 1880s, had limited finances to send her children to university, yet her four sons did win scholarships to both Cambridge and Oxford Universities. Although his brother, Arthur, died while 'an undergraduate student at Oxford',[9] he and his two other brothers – Reginald and Willoughby[10] – 'all went on after graduation

---

5. Ibid.

6. Ibid., 12.

7. Many relatives of hers were Plymouth Brethren, yet, she 'was not of the Brethren'; Ibid., 12-13.

8. 'Allen. – REV. ROLAND ALLEN, The Vicarage, Chalfont St Peter; son of the Rev. Charles Fletcher Allen; born December 29th, 1868; educated at Bath College, and Bristol Grammar School; Scholar of St. John's College, Oxford; 2nd Class Mods., Classical, 1889; Lothian Prize, and BA, 1891, and Leeds Clergy School, 1892. Ordained Deacon, 1892, and Priest, 1893, by the Bishop of Durham; Curate of St John the Evangelist, Darlington, 1893-94; Principal of the Theological School, North China Mission, and Acting Chaplain at the British Legation, Peking, 1895-1900; Priest-in-Charge at Yung Ching, North China, 1902; Chaplain to the Bishop of North China, 1898-1903; Vicar of Chalfont St Peter, 1904; author of "The Siege of the Peking Legations". Married, in 1901, Mary Beatrice, daughter of Admiral Sir John Walter Tarleton, K.C.B.' (On the right side of the photo of Roland Allen are the following words: Amico meo Rolando Allen Donum Dedi XVI Kal: Nov: 1901, "Lumen ad revelationem gentium") Box 1, File A, Oxford, Bodleian Library, Roland Allen archives, USPG X622.

9. Arthur, a fourth brother, drowned while 'skating on the River Cherwell', Ibid., 15.

10. Ibid.

to take Holy Orders in the Church of England'.[1] The Allen's had two
daughters – Catherine and Ellen, and also, another son, Ernest, who died
in the same year he was born (1865).[2]

St John's College, Oxford (1887-92)[3]

Before Roland went to University, he attended Bath College School
and then went on to the Bristol Grammar School (1884-87) 'where he
was in the Classical VI'.[4] Subsequently, he entered St John's College,
Oxford (1887)[5] having received 'the Bristol Grammar School's closed Sir
Thomas White Scholarship' and later, 'the University's Lothian Prize'
due to the evaluative essay he wrote on Pope Silvester II.[6] He achieved

---

1. Ibid. To digress, Reginald served 'the Gloucestershire parish of
   Blakeney . . . [later] was chaplain of a school for European boys at Bournabat,
   near Smyrna in Turkey . . . [and] a few years after the war [was] chaplain
   to the British community at Dinan, near St Malo in Brittany' (Hubert Allen,
   Roland Allen, 15-16). Willoughby later was 'both Archdeacon of Manchester
   and Principal of the Egerton Hall theological college . . . [and later] became
   simultaneously Rector of Chorley, Archdeacon of Blackburn, and an army
   chaplain,' Hubert Allen, *Roland Allen*, 16.
2. Ibid., 178-79.
3. The official name is S. John Baptist College, Oxford.
4. Ibid., 17: 'Information supplied to David Sanderson by the Bristol Grammar
   School's Archivist through Dr John McKay' (page 29, footnote 6).
5. Ake Talltorp corrects Hans Wolfgang Metzner's claim that Allen began
   studies at St John's in '1889.' My archival research verified that Talltorp
   was accurate in pointing out that Allen's enrollment at St John's was in
   fact '1887' after viewing the biographical register of members at St John's
   College [1875-1919]; access to information granted by Michael Riordan,
   St John's College archivist (14 and 16 November 2012). See David Paton,
   Reform of the Ministry: A Study in the Work of Roland Allen (London: The
   Lutterworth Press, 1968) 14; also, Ake Talltorp, Sacrament and Growth: A
   Study in the Sacramental Dimension of Expansion in the Life of the Local
   Church, as Reflected in the Theology of Roland Allen (Uppsala: Swedish
   Institute of Missionary Research, 1989) 72; Hans Wolfgang Metzner's
   Roland Allen Sein Leben und Werk: Kritischer Beitrag zum Verstandnis
   von Mission und Kirche (Gutersloh: Gutersloher Verlagshaus Gerd Mohn,
   1970) 16.
6. Allen's essay was his 'first' publication printed in the journal The English
   Historical Review, vol.7, London, October 1892, Pusey House Library,
   Oxford, S:59.00.c2, Miscellania: Hagiology. My research at Pusey House
   confirmed the publication date as October 1892. Hans Metzner argued that
   Cornelius van Heerden assumed 1901 to be Allen's first publication, i.e., The

'Second Class Honours – both in Classical Moderations in 1888, and in
the Final School of History'[7] in 1890. In sum, Allen studied at St John's
College from 1887 until 1892. Archival records from St John's College
give this information:

ALLEN, Roland (1887-); b. 1869 [1868], s. of Charles Fletcher
Allen, clerk. Educ. Bristol S. Sir Thomas White sch.; Lothian
Hist. Essay Prize 1891. 2nd Class. Mods. 1889; 2nd Mod. Hist.
and BA 1891; MA 1901. Mem. Debating Soc.; Essay Soc. (vice-
pres.). Leeds Clergy sch. 1892. HO (d. 1892; p. 1893): C. St. John
Evang., Darlington 1892-[4]; Mission SPG at Peking 1895-1903;
Chapl.to Bp. Of N. China 1898-1904; V. Chalfont St. Peter 1904-
[0]7; Actg. Naval Chapl., HM Hospital Ship 'Rohilla' 1914; in
Kenya in 1937; author. Publ.: 'The Siege of the Peking legations'
(1901); 'Missionary methods' (1912); 'Missionary survey' (1920);
'Voluntary clergy' (1923); 'Sidney James Wells Clark' (1937); etc.
etc. D. 1947.[8]

In addition, the archives disclose the various business meetings he
attended for the St John's College Essay Society, of which he also served
as vice-president.[9] Also, Allen read two significant essays entitled 'The
Jesuits in Asia' and 'French Schools in Xth Century'.[10] His essay on 'The

Siege of the Peking Legations, Being the Diary of the Rev. Roland Allen
(London: Smith Elder & Co., 1901); see Hans W. Metzner, 22, 24, 280 in
reference to Cornelius van Heerden's Die spontane uitbreiding van die Kerk
by Roland Allen, I.H. Kok, N.V. Kampen OJ; see also Hubert Allen, *Roland
Allen*, 18.

7. Ibid.
8. Biographical register of members at St John's College [1875-1919] (14 and
16 November 2012).
9. Jan. 20, 1889 (Lent Term); April 28, 1889 Allen 'seconded' a motion (Summer
Term); April 27, 1890 Allen 'seconded' a motion (Summer Term); October 12,
1890 Allen 'seconded' a motion (Michaelmas Term); April 19, 1891 (Summer
Term, Allen proposed a motion); June 27, 1891, 'Mr R. Allen was elected Vice-
President for the ensuing term' (Michaelmas Term); 'R. Allen retired March
13, 1892'; 'A unanimous role of [?] was passed to the late Vice-President, Mr
Allen' (Lent Term, 1892); Biographical register, St John's College (14 and 16
November 2012).
10. 'Mr R. Allen read a paper on 'The Jesuits in Asia', June 2, 1889, Summer
Term; 'Mr R. Allen read an essay on French Schools in the 10th Century
followed by a somewhat desultory discussion on arithmetic harmony and
astronomy,' October 26, 1890, Michaelmas Term; Biographical register of

Jesuits in Asia' is the earliest evidence revealing his interest in Christian missions in Asia preceding his missionary work in China.

While at St John's College, he carved out his own place for demonstrating his debating skills. Hubert Allen stated:

> in a debate between *Total Abstinence and Temperance*, Roland spoke in favour of temperance – the winning side. In other debates he voted in favour of motions that *Free Schools would be for the advantage of the nation*, and *Thackeray was a better writer than Dickens* – Roland supported Dickens (who won, 20-10). He is also recorded as speaking in a debate between *Free Trade and "Fair Trade"*; and, as an Old Boy, returned to move – successfully – that *Britain's national defenses are inadequate* [original emphasis].[1]

The 'minute book' for the Members of the St John's College Debating Society discloses how Roland frequently expressed his opinions during committee meetings.[2] He also served as 'a founder member and secretary of the undergraduate theological study group, the Origen Society'; of which, almost a century later, Hubert's son, Roland's 'great-grandson (another Roland Allen) was to be the *last* Secretary of the Origen Society.'[3]

Hutton, Murray, Waggett, Brightman and Gore

The influence of the Oxford Movement left its 'High Church' mark upon St John's College and another notable institution that Allen frequented – Pusey House. His spiritual formation was shaped by men from both of these Oxford institutions. The Rev. W.H. Hutton (1860-1930), both a historian and biographer, served as his primary mentor and benefactor during his education at St John's College. Hubert Allen believes that

members at St John's College [1875-1919], (14 and 16 November 2012).

1. Hubert Allen, *Roland Allen*, 17.
2. 'The 9th Meeting of Term, & the 164th of the Society, (March 12th) Messrs. Poynder, & R. Allen also spoke . . .'; '2nd meeting . . . the 183rd of the Society . . . against (the motion) . . . Mr R. Allen'; '3rd meeting . . . the 184th of the Society . . . Mr Allen supported the Amendment . . .'; '6th meeting . . . the 187th of the Society (Monday Nov. 18th) . . . In Public Business Mr R. Allen [made a proposal] . . . after a ballot Mr Allen was elected' on the committee (Lent Term 1890). Biographical register of members at St John's College [1875-1919]; access to information granted by Michael Riordan, St John's College archivist (14 and 16 November 2012).
3. Hubert Allen, *Roland Allen*, 18.

Hutton's influence provided Roland with a thorough Oxford education.[4] Hutton's influence at St John's College and within the Church of England is quite remarkable, not only as a fellow tutor, precentor, examining chaplain to the Bishop of Ely, and librarian of St John's, but also for his historical contribution – *S. John Baptist College* – an exhaustive account of St John's history.[5] Archival research within the historical records of the minutes for both St John's College Essay Society and St John's College Debating Society disclose Hutton's involvement within the lives of the students as tutor, mentor and facilitator of various meetings, including his own essays which he presented periodically for the students.[6]

The recorded archival minutes from the Essay Society and Debating Society unveil his consistent involvement within both of these societies and it is safe to assume that Hutton would have inter-related with him on numerous occasions, which would account for his adeptness for historical context within his writings.[7]

Another professor who had an influence on Allen was Gilbert Murray (1866-1957). When discussing Murray with Hubert Allen, he remarked:

Gilbert Murray wasn't a theologian, he was a classical scholar. He may have taught Granfer Greek and/or classical history, but he was at New College when he was first a don (and for only one year 1888/89) and for the next ten years at Glasgow as Professor of Greek (later 1908-1936, Regius Professor of Greek at Oxford). Their friendship arose from the childhood friendship of their *wives*

---

4. Interview with Hubert Allen on 4 February 2011.

5. William Holden Hutton, *S. John Baptist College*, Oxford University College Histories (London: F.E. Robinson, 1898); access to information granted by Michael Riordan, St John's College archivist (14 and 16 November 2012).

6. The minutes from the Members of the St John's College Debating Society, UGS V.1; and also, the minutes from St John's College Essay Society, UGS VI.1, St John's College, Oxford archives; interview with Michael Riordan, archivist (16 November 2012).

7. Business meetings Roland Allen attended for the St John's College Essay Society (20 Jan. 1889, Lent Term); Allen 'seconded' a motion (28 April 1889, Summer Term); Allen 'seconded' a motion (27 April 1890, Summer Term); Allen 'seconded' a motion (12 October 1890, Michaelmas Term); Allen proposed a motion, (19 April 1891, Summer Term); 'Mr R. Allen was elected Vice-President for the ensuing term' (27 June 1891, Michaelmas Term); 'R. Allen retired 13 March 1892'; 'A unanimous role . . . was passed to the late Vice-President, Mr Allen' (1892, Lent Term); minutes from St John's College Essay Society, UGS VI.1, St John's College, Oxford archives; interview with Michael Riordan, archivist (16 November 2012).

– Beatrice and Lady Mary [original emphasis].[1] This subsequent friendship between their wives remained[2] but there is no archival evidence[3] for any ongoing correspondence between Murray and himself. As to whether Murray was his tutor in Greek, the archival evidence is silent. And yet, whoever his tutor was it is interesting to note that for years Allen's sermons and teachings disclose continued use of the Greek text of the New Testament.[4]

Why did Allen walk across the street from St John's College to visit the Anglo-Catholic fathers at Pusey House? What compelled him to be influenced by – Charles Gore (1853-1932), Philip Waggett (1862-1939) and F.E. Brightman (1856-1932) – High Anglican and Tractarian churchmen?

[Allen] was particularly influenced by Pusey's librarian, the great liturgical scholar F.E. Brightman, whom he later referred to as his dear Father in God. One of Brightman's particular interests was the spirituality of the Eastern Churches, and it has been argued that this may account for Roland's own very Church-centred view of mission.[5]

Allen received assistance from Brightman when arranging his 'first' (previously mentioned) publication, 'Gerbert, Pope Silvester II' (1892).[6] At the end of his thesis, he notes these words: 'For the collation of this stone [marble slab which covered the tomb of Gerbert] I am indebted to the kindness of my friend the Rev. F.E. Brightman, of Pusey House, Oxford.'[7] This dissertation cites significant medieval scholarly works from Latin texts and exposes the 'fingerprints' of someone with unique liturgical and Church history knowledge, that being, Pusey House's librarian – F.E. Brightman. This is obvious. Examination of this work,

1. Interview with Hubert Allen on 4 February 2011 and subsequent email correspondence.
2. Hubert Allen, *Roland Allen*, 110.
3. Roland Allen's archives, Special Collections & Western MSS, Bodleian Library of Commonwealth and African Studies, USPG X622, Box 6, Files K-M, Oxford, Bodleian Library.
4. Ibid., USPG, Box 5, Oxford, Bodleian Library.
5. Hubert Allen, *Roland Allen*, 18-19.
6. Roland Allen, 'Gerbert, Pope Silvester II,' *The English Historical Review*, vol.7, (London, October 1892. Repr., London: Spottiswoode & Co., 1892) Pusey House Library, Oxford, S:59.00.c2, Miscellania: Hagiology.
7. See Roland Allen, *Gerbert, Pope Silvester II*, 46 (footnote no. 264).

while performing research at Pusey House,[8] uncovers a great deal about how much Brightman actually influenced Allen's thinking about medieval Christianity and Gerbert's pontificate. This essay won him the University's '1891 Lothian Prize',[9] and was published in 1892. Talltorp correctly points out that 'existing bibliographies have to be corrected and re-dated by almost a decade from 1900 to 1892',[10] especially Hans Wolfgang Metzner's assumption that Allen's published works commenced in 1900.[11]

The friendship with Brightman remained strong over the years. In 1901, during a time of furlough from China (after the Boxer Uprising), Roland asked his dear 'father in God' to be the 'celebrant' for an important Eucharistic service. He was to be the celebrant at the wedding of Roland Allen and Mary Beatrice Tarleton. Brightman accepted and presided at the Eucharist.[12]

Around the time when Allen was finishing his time at St John's College he established a friendship with one of the newly appointed Cowley Fathers, Philip Napier Waggett, who was 'clothed as a novice in this Society in 1892.'[13] According to Hubert Allen, 'Father Philip Waggett, SSJE, an eminent sacramental theologian, was another inspiration for Roland."[14] It appears that both men maintained a lasting friendly relationship with each other, which is demonstrated by the disclosure of three letters between them even as late as 1925.[15]

In Allen's original publication of *Missionary Methods: St Paul's or Ours?* (1912) he gives recognition to Waggett in his preface: 'My most sincere and grateful thanks are due to the Rev. Father Waggett, SSJE, for valuable assistance in forwarding the publication of this book. . . . '[16]

8. The librarian of Pusey House photocopied this work for my research.

9. Ake Talltorp, *Sacrament and Growth: A Study in the Sacramental Dimension of Expansion in the Life of the Local Church, as Reflected in the Theology of Roland Allen* (Uppsala University, 1989: 11); Hubert Allen, *Roland Allen*, 18.

10. Ake Talltorp, *Sacrament and Growth*, 11.

11. Hans Wolfgang Metzner, *Roland Allen Sein Leben und Werk*, 22, 24, 280; cf. Talltorp, *Sacrament and Growth*, 75.

12. Hubert Allen, *Roland Allen*, 69.

13. John Nias, *Flame From An Oxford Cloister: The Life and Writings of Philip Napier Waggett SSJE Scientist, Religious, Theologian, Missionary Philosopher, Diplomat, Author, Orator, Poet* (London: The Faith Press, 1961) 49.

14. Hubert Allen, *Roland Allen*, 18-19.

15. 12 June 1925 draft letter (no. 36) from Allen to Waggett, along with copy of a draft intended for I.R.M.; 15 June 1925 letter (no. 37) from Waggett to Allen; 16 June 1925 draft letter (no. 38) from Allen to Waggett, Box 6, File K: 36-38, Oxford, Bodleian Library, Roland Allen archives, USPG X622.

16. Roland Allen, *Missionary Methods: St Paul's or Ours? A Study of the Church in the Four Provinces* (London: Robert Scott, February 1912. Repr., October

Robert Jeffrey seems to think that Allen's thesis in *Missionary Methods* was directly influenced by Waggett, and another Cowley colleague, i.e., Richard Meux Benson (founder of the Cowley Fathers), who, Jeffrey claims, when unpacking 'the indwelling power of the Spirit', his thinking carries the influence of 'Benson's notes on the Acts of the Apostles'.[1] Furthermore, Benson, though a High Anglican, had an anti-ritual tendency, de-emphasized the necessity of church buildings, did not believe there should be any 'priestly caste' and emphasized the ministry of the laity as 'agents of the Spirit in the world'.[2] These similar ideas are rooted in Allen's ecclesiology.[3] It is more than likely that Benson had an indirect influence on him through his friendship with Waggett. One of his sermons contains a quote that he had used from Waggett:

> A reality which is spiritual is not on that account of necessity unconcerned with matter. A process of healing, e.g. is not in the least degree more spiritual because it does not use what are called means – our sleep is not less a spiritual refreshment and dependent upon spiritual dispositions because it accompanies and depends upon a change in the condition of the body.[4]

Waggett's incarnational and sacramental theology obviously influenced Allen's thought. This is evidenced in his *Missionary Principles – and Practice.*[5]

1913. Revised edition published by World Dominion Press, 2nd edition August 1927. Repr. 1930, 1949, 1956. Reset – with memoir by Alexander McLeish – Grand Rapids: Eerdmans, 1962. Repr., 1993. Repr., Cambridge: The Lutterworth Press, 2006) *New Foreword*: Bishop Michael Nazir-Ali, III-IV) the Library of Historic Theology. Hereafter, this book will be referred to as *Missionary Methods*.

1. Interview with Robert Jeffrey, Oxford, UK (3 October 2012). The quote (above) is from an unpublished paper Jeffrey presented on 'Richard Meux Benson, 1-9 (6).

2. Interview with Robert Jeffrey, Oxford, UK (3 October 2012). The quote (above) is from an unpublished paper Jeffrey presented on 'Richard Meux Benson, 1-9 (4-5); see *Further Letters of R.M. Benson* (Mowbray, 1920) 95; A.M. Allchin, *The Spirit and the Word* (Faith Publications, 1963) 46.

3. Allen, *Missionary Methods*, 2006, 55-58.

4. Philip Waggett, 'Criticism and Faith,' as quoted in Roland Allen, Sermon no. 273, USPG X622, Box 5, Oxford, Bodleian Library.

5. Roland Allen, *Missionary Principles – and Practice* (1st edition [Roland's handwritten marked copy] entitled *Foundation Principles of Foreign Missions*, Bungay, Suffolk: Richard Clay & Sons, May 1910. Repr., Cambridge: The

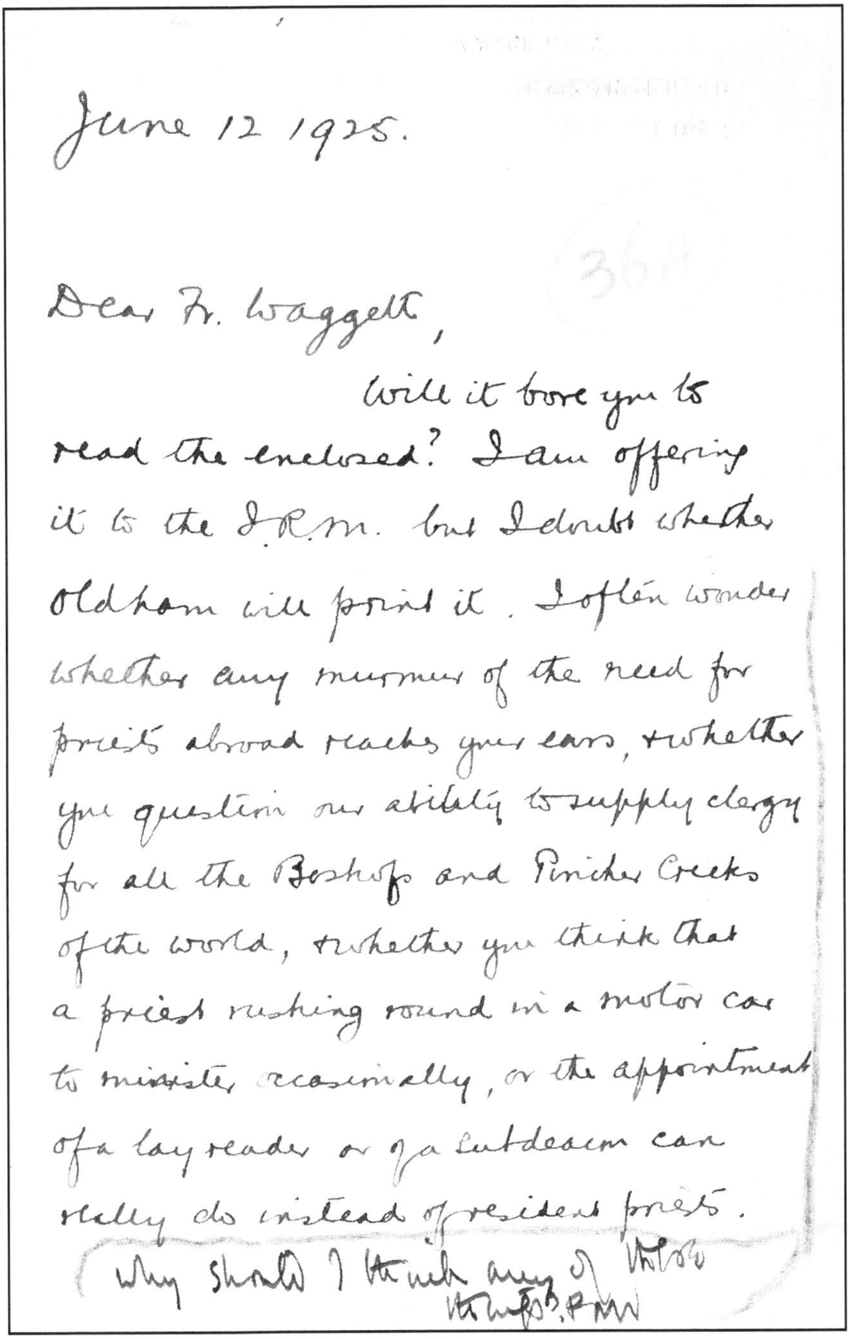

June 12 1925.

Dear Fr. Waggett,

Will it bore you to read the enclosed? I am offering it to the I.R.M. but I doubt whether Oldham will print it. I often wonder whether any murmur of the need for priests abroad reaches your ears, + whether you question our ability to supply clergy for all the Bishop and Pincher Creeks of the world, + whether you think that a priest rushing round in a motor car to minister occasionally, or the appointment of a lay reader or of a catechism can really do instead of resident priests. (Why should I think any of ...

Figure 2. Rough draft letter from Roland Allen to Fr Waggett (12 June 1925).

Only by spiritual means can spiritual results be effected . . . the Spirit works through the material. . . . There is in Christ no ignoring of the outward material form. The whole world is sacramental and Christ is sacramental.[1]

Roland's admiration of Waggett's spiritual insight continued for many years and, at times, he pursued critical dialogue with him. Waggett was noted for blending both science and theology as shown in his publication *Religion and Science* (1904)[2] and yet, there does not seem to be any evidence of dialogue concerning Waggett's Darwinian ideas.[3] This may be due to the influence of Roland's mother, who 'had little patience with "free thinkers".'[4] Hubert Allen explained what his grandmother meant: 'By "free thinkers" I imagine Great-Granny was thinking of the humanists and Darwinists of her time.'[5]

Another important Anglo-Catholic that he, as a young man, respected in Oxford was Charles Gore. He served as the Principal of Pusey House during the time of Allen's many visits, and was 'later Bishop of Oxford, and one of the founders of the so-called "Liberal Catholic" tradition among High Anglicans [and also] edited the seminal collection of studies, *Lux Mundi* (1889)'.[6] The archives reveal no evidence of letters between both men, however, Allen did take the initiative to ask Gore to review his thesis and write the introduction for his *Educational Principles and Missionary Methods: The Application of Educational Principles to Missionary Evangelism* (1919).[7] It was generally his custom to have a bishop critique

---

Lutterworth Press, 1913, entitled *Essential Missionary Principles*; Grand Rapids, Michigan: Wm. B. Eerdmans, 1964; London: World Dominion Press, 1964, Cambridge: The Lutterworth Press, 2006). Hereafter referred to as *Missionary Principles*.

1. Allen, *Missionary Principles*, 69.

2. Philip Napier Waggett (SSJE) *Religion and Science: Handbooks for the Clergy*, A.W. Robinson (Longmans, 1904).

3. Philip N. Waggett in John Nias, *Flame From An Oxford Cloister*, 107, 112.

4. Hubert Allen, *Roland Allen*, 12.

5. Interview with Hubert Allen on 18 October 2010 and subsequent email on 1 November 2010.

6. Ibid., 18-19. See Charles Gore (ed.) *Lux Mundi: A Series of Studies in the Religion of the Incarnation* (London: John Murray, 1890); also, Charles Gore, *Dissertations: on Subjects Connected with the Incarnation* (London: John Murray, 1895).

7. Roland Allen, *Educational Principles and Missionary Methods: The Application of Educational Principles to Missionary Evangelism* (London: Robert Scott, 1919) Introduction by the Right Rev. Charles Gore, vi.

his work. Gore's comments are revealing in that, although, on one hand, he welcomes this book, but also underscores that some of Allen's 'views of education' are 'rather seriously one-sided' and that [Gore said] 'I am not wholly converted myself' of his arguments.[8] On the other hand, he asks missionaries 'to refrain from criticizing it and pointing out its weak points [and that] they should give it sympathetic attention and consider how vast and how important is the element of truth which the author's view contains.'[9] Allen was pleased to have the bishop's endorsement. Conversely, years later Allen critiques some of Gore's published work on apostolic succession.

Leeds Clergy Training School

After Allen's Oxford classical education at St John's College was completed and the experience of paleo-orthodox spirituality, which shaped his theology due to the influence of the Tractarian mentors at Pusey House, he then matriculated to the 'High Anglican clergy training school in Leeds' called the Leeds Clergy Training School.[10] Ake Talltorp points out that this school was founded by John Gott, vicar of Leeds, 'to train candidates for curacies in town parishes, and its theological profile was Tractarian'.[11] Moorman explains the daily spiritual formation that Leeds required of these ordinands, e.g., 'Mattins and Compline were obligatory, Sext and Evensong voluntary. Holy Communion was administered three days a week and Saint's Days.'[12] The frequent Eucharist celebration, as evidenced at Leeds and Pusey House, continued to remain a constant practice for Allen throughout his life and ministry.[13] For him, as an Anglican, he was both 'Catholic' in churchmanship and 'Evangelical' in his missionary approach to gospel ministry. How did Allen's churchmanship engage with the combination of both Catholic order and an Evangelical faith?

Firstly, during Allen's training at Leeds he was influenced by E.S. Talbot, the residential vicar for the school and also one of the authors of

---

8. Ibid., vi.

9. Ibid.

10. Hubert Allen, *Roland Allen*, 17.

11. Talltorp, *Sacrament and Growth*, 12; cf. Moorman, J.R.H., *A History of the Church in England* (London, 1986) 373.

12. Moorman, *History of the Church*, 373.

13. See Roland Allen, *Diary of a Visit in South India* (unpublished) USPG X622, Box 7, File N: 30-34, Oxford, Bodleian Library.

Anglo-Catholic sacramental thought (located in the volume *Lux Mundi*)[1] that, according to Talltorp, 'helped to form the theological conceptions of the students'[2] preparing for ordination. Within this theological environment, he appeared to fine-tune his 'spirituality', which embraced an understanding of how the Church viewed life as sacramental. He believed that the Holy Communion provided a context for the Church to encounter Christ spiritually. And, at Leeds, his theological understanding on the centrality and frequency of Eucharistic practice was reinforced. For him, this understanding was rooted in biblical veracity and the patristic fathers. David Paton was correct in identifying this understanding of Allen as 'old-fashioned Anglican Catholicism – sober, restrained, scholarly, immensely disciplined'[3] as evidenced through his own incarnational and sacramental emphasis, which eventually shaped his missionary theology. This meant that he advocated the belief that the spontaneous expansion of the Church naturally occurs when the Eucharist is central in the life of the community of faith because it promotes a holistic approach of faith and practice.

1. E.S. Talbot, 'The Preparation in History for Christ' in Charles Gore (ed.) *Lux Mundi*, 127-78.
2. Talltorp, *Sacrament and Growth*, 12.
3. David Paton, *Reform of the Ministry: A Study in the Work of Roland Allen* (London: The Lutterworth Press, 1968) 24.

2. Missionary Experiences in China
Life as an Anglican Missionary in China

Towards the conclusion of Roland Allen's ministerial training at Leeds, he attempted to apply for missionary work with the Society for the Propagation of the Gospel (SPG)[1] but to no avail. In fact, he sent two letters to the Secretary of the SPG[2] in 1892 to seek application to serve as a missionary, only to find out later that he was declined due to 'his mysterious heart ailment'.[3] Winfred Burrows (Principal) of Leeds Clergy School defended Allen by sending them a letter.[4] Burrows' letter appealed for him to possibly serve within the SPG and said that he was ' . . . a refined intellectual man, small not vigorous, in no way burly or muscular . . . academic and fastidious rather . . . learning and civilization are more to him than to most men'.[5] In addition to Burrows' previous advocacy letter to the SPG, Allen made application in 1893 to another mission agency, the Church of England Mission to North China.[6] During this waiting period, he was ordained as Deacon (1892) and Priest (1893) by Bishop Westcott of Durham, who subsequently authorized him to serve as curate at the parish of St John the Evangelist, Darlington (1893-94).[7]

---

1. Letters (handwritten) from Roland Allen to Mr Tucker, Secretary of the SPG, 12 September 1892 and 18 September 1892, D Series: 121a, 'Letters Received', Asia 2,77, Oxford, Bodleian Library, Roland Allen archives, USPG X622; see also, Talltorp, *Sacrament & Growth: A Study in the Sacramental Dimension of Expansion in the Life of the Local Church*, *as reflected in the Theology of Roland Allen* (Uppsala: Swedish Institute for Missionary Research, 1989) 11, 12, 75, 76.
2. Ibid.
3. Hubert Allen, *Roland Allen*, 22.
4. Winfred Burrows' letter to the SPG (1892) supporting Roland's desire to serve in the SPG. Cf. Hubert Allen, *Roland Allen*, 19.
5. Ibid.
6. Interview with Hubert Allen on 4 February 2011.
7. Amico meo Rolando Allen Donum Dedi, XVI Kal: November 1901 'Lumen ad revelationem gentium', USPG X622, Box 1, File A, Oxford, Bodleian Library.

While Allen faithfully served this curacy, undeterred by what seemed to be the inevitability of never becoming a foreign missionary, he was suddenly overwhelmed by a turn of events when he received word that the Church of England Mission to North China considered him to be sent to North China in 1895.[1] However, this decision was not formed without reservation. The representatives of the Mission to North China were still concerned about his heart ailment. Hubert Allen's biography reveals his grandfather's defense: '*If, as you say*, he challenged the examining doctor, *I have so bad a heart that I am likely to die soon, can you tell me why I should be likely to die sooner in China than in England?*[2] While awaiting the Mission's final decision, he continued to serve his curacy. Final approval came from the Mission for him to leave England for China at the end of January, 1895, and then on 22 March he arrived in Tientsin.[3]

What evidence is there to explain Allen's interest in China in the first place? The archival records at St John's College, Oxford, disclose an interesting essay that he presented to St John's College Essay Society during the Summer Term. On 2 June 1889, the Society's minutes read thus 'Mr R. Allen read a paper on "The Jesuits in Asia".'[4] To date (as mentioned in the previous chapter), the only written evidence that specifically unveils his interest of Christian missionaries in Asia prior to his clergy training at Leeds is located within the handwritten minutes from St John's College Essay Society. This evidence discloses his early interest in understanding how the Jesuits, in general, functioned as missionaries in Asia, and also serves as a backdrop for his later analysis of Roman Catholic influence, in particular, amongst the Chinese.[5]

Now that Allen's desire had become a reality, he was financed by a small stipend 'as acting chaplain to the British Legation', and according to Hubert Allen, finally 'taken onto the payroll by [the] SPG'[6] after

[handwritten margin note: does not say what is prob meant]

1. Hubert Allen, *Roland Allen*, 22.
2. Ibid.
3. Ibid.
4. St John's College Archives: Minutes from the *Members of the St John's College Essay Society*, UGS VI.1, and interview with Michael Riordan, archivist (16 November 2012) St John's College, Oxford.
5. 'Of Some of the Causes Which Led to the Preservation of the Foreign Legations in Peking', the Church of England Mission, *The Cornhill Magazine*, no.53/491 (November 1900) 676-677, USPG X622, Box 2, File J: 1, Oxford, Bodleian Library; and also, 'The Development of Independent Native Churches and their federation in union with the Church of England', paper read to a clerical Society in East London, (1901) 6, USPG X622, Box 3: 1, Oxford, Bodleian Library.
6. Hubert Allen, *Roland Allen*, 22.

Figure 3. Photograph of the Rev. Roland Allen.

that first year. Further elaboration of this second year of missionary service subsequently follows but now the focus turns to the preliminary background, which preceded his first year of service, with the Church of England Mission to North China.

Some twenty years prior to Allen's arrival in China there were two men – Charles Perry Scott and Miles Greenwood (curate of Padiham) – who were chosen to be sent as missionaries to China by the Society for the Propagation of the Gospel (SPG). H.P. Thompson wrote that:

on St. Peter's Day, 1874, [they] were sent forth to their work followed by the prayers and gifts of the St Peter's Missionary Guild, from which grew the North China (and Shantung) Missionary Association.[1]

Scott was consecrated bishop on 28 October 1880 for North China together with 'G.E. Moule as Bishop of Mid-China, in succession to Russell'.[2] Scott served as the bishop in North China for fifty-three years.[3] Thompson said that Scott's diocese covered the six northern provinces – Chihli (or Hopei), Shantung, Honan, Shansi, Shensi and Kansu – an immense area, stretching to the frontiers of Korea, Mongolia and Tibet; and he faced it with a staff of two, Greenwood at Chefoo, and William Brereton, a C.M.S. missionary in Peking, who was now transferred to the S.P.G. list.[4]

When Roland Allen arrived in China (1895) Scott appointed him to 'the training of Chinese workers'.[5] It was through Scott's influence that he had first begun to understand the missionary theology behind indigenous church-planting. Scott's understanding of this form of missiology stemmed from engaging with his good friend, John L. Nevius,[6] an American Presbyterian missionary serving in Chefoo, whose writings on and application of the 'three selfs'[7] approach to indigenous

1. H.P. Thompson, *Into All Lands: The History of the Society for the Propagation of the Gospel in Foreign Parts 1701-1950* (London: SPCK, 1951) 442.

2. Ibid., 443.

3. The Rt. Rev. Montgomery, *Charles Perry Scott: First Bishop in North China* (Westminster: The Society for the Propagation of the Gospel in Foreign Parts, 1928). See Robinson, Charles Henry, *History of Christian Missions*, International Theological Library [editorial secretary of the Society for the Propagation of the Gospel in Foreign Parts], (New York: Charles Scribner's Sons, 1915) 190.

4. Ibid.

5. Ibid., 444.

6. John L. Nevius, *The Planting and Development of Missionary Churches* (Shanghai: Presbyterian Press, 1886. Repr., Hancock: Monadnock Press, 2003).

7. This means indigenous self-governing, self-supporting and self-extending Christian churches and is *distinguished from* the 'Party controlled Protestant Three-Self Patriotic Movement' of the People's Republic of China (D. Aikman, *The Beijing Factor: How Christianity is Transforming China and Changing the Global Balance of Power*, (Oxford/Grand Rapids, 2003, 53f. Also see Jin Huat Tan, *Planting an Indigenous Church: The Case of the Borneo Evangelical Mission* (Oxford: Regnum, 2011). Tan identifies this 'three self'

church-planting, challenged Scott to apply these principles to his diocesan ministry, especially by making use of Allen's ministry gifts. Further details concerning Scott's and Nevius' missiological influence on Roland's life will be extensively discussed later with a disclosure concerning a certain shift within Allen's understanding and where he argued that the *missionary methods* and *systems* generally practised by Western missionary societies of his day appeared to create a *dependency system* for their converts, contrary to St Paul's *apostolic principles* that, he believed, methodically *empowered churches* towards independence. This shift in Allen's thinking began to emerge prior to the experiences he encountered in the Boxer Rebellion of 1900 in Peking (Beijing).

The Siege of the Peking Legations: Being the Diary of Roland Allen (1901)[8]

The formation of this publication originated from Roland Allen's personal diary being an eyewitness to the events that occurred in Peking (Beijing) in 1900. He said that this account is not designed to be a historical analysis but that it was an attempt 'to give as true and clear an account as I can of the general course of events, and of the effect which they produced upon the besieged community as reflected in our mind.'[9] The book consists of nine chapters, including maps and plans.

In the opening chapter, he describes how the 'society of Boxers first became widely known in England by the murder of the Rev. Sidney Brooks, of the Anglican Mission, on December 31, 1899.'[10] There was growing 'violent anti-foreign agitation', which was infecting the Chinese population against the foreign presence of missionaries, traders, soldiers and other professional workers who were British, American, Dutch, German, Italian, Spanish, French, Austrian, Russian and Japanese. The Chinese tendency was to view all foreigners as 'Christians'.[11] On 30 January, Bishop Charles Perry Scott told his diocesan missionary priest, Roland

---

methodology with Nevius (page 2) and yet, attributes how this method was applied to the Borneo Evangelical Mission more through the influence of Roland Allen, who, he frequently cites (pages 2, 100-102, 121, 170, 173, 175, 177, 182, 245, 276, 320, 327).

8. Roland Allen, *The Siege of the Peking Legations: Being the Diary of the Rev. Roland Allen* (London: Smith Elder & Co., 1901; further editions, patented 'print on demand' technology).

9. Ibid., 1-2.

10. Ibid., 3.

11. Ibid., 4.

Allen, 'that things had never before been in quite such a dangerous state' because the 'Boxers were openly preaching destruction to foreigners in the city'.[1] He gives an account of how Boxer 'superstitious frenzy' was evident due to their belief in demonic supernatural powers; thus, they would rave 'like lunatics'.[2]

Allen describes the topography of Peking, especially the 'great Altar of Heaven', Temple of Agriculture, Legation Street, Hanlin Library, British Legation, and various Christian missions.[3] He later relates how there was a gathering of missionaries, converts, and others into the protected area especially when the British Legation gave instructions to all women to gather at the Anglican mission (7 June)[4] where Allen served daily. Hubert Allen says that at 'the Legation, of course, Roland already had the status of Chaplain to the British diplomatic mission'.[5] His responsibilities with the Anglican mission, British Legation and his Chinese theological students kept him actively involved within the city and even though he was 'walking unarmed through crowds of Chinese' he remained safe.[6] He goes on to describe how the Boxer attacks caused the 'whole city' to be in 'uproar' with the burning of buildings while 'its peaceful inhabitants were being massacred'.[7] Dr Morrison brought 'a large convoy of Roman Catholic Christians' in for refuge after escaping the area around the South Cathedral where the Boxers were 'going from house to house cutting down every Christian they could find', and he said, 'the place was running with blood.'[8]

Allen's diary discloses how the Boxers' worldview incorporated a spirituality of demon possession. They believed that by their 'incantations' they could selectively bring destruction, for example, to one house and 'confine the fury of the flames' so that other houses were not affected.[9] They said that with 'tears we announced the war in the ancestral shrines' because 'our trust is in Heaven's justice' and they believed the 'gods have answered our call'.[10] Basically, the Boxers believed that once the demons possessed them, they would experience supernatural strength for warfare

---

1. Ibid., 7.
2. Ibid., 10-12.
3. Ibid., 14-18.
4. Ibid., 29.
5. Hubert Allen, *Roland Allen*, 44.
6. Allen, *The Siege*, chapter three.
7. Ibid., 29-33.
8. Ibid., 34.
9. Ibid., 35.
10. Ibid., 54.

and they would experience only success in battle. Another example that he gave described a story 'that a spirit had ridden through a little village called Hai Tien' on a donkey and that this spirit 'had not been seen since the foundation of the dynasty', thus, implying that the 'reappearance' of the spirit signified 'fearful things' were to transpire.[11] Also, he wrote how a story had emerged, which described that, when 'The Empress' was staying at the Summer Palace, she 'had heard spirits in the night crying "Kill! Kill!" though who was to be killed did not appear'.[12] His mention that the Boxers believed 'The Empress' encountered such a supernatural event shows how far they would go to justify their belief in destructive spirits. Stephan Feuchtwang argues that, normally, 'those in positions of authority within the system of actual imperial or indeed republican rule decry' superstitious offerings, 'territorial guardian carnivals and processional pilgrimages to regional temples' in order to deal with the 'non-human agency in Chinese religious cosmology', especially to appease or summons the demonic.[13] Allen's reference to this story said that it appeared not to affect 'the political situation', but that it did illustrate 'the state of men's minds'.[14] The diary records how he described the Boxers as 'the enemies' and this terminology he used frequently.[15]

The Boxer siege of Peking lasted for two months and his daily account of the events included information, such as: his responsibilities at the Anglican mission and Chaplaincy with the British Legation;[16] his Chinese theological students;[17] how his friendship with the American Presbyterian missionaries deepened;[18] that in spite of the difficulties for lack of food, living conditions and various attacks, he was thankful for the preservation 'from disease' and wrote 'it can yet only be accounted for as the work of God's good Providence';[19] how the women serving in the hospital were respected with 'double honour' by everyone;[20] how the

---

11. Ibid., 29.

12. Ibid., 29.

13. Stephan Feuchtwang 'Chinese religions', in Linda Woodhead, Hiroko Kawanami and Christopher Partridge, (eds) *Religions in the Modern World: Traditions and Transformations* (London and New York: Routledge, second edn, 2009) 131-32.

14. Allen, *The Siege*, 29.

15. Ibid., 53, 54, 57, 67, 69, 72, 73, 75, 77, 80, 81, 91, 102, 103.

16. Ibid., 18.

17. Ibid., 25.

18. Ibid., 18, 75, 83.

19. Ibid., 69.

20. Ibid., 66.

Chinese feared Western civilization;[1] and how the unity experienced in the British Legation between all the denominations and races represented during the siege caused them to worship together.[2] These experiences with Christians from other denominations in Peking helped to shape Allen's developing ecumenical understanding and influence his practice.

He brought clarity to the situation by differentiating between the 'enemies' – the Boxers – and the peaceful common Chinese people.

> In the face of that incomprehensible background of thought in the Chinese mind I felt doubly disgusted when I heard people talk of the Boxers and the Chinese in one sweeping denunciation as devils and monsters of iniquity. They seemed to me to have done nothing morally worse than the French did at the Revolution, nothing morally worse than we ourselves did when we burnt witches alive; yet no one would feel justified in condemning the whole French race as a race of devils or the whole English race as a race of monsters because in their ignorance they thought such iniquities to be just and lawful. . . . It is great injustice to judge a race by standards of morality of which they are totally ignorant, from a level of education to which they are utter strangers. Yet at that time if a man ventured to suggest such a thought there were people in the Legation who would refuse to speak to him.[3]

The diary entry sheds light on this missionary's attempt to understand why the Boxers reacted to the foreigners so viciously and yet the entry does not dismiss this uprising as something unprovoked by the foreigners' presence or anything different from other ethnic revolts of the past. Robert Young identifies how similar concerns were developing within the British colonies and that between William Gladstone's 'anti-imperialist' sentiments in 1846,[4] and, Adam Smith's earlier 'long-standing moral and humanitarian objection to colonialism and colonial practices' in 1776,[5] both men argued for 'establishing free trade' as a way to 'restore [the peoples'] integrity, equality and power'.[6] The problem that Allen observed

---

1. Ibid., 96.
2. Ibid., 47, 70, 75, 76, 99, 102-104, 108-111, 114.
3. Ibid., 84-85.
4. Robert Young, *Postcolonialism: An Historical Introduction* (Oxford and Malden: Blackwell Publishers, 2001) 93.
5. Ibid., 82-85; see Adam Smith, *Wealth of the Nations* (London: Dent [1776], 1910) 2 Vols.
6. Young, *Postcolonialism*, 84.

was not due to economic trade issues with the Chinese, but rather because the socio-religious dynamic of ancient Chinese belief was in decline, and, with the reintroduction of Christianity by foreign missionaries this time from the West,[7] the Boxers sought to bring a renewal of the ancient faith. On one hand, Allen believed that the Western missionaries had a legitimate right to evangelize the Chinese and to plant churches. On the other, he believed that these churches must be independent of foreign control. His desire to be fully immersed in Chinese culture led him to be 'the Chinese-speaking British chaplain' and to receive instruction from 'an elderly Confucian' who met with him daily in order to help him understand the 'classical Chinese texts'.[8] His practice discloses evidence for an emerging theology of cross-cultural mission. Allen's attention to the *imago Dei* blends with his missionary theology and appears to give a glimpse of how his missionary ecclesiology began to take shape early on in 1900.

On 13 August, 'the firing upon the Legation had been heavy' and so it was necessary that by 9:00 P.M., as 'the bell rang furiously', everyone rushed to the Bell Tower and was 'given his post'.[9] The diary states that every single weapon inside the Legation 'was handed out' and that 'Norris and myself [Roland], who had never been armed before, were provided with revolvers' in expectation of another 'grand assault'.[10] Next, Allen ran to the hospital in order to see if he 'could be of any use' and stayed with the deaconesses during all 'the deafening noise of the rifles and guns'.[11] Early in the next morning, the 'last effort of the enemy had failed'[12] and Allen went back to writing in his diary and 'meditating on the wonderful events which had occurred and of the events still more wonderful which might follow the end of the war.'[13]

Since the allied troops had arrived, everyone was overwhelmed with thankfulness and joy. Allen writes that on Sunday, 19 August, 'all the besieged met together at 9 A.M. outside the chapel in the broadway

---

7. Justo Gonzalez comments that the Nestorian Christians sent missionaries 'for a time in the Middle Ages [when] this church was numerous, and its missions extended into China. . . . ', Justo L. Gonzalez, *The Story of Christianity* (Peabody: Prince Press, 2004) 343.

8. Hubert Allen, 'Would Roland Allen still have anything to say to us today?', *Transformation* (July 2012) 29(3) 179-185 (182).

9. Roland Allen, *The Siege of the Peking Legations*, 102.

10. Ibid., 102.

11. Ibid., 102.

12. Ibid., 103.

13. Ibid., 103.

leading from the Bell Tower to the Great Gate to return thanks for our deliverance.'[1] As they gathered for worship they 'sang a few hymns and the *Te Deum*' and then various leaders among them, such as, 'Norris read some appropriate prayers', and also, the author Dr Arthur Smith 'delivered an address, in which he summed up the events of the siege, in which the protection of our God was most manifest.'[2] Interestingly, after Smith's address, Allen wrote that for whatever reason 'he', that is, Smith, 'rather took the services of the Marine guards for granted' and later one of the Marines commented: 'And where do I come in?'[3] Allen's assessment of this situation provides a glimpse into his ideas on the sacramental nature of the 'natural' and the 'spiritual' as not being in opposition to each other but rather as complementing each other. His thought on the Marine's comment is as follows:

> It emphasized the mistake of neglecting the natural in filial recognition of the supernatural. The supernatural over-watching care of God ordering events for His good purpose is commonly revealed through the success of the natural care and labour of men would obviously have been in vain if the favour of God had not aided their efforts. And never before in the lives of those present had that truth been more unmistakably proved.[4]

Allen seemed to be able to make sense of how the 'ordering events for His good purpose' *supernaturally* worked in and through the 'natural' efforts of the Marines. His grasp of divine providence discloses an Augustinian influence on his theology. When it became safe for the people to begin to leave his diary stated that they were 'glad to be on the way home free from the horrors of Peking.'[5]

> So we arrived about 7 o'clock A.M. made our way to the Mission, greeted our friends, and, going into the little church together, returned thanks to Almighty God. To Whom be glory forever.[6]

The missionaries sought to demonstrate forgiveness afterwards, as Thompson discloses, in the fact that the Chinese 'Government offered

1. Ibid., 108.
2. Ibid., 109.
3. Ibid.
4. Ibid.
5. Ibid., 112.
6. Ibid., 114.

reparation, but the S.P.G. refused to put in any claim or accept any compensation for loss of life or property, and the missionaries tried to check revengeful claims by their Chinese converts.'[7]

W.R. Williams recorded that throughout China, at the time of the Boxer Rising, 'well over 30,000 Christians perished, including 135 missionaries . . . with over 50 of their children'.[8] And also, that during the actual time of the Siege '90 had been killed and over 130 wounded'.[9] Niall Ferguson said that when the 'xenophobia erupted once again in the Boxer Rebellion, as another bizarre cult, the Righteous and Harmonious Fist (*yihe quan*), sought to drive all "foreign devils" from the land' and that there were 'fifty-eight CIM[10] missionaries [who] perished, along with twenty-one of their children'.[11] An interesting fact is stated by Hubert Allen: 'Roland and his mission companions had all survived.'[12]

lot the reader decide

Allen's Engagement with Chinese Culture

The culmination of Allen's studies of Confucianism and Taoism caused him to write various articles to help Christians understand the presuppositions held within Chinese culture. However, in 1909, he produced his Christian 'apologia' to what he believed was the religious system of Confucianism entitled: 'The Message of the Christian Church to Confucianists'.[13] Specific attention was given in the Introduction to articulate the *statement of the problem* concerning the contextualization of a missionary theology, which Allen believed was universally applicable to any ethnic *milieu*. He attempted to put into effect what he believed was a missiological philosophy of the kingdom of God, which enhanced an indigenous response to the Christian faith in every area of life. Another article entitled 'The Work of the

7. Thompson, *Into All Lands*, 676.
8. W.R. Williams, *Ohio Friends in the Land of Sinim*, Mount Gilead, Ohio: 1925, chapter VI, – 'China in Crisis', as cited in Hubert Allen, 55.
9. Williams, *Ohio Friends in the Land of Sinim*, chapter VI, – 'China in Crisis'.
10. The China Inland Mission (CIM) was founded by James Hudson Taylor in 1865. See Dr and Mrs Howard Taylor, *Biography of James Hudson Taylor* (London: Overseas Missionary Fellowship, 1965. Repr, 1972) 164-81; also, Dr and Mrs Howard Taylor, *Hudson Taylor's Spiritual Secret* (London, Philadelphia, Toronto, Melbourne, Shanghai: China Inland Mission, 1932).
11. Niall Ferguson, *Civilization: The Six Killer Apps of Western Power* (London: Penguin Books, 2011) 282-83.
12. Hubert Allen, *Roland Allen*, 55.
13. Roland Allen, 'The Message of the Christian Church to Confucianists', *The East and The West*, October 1909, 437-452, USPG X622, Box 2, File J: 7, Oxford, Bodleian Library.

The Imperialism of Missions in China

By the Rev. Roland Allen

IN HIS recent book, *China: A Nation in Evolution* (Macmillan, $3.50), Chapter XI, Dr. Paul Monroe gives us a most instructive analysis of the sources of the Chinese conviction that missions in their country are imperialistic. "Anti-imperialism," he says, "has now become the great national force among the student body; and unfortunately, imperialism has been identified with the Christian nations chiefly, while—far more regrettably—the Christian missions have become identified with the imperialistic interests." And then he proceeds to discuss the question: "How did the mission interests become identified in popular Chinese thought with imperialistic interests?" His conclusions may be summarized as follows:

1. The missionaries have penetrated the country more thoroughly than have business men or other foreigners, and are thus the foreigners with whom the great masses of the people are familiar; they are identified with foreign civilization in general; their compounds are identified with the concessions, because the fact that they carry some special protection is well known to all Chinese, and their very prominence as the most conspicuous and substantial buildings in many places, furnishes the most visible evidence of the domination of the foreigner over the native.

2. In the mission schools compulsory instruction in religion and compulsory attendance at religious exercises suggest imperialism to the Chinese. "Any action on the part of the foreigner which forces the Chinese to do or think as the foreigner wishes . . . becomes imperialism. So the mission schools, by their very nature, are imperialistic." "The foreigner is free to hold his religious beliefs and to propagate them through religious activities. But education is a function of the State; and if delegated to private agencies must be carried on as educational, not as religious, activities." "The missionaries in general have long objected to this, on the ground that their schools had as their chief purpose the propagation of religion. Then, the Chinese educational authorities maintain, such institutions are not schools"; and "the attempt to urge the Anglo-Saxon view of mission schools against the Chinese view is but another evidence of imperialism." On this Dr. Monroe remarks: "The logic of the case lies with the Chinese authorities."

3. The "constant attempt to dominate, even in the sphere of religious belief and practice, appears to the non-Christian as a form of foreign tyranny or imperialism." "This impression—that the missionary is unwilling to trust the Chinese Christian—cuts far deeper than most Christians realize." Here Dr. Monroe cites the unwillingness of many missionaries to accept the demand for government registration and inspection of schools, or to admit Chinese to the boards of control.

4. "The failure to make adequate use of the Chinese in the activities of the missions." "Now that the present crisis has arisen there is a great demand for able Chinese to fill administrative positions, but they cannot be found in sufficient numbers because they are in demand by their own people." Again Dr. Monroe draws his illustration from an educational institution.

5. "An unconscious Anglo-Saxon masterfulness that may be Anglo-Saxon efficiency, or may be nothing more than the customary way of doing things with directness, but which offends the Chinese respect for form." Again Dr. Monroe is thinking of educational institutions, for he proceeds: "The missionary is in charge: he is there to run the school or to teach. He does this in the English way, or the American way, either of which has little consideration for the Chinese way."

NOW, it will be at once recognized that of these five poi... all but the second have a much wider bearing than th... educational controversy in which Dr. Monroe is particularly ... terested. The reason why he writes almost entirely in terms... schools is that, as he says: "The chief strength of the oppo... tion now centers on the mission schools," and "The imperialis... aspect of Christianity is found primarily in its schools." It m... well be true, but it does not follow that the point on which t... Chinese seize today is the most important point, nor the c... on which we ought to concentrate our attention; like the b... barian fighters at whom the Greek laughed, saying that th... hands flew to the place where they had received the last blo... There is more here than a controversy over schools and sch... administration. That is simply a detail. The matter of imp... tance is the charge that missionaries manifest an imperialis... spirit. I pass, then, from the consideration of the schools, o... pausing to call attention to two remarks which Dr. Mon... makes about missions in t... chapter: (1) "To a very la... extent in recent years Pr... estant mission work has... come a cultural mission rath... than a religious mission in... narrow sense"; and ... "Nearly all the difficulties ... the missions center arou... their material property"; t... profoundly important and s... nificant statements.

I return to the manifes... tion of the imperialistic spi... As I said, of the five poi... made by Dr. Monroe, fo... have a bearing much wid... than school administrati...

and I want to add another which seems to me the most significant of all. It is the unwillingness of the missionaries to ... tablish the Chinese Christians as a body in the place whe... they reside with the full authority and power to carry on th... own Church life.

Nearly all the larger missions, and a great many of t... smaller, believe that a Christian Church should be guided a... led by ordained ministers; and it is a most remarkable and ... portant sign of the imperialistic spirit in the missionaries th... they have retained that power to ordain ministers in their o... hands to such an extraordinary degree, and only in a ve... few cases, comparatively, have committed it to native Chine... Churches. That is an action which forces all Chinese to lo... on their work as imperialistic. Almost universally men belie... that a Christian minister must be so appointed that all t... Christians, at least of their own denomination, will recogn... him as a true minister. The missionaries have never trust... their Chinese Christians enough to put that power wholly ... unreservedly into their hands. The battle against missiona... domination has hitherto been waged over positions in co... ferences, or on boards of school or hospital management; ... one day it will be waged on this ground.

And I do not see how the missions can escape from the ... sault. "You held all spiritual authority in your own hands ... long as possible, and conferred it grudgingly and only to m... whom you had trained to exercise it as *you* thought that ... ought to be exercised. You did not trust the Chinese with f... authority to direct their own Churches; and you maintai... your position by insisting upon the payment of stipends a... that were a part of the Gospel. Many of you declared that y... did not believe that you had any spiritual authority to conf... but you exercised it as if you had. Subtly, without words, y... persuaded your converts that they could not go to the ne... village and establish a church which you would recognize a... church unless you were consulted both in the baptism of f... first converts and in the organization of the body there w... its ministers. In some way it must be connected with you, a...

Figure 5. A critique of Allen's article in *The Living Church* (13 April 1929).

ng Church: 1801 Fond du fac Avenue,
Milwaukee, Wis, U.S.A.

APRIL 13, 1929   THE LIVING CHURCH   833

CORRESPONDENCE

All communications published under this head must be signed by the actual name of the writer. The Editor is not responsible for the opinions expressed, but reserves the right to exercise discretion as to what shall be published. Letters must ordinarily not exceed five hundred words in length.

"THE IMPERIALISM OF MISSIONS IN CHINA"

To the Editor of The Living Church:

A MISSIONARY who proposes to answer the Rev. Roland Allen's article on The Imperialism of Missions in China [L. C. January 26th] is practically out of court from the start. If he defends anything at all he is an "imperialist."

The article is unfair in its title. Mr. Allen is a protagonist for the ordination of self-supporting ministers. No one questions his right to argue his case; but one-sided criticism is not argument, and labels prove nothing. The proper meaning of the word "imperialism" is the desire and effort to extend national interests in external fields. Mr. Allen extends it to cover practically any holding of property or exercise of discipline by missionaries in China whatsoever. . . .

The missionary body in China is, flatly, not imperialistic. A large part of it has done everything but change the color of its skin in the effort to be what Chinese super-nationalism thinks it wants. The movement to turn things over to Chinese control is far in advance of the inherent rights of the situation. The men and women who are the backbone of the Chinese churches freely recognize this.

Every imaginable scheme for making Christianity "native" and free in China has been tried. But a tyro in China knows that loose ordinations do not make for Christianity, but for financial gain and political sedition under cover of religion. That is what the majority of non-Christian Chinese think a *hiao* or religious organization is for. You've got to convert, train in the Christian faith, and settle and test in Christian habits before you can leave a young church to free native leadership. May I quote from the last issue of the National Christian Council Bulletin, from the report of one of its secretaries—himself an English Quaker, and a man hardly in favor of unnecessary supervision?

"Traveling in China during the last few months not only I but others have been grieved, if not alarmed, to find a low level of spiritual life among the churches. In many places active opposition has died down, and there is a fine field for fresh endeavor. But in not a few cases the desire and passion to enter into such a field is lacking or confined to very few. In other cases extremists with queer unbalanced ideas are coming in, emphasizing a single and perhaps a distorted aspect of truth and by their evident enthusiasm and devotion deceiving 'the very elect.' "

This is plainly written of places where the missionary is very little in control. Is it either catholic or Christian sanity to suppose that a bit of preaching, accompanied by passing out the Bible and an ordination, is going to plant a *Christian* church? The plain fact is that the missionary has a duty to see that so far as in him lies the true faith is taught and a regulated ministry set up. If you want us to ordain at random and have heresy and immorality representing the Christian name in China, please tell us so.

Dr. Monroe is quoted extensively about imperialism in Christian schools. Many of his statements are just; but Dr. Monroe would, I am sure, readily admit that the problems he sees are no less clearly seen by missionary educators themselves and that things have moved very much since he wrote. Moreover the statement: "Any action on the part of the foreigner which forces the Chinese to do or think as the foreigner wishes . . . becomes imperialism" represents the situation in China exactly; but it burks the whole question of right or wrong. Imperialism means "what the Chinese don't like." The Nationalist government has just issued an order which states that students are to study, not to engage in political activities, and that school heads are to see that discipline is more thoroughly enforced. This is exactly the imperialism for which St. John's University and the schools of this diocese have been under bitter attack for the past three years. It is good to see signs of its passing away.

There is distinct evidence that an effort is being made to set up Dr. Sun Yat-sen as a god in China. I quote from the address of a Chinese officer made to a mission school in Chefoo January 30th: "You gentlemen believe in God. You must have the same belief in our saviour Dr. Sun and with all your strength forward the cause of the Revolution." Another official has been quoted as saying that since the Chinese as a people are not yet up to abstract patriotism, they need a personal center for devotion and therefore Dr. Sun must be made a god. The power of Christianity and Japanese emperor worship are both back of this idea. The proponents are extreme men, but they count. Are we missionaries to turn schools over to this sort of thing, or to oppose and be transfixed on Mr. Allen's imperialistic dart, or what?

That there are dominating missionaries, that we are foreigners and aliens, that property and salaries make trouble is all true, and we live in the midst of problems. But mere faultfinding from a London arm-chair does not help. And I think Mr. Allen's unbalanced criticism is not unfairly met by a somewhat categorical reply. His concluding paragraph about Anglican bishops ordaining native unpaid bishops is simply fantastic.
                                        (Rev.) JOHN W. NICHOLS.

St. John's University, Shanghai, China.

Missionary in Preparing the Way for Independent Native Churches',[1] attempted to contextualize this faith for winning Chinese converts wherein, he said, 'I mean Converts who are not semi-Europeanized by conversion'.[2] For him, imposing one's customs on foreigners to whom he served was not biblical evangelism, he believed, but rather a form similar to what the apostle Paul addressed in his letter to the churches of Galatia when addressing Judaizing practices.[3] As a British missionary, he made distinctions between personal customs, which he attempted to keep to himself, and the customs of those to whom he ministered. However, how could he – as a Church of England missionary and Chaplain to the British diplomatic mission –[4] function within a branch of Christendom without imposing foreign customs on the Chinese? What influences contributed to his analysis of Chinese religious faith and his conscious response to it, which was formed through a proactive missional and global Christian faith, designed to be contextualized into its cultural framework? The following information will attempt to address these important questions.

The people within the Chinese culture who influenced Allen's missionary theology were missionary colleagues (1895-1903), Viceroy Chang Chih Tung, in addition to various Chinese scholars, such as, Jan Jakob de Groot (Dutch sinologist and historian of religion), James Legge (Scottish sinologist and first professor of Chinese at Oxford), and Joseph Edkins (English sinologist and missionary). As a missiologist, he remained quite eclectic and this influenced his style of critical analysis. Therefore, this diverse group of people contributed to the way he articulated a missionary theology that engaged Christianity within Chinese culture.

For example, in an article for the *The East and West* (1909) Allen assessed the Chinese religious culture, in which he previously served as a missionary, by acknowledging the lack of agreement among scholars when defining Confucianism and its 'fundamental characteristics'.[5] He had already recognized the changing nature of this system when he wrote about it in 1909. Years later, Ninian Smart (1989) similarly commented

---

1. Roland Allen (Chaplain to the Bishop of North China) 'The Work of the Missionary in Preparing the Way for Independent Native Churches,' a paper read before the Federation of Junior Clergy Missionary Associations in connection with the SPG, Resume of Proceedings at the 19th Conference of Delegates, John Rylands Library, Manchester (11-12 November 1903) 8, USPG X622, Box 2, File J: 4, Oxford, Bodleian Library.

2. Ibid.

3. See Galatians 1:1-9; 2:11-3:14; Ibid., 11.

4. Hubert Allen, *Roland Allen*, 44.

5. Allen, 'The Message of the Christian Church to Confucianists', 437.

on Confucianism as the 'official cult which disappeared with the revolution of 1911, and has had no basic significance since then.'[6] That said, Allen thought that this system's influence on Chinese culture stemming from the 6th century BC – even with its variations – had fashioned into a worldview. For the sake of clarity, he maintained that the followers of Confucianism could be categorized into 'three classes' by those who teach:

(1) a pure moral philosophy separated from all religion
(2) the form of certain Chinese characters, the use of certain expressions in the Imperial worship, and hints which are to be found of early religious practice [and]
(3) the Rites practised by the Chinese people, and the Classical Books are interpreted by them. Confucianism is represented as a purely animistic religion. In this school no sharp line of division is drawn between Confucianism and Taoism.[7]

These three classes summarize the basic divisions within Confucianism so-called and Allen's proposed understanding of this belief system. He described this religious system to be a synthesis of 'the fundamental principles of Taoist demonolatry . . . whose Bible is the Confucian Classics . . . whose worship is a worship of spirits'.[8] Allen also believed the Confucian worldview to be deficient when defining the disciplines of theology, cosmology, anthropology and eschatology. By way of analysis, he engages with the writings of de Groot, Legge and Edkin. Firstly, the Chinese theory and explanation of cosmology, Allen discloses, stems from the source which he identifies as the 'most important text on the constitution of the world . . . found in an Appendix ascribed to Confucius himself' on the Classic called "I Ching" or "The Book of Change".[9] This text teaches 'the Great Ultimate Principle . . . T'ai Chi' as a transmutation within 'the system of I' which produces 'two regulating Powers . . . Yin and Yang' and then doubles into 'Forms' and yet again doubles into what is called 'Trigrams'.[10] It is from these Trigrams that 'good and evil' are determined identifying Confucian thought of the 'world' as definitely 'Taoistic',[11] according to Allen's understanding. The sinologist, de Groot, described this viewpoint of the world as a peculiar place, full of spiritual powers which bring good

---

6. Ninian Smart, *The World Religions: Old Traditions and Modern Transformations* (Cambridge: Cambridge University Press, 1989) 104.
7. Allen, 'The Message of the Christian Church to Confucianists', 437-438.
8. Ibid., 438-39.
9. Ibid., 439.
10. Ibid.
11. Ibid.

or evil fortune.[1] Yet these 'spirits' cannot execute their powers arbitrarily for they are restrained and directed by 'a higher power – Heaven', which signifies 'the Divine Will, the Creator'.[2] This understanding from the text somehow was blurred by the throng of spirits as the Chinese were doing theology. It is here that Allen assesses their culture's lack of contribution to the 'scientific knowledge of the world' due to their worldview, which embraced a 'world as under the control of capricious and unintelligible spirits'.[3] On one hand, in another article entitled 'The Progress of Education in China',[4] he engages with Chang Chih Tung's assessment that both Taoism and Buddhism were 'decaying and cannot long exist' and had little to offer in contrast with the scientific advancement produced through 'Western learning'.[5] Chang Chih Tung believed that the only way to reform the Chinese culture from its educational lethargy and stagnancy was to make a major shift by advancing Western education. He said: 'Convert the temples and monasteries of the Buddhists and Taoists into schools [and] that seven temples with their land, &c., out of every ten be appropriated to educational purposes [because] Buddhism is dead, Taoism is dead [and] Confucianism is in peril'.[6] Chang Chih Tung's concern that Chinese religion was in decline and that it was not adequately addressing various cultural problems motivated him to, 'in spite of his advanced age, he resigned his vice-royalty in order to undertake the task of establishing a system of universal education'[7]. On the other hand, Chang Chih Tung, although willing 'to tolerate Christianity' was not willing to eliminate Confucianism within Chinese culture, for he believed, as Allen points out, that 'the overthrow of Confucianism would mean the overthrow of all moral sanctions'.[8] He stated that Chang Chih Tung came to this conclusion by assuming that 'Western learning' was basically 'practical' whereas

1. Jan Jakob de Groot, *The Religious System of China, its ancient forms, evolution, history and present aspect, manners, custom and social institutions connected therewith*, iv (1st edn [Taipei: Ch'eng Wen Publishing, 1892. Repr, 1976]; Leiden: E.J. Brill, 1907) 431.

2. Allen, 'The Message of the Christian Church to Confucianists', 440.

3. Ibid.

4. Roland Allen, 'The Progress of Education in China', *Cornhill* (November 1908) USPG X622, Oxford, Bodleian Library.

5. Ibid., 658.

6. Roland Allen refers to this as 'a little book written by Chang Chih Tung'. When he cites the book it is referred to as *Woodbridge's Translation*, pp. 74, 75, 85, 103, 104.

7. Allen, 'The Progress of Education in China', 658.

8. Ibid.

'Chinese learning is moral'.[9] Allen's answer to that assumption was that the
'first and deepest wish of every friend of the Chinese nation must be that
the Chinese should unlearn that lesson'.[10]   ⟋ Mission?

Allen's impetus for doing missiology within the Chinese culture |
was his conviction of presenting the uniqueness of Christ and, to this
end, he wrote another article earlier entitled 'The Chinese Character
and Missionary Methods'.[11] The purpose for the article hinged on his
incessant belief in an indigenous Chinese Church, in which 'Chinese
thought is permeated with Christian doctrine and belief'.[12] This view was
pre-eminent in his missiology, although today critics would probably
interpret his posture as religiously narrow and intolerant.[13] Given that
Allen's counter-cultural evangelism among the Chinese was rooted in
an evangelical and catholic understanding of the Christian religion,
which he believed was called to challenge any religious culture with the
claims of Christ's uniqueness as revealed through biblical revelation.
This was always Allen's approach. Throughout his life he maintained the
uniqueness of Christ and his sermons truly exemplify this strength of
belief. Consider these words from a few of his sermons:

> Read the best books of other men [and] then turn to the Gospels.
> What a change! What a difference! It is a difference of the Person
> who speaks (15 February 1920). . . . Men without faith in Xt.
> [Christ] are still lost & [and] condemned . . . You may say that this
> is not the meaning of the words of the Creed [i.e. The Athanasian
> Creed]. . . . It was a great element in the zeal of the early Ch.
> [Church]. Knowing the terror of the Lord we persuade men. It is
> the man who knows that he is lost but in Xt. [Christ] that cares
> for the salvation of others (June 1921).[14]

9. Ibid., 657.

10. Ibid., 665.

11. Roland Allen, 'The Chinese Character and Missionary Methods', *The East
and The West* (July 1903) Oxford, Bodleian Library, USPG X622.

12. Ibid., 320.

13. John Hick, *God Has Many Names: Britain's New Religious Pluralism* (London/
Basingstoke: The MacMillan Press, 1980) 4-5, 59-79. See Johannes Christiaan
Hoekendijk, *The Church Inside Out* (Philadelphia: Westminster, 1966); and,
Johann-Baptist Metz, *Theology of the World* (New York: Herder & Herder, 1969).

14. Cf. Allen's sermons: 'Never man spoke like this man', St John 7:46, 15 February
1920: 9; Sermon on St John 3:35-36 and Ephesians 2:11-12, June 1921: 351;
see also sermons 13, 106, 117, USPG X622, Box 5, Oxford, Bodleian Library.
See John R.W. Stott, *Christian Mission: in the Modern World* (Downers Grove:
InterVarsity Press, 1975) 35-57.

To characterize him as intellectually clueless, however, to the *common ground* beliefs found in 'the filial piety of the Chinese' misrepresents his reasonable engagement 'that Christianity and filial piety are not antagonistic'.[1] Allen recognizes some levels of compatibility:

> That there is in the Chinese Classics and in the teaching of the Confucian School much that is admirable, little that is incompatible with Christian teaching, is, I am sure, true, but the explanation, the illumination is everything. I can quite conceive that the Chinese Church of the future may express its filial piety in services and prayers offered on behalf of its dead, but these things when so transformed will not and cannot be the Confucianism of to-day.[2]

Allen's developing *missionary ecclesiology* sought to engage with Chinese culture, not negate it. This meant, however, that his missionary theology was concerned to make distinctions rooted in and developed from his evangelical understanding of biblical revelation which necessitated a belief in, for example, the story of creation where 'the simplicity of the first sentence of the Book of Genesis'[3] asserts God as Creator, in contrast to the Chinese system of thought concerning 'a source of Creation which is extremely vague, working by a law which is unintelligible, through innumerable agents whose conduct can neither be anticipated nor understood... for no intelligent purpose.'[4] His pithy answer to the Chinese system of what he believed to be 'chaos' was that 'Christianity brings order'[5] to the whole discussion of creation. He believed the religious system of Chinese culture prevented a purposeful direction of society, that being, a static approach to life, whereas the Christian faith declared the 'restoration of harmony by submission to Christ's control',[6] which in his opinion was the 'element which makes for stability' in any culture for it establishes an 'orderly progress' and which provides a basis

1. Allen, 'Message of the Christian Church to Confucianists', 452. See Hendrick Kraemer, *The Christian Message in a Non-Christian World* (Grand Rapids: Kregel Publications, 1969) 338-52.
2. Allen, 'Message of the Christian Church to Confucianists', 448, Oxford, Bodleian Library, Roland Allen archives, USPG X622.
3. Ibid., 449.
4. Ibid., 448.
5. Ibid.
6. Roland Allen, Epiphany sermon on Matthew 8:23, Box 5, Sermon no. 13, (1905) Oxford, Bodleian Library, Roland Allen archives, USPG X622.

for 'the moral support which is so grievously needed' in China.[7] His belief in the pre-eminence of Western learning to advance the Chinese culture differed from that of Chang Chih Tung's. Even though Chang Chih Tung embraced the 'practical' side of Western learning, he did not make the connection of what constituted its significance. Allen pointed out that:

> Western learning is not based on materialism, nor is the greatness of Western nations. Western civilization is rooted in Christian faith and Christian morals. That is the lesson which the East needs to learn.[8]

Here is evidence for Allen's unique contribution to Western civilization's significance in the global context because of its rootedness in the Christian faith. Even though Chang Chih Tung did not fully recognize the significance of how the Christian faith and morals advanced Western learning during the latter years of the ninteenth century, yet in 2011, more than a century later, a similar analysis was made by the historian Niall Ferguson when he assessed the research conducted by Liu Peng and Dunhua Zhao[9] where 'after much hesitation, at least some of China's communist leaders now appear to recognize Christianity as one of the West's greatest sources of strength.'[10] Ferguson (and Lord Jonathan Sacks) similarly concluded what Allen's assessment was of the West's rootedness in Christianity, and yet, both men go further to cite Aikman's *The Beijing Factor: How Christianity is Transforming China and Changing the Global Balance of Power.*[11] Ferguson says that a particular scholar from the Chinese Academy of the Social Sciences said:

---

7. Allen, 'Progress of Education in China', *Cornhill* (November 1908) 665, Oxford, Bodleian Library, USPG X622.

8. Ibid.

9. Liu Peng, 'Unreconciled Differences: The Staying Power of Religion', in Jason Kindopp and Carol Lee Hamrin (eds) *God and Caesar in China: Policy Implications of Church-State Tensions* (Washington, DC: 2004) 162f; Dunhua Zhao, 'Recent Progress of Christian Studies Made by Chinese Academics in the Last Twenty Years', in H. Yang and Daniel H.N. Yeung (eds) *Sino-Christian Studies in China* (Newcastle, 2006) 252-64.

10. Niall Ferguson, *Civilization: The Six Killer Apps of Western Power* (London: Penguin Books, 2011) 286-87; Peng, 'Unreconciled Differences', 162f; Zhao, 'Recent Progress of Christian Studies', 252-64.

11. D. Aikman, *The Beijing Factor: How Christianity is Transforming China and Changing the Global Balance of Power* (Oxford/Grand Rapids, 2003).

We were asked to look into what accounted for the . . . pre-eminence of the West all over the world. . . . At first, we thought it was because you had more powerful guns than we had. Then we thought it was because you had the best political system. Next we focused on your economic system. But in the past twenty years, we have realized that the heart of your culture is your religion: Christianity. That is why the West has been so powerful. The Christian moral foundation of social and cultural life was what made possible the emergence of capitalism and then the successful transition to democratic politics. We don't have any doubt about this.[1]

When these Chinese scholars began to analyze the gathered evidence, they concluded – similar to Allen's analysis – that it was the 'Christian faith' which provided the impetus for Western exploration and expansion. An argument can be made for him making distinctions, on one side, in situations in which Western Christianity brought freedom to the oppressed in many ways, and in particular, by providing vernacular translations of the Bible for indigenous people groups; while, on the other, during times when certain aspects of Western expansionism had been put into effect, the systems carved out became hegemonic, which oppressed some people groups. In other words, he did *not* lump Western expansionism as 'all bad' or 'all good'. The introduction and spread of the Christian faith within China, he believed, would provide a moral framework to serve the culture with a value system that could enhance its cosmology and anthropology. These contemporary scholars likewise accept this perspective. Of course, at the core of his analysis of the West's prominence are the Church and her ability to adapt faith to any indigenous context. For him, Christianity's expansion stems from the pneumatological dynamic experienced by the faith community – the Church – when Christians engage with the transcendent values of freedom, equality and justice. Another historian, Lamin Sanneh comments on Allen's missionary engagement with China:

That was the vision Allen had of China, so that 'in every market town in China, in every centre of population all over the world [there would be] the Church which could grow and expand without any direction from foreigners. . . . As a contemporary of the pivotal

---

1. Aikman, *The Beijing Factor*, 5; Niall Ferguson, *Civilization*, 287; Lord Jonathan Sacks, *The Times*, 21 May 2011, 86. See Philip Jenkins, *The Next Christendom: The Coming of Global Christianity* (Oxford/New York: Oxford University Press, 2002) 69-70.

changes in China underwent in the Communist revolution, Allen was surprisingly tight-lipped on Christianity's encounter with Marxism.... For Allen, however, Christianity was a world religion because Christianity had real and present worldwide appeal, not because it had a Western mandate.... His confidence in the future of the church was bound up with his theological conviction about faith as local embodiment, and that carried an implicit rejection, for example, of the merits of a foreign Marxist ideology.[2]

Firstly, Sanneh's comment of how Allen appeared to be 'tight-lipped on Christianity's encounter with Marxism'[3] was due to his primary focus on critiquing the imposition of certain foreign forms of Western colonial customs rather than the imposition of foreign forms of Marxism on China's context. In all fairness to Allen, by the time Mao Tse-tung and his friends in Yenan jointly published *The Chinese Revolution and the Chinese Communist Party* in December 1939, Allen was already in his early 70s, living in Kenya, and spending most of his time writing about issues within the African context. To digress for the sake of clarity, Hubert Allen recently clarified how his grandfather's ministry in Africa included things such as 'in the 1930s he acted as an up-country locum during his retirement in Kenya, where during the War he ministered to Germans interned in prison camps.'[4] By him serving as a priest to the marginalized 'interned' Germans in Kenya shows the 'pastoral' side of Allen and his willingness 'to reach across the aisle' without any fear of guilt by association. In fact, in 1943 he was criticized in the editorial section of the *East African Standard* after writing and being critiqued by advocates for the extermination of all Germans in Kenya. One such example is E.W. Ashe's comment:

> Peace and goodwill is a very good motto at any time and the best way to make it reasonably sure is to exterminate – as far as possible – the race of ruffians that has been its chief disturbers for the past hundred years and more.[5]

---

2. Lamin Sanneh, *Disciples of All Nations: Pillars of World Christianity* (Oxford/ New York: Oxford University Press, 2008) 233-34.

3. Ibid., 233.

4. Hubert Allen, 'Would Roland Allen still have anything to say to us today?' in *Transformation: An International Journal of Holistic Mission Studies*, vol.29, no. 3 (July 2012) 179-85.

5. E.W. Ashe's letter to the editor of *East African Standard* (4 January 1943) Oxford, Bodleian Library, USPG X622, Box 7: 51.

Allen's response in the editorial page the next day was:

> Mr Ashe . . . makes no bones about this doctrine of "Peace through extermination". . . . Does he think "the extermination of a race of ruffians" by which he clearly means the Germans, an easy matter? Hitler declared precisely the same object in his attack upon the Jews. . . . Does he think that the Americans will wholeheartedly support a policy of "extermination" . . . does our King? . . . You and I, sir, know that any policy of "extermination", even "as far as possible" is quite unreasonable, as well as Anti-Christian.[1]

Here, again, we see Allen's tenacious style to defend the Christian community, and, in particular, the German Christians in Kenya, as part of the Church catholic. And, this letter to the editor gives a hint concerning his position of 'Peace through goodwill,' especially when it came to the way the British and American forces were to deal with German imperialism.[2] Here is an example of a priest whose decision to serve the interned German Christians in Kenya kept him focused on the African situation rather than the situation of Marxism in China. It was an Anglican bishop – K.H. Ting (Nanjing, China) – who referred to David Paton as one who 'belongs to the school of missiological thinking with Roland Allen' that actually engaged this issue by writing about Marxism and Christianity in his book *Christian Missions and the Judgment of God.*[3]

Secondly, Allen did not soft-peddle his words when describing events that preceded the Boxer movement and its successive reactions against Christian missionaries, as referred to earlier in *The Siege of the Peking Legations.* Within his archives are copies of articles he read, analyzed and occasionally 'underlined' for critical purposes. One article entitled 'China: The Outbreak and the Outlook (1901)'[4] underlined comments by the Chinese Viceroy who argued for religious toleration since 'Buddhism and Taoism are decaying . . . while the Western religion is flourishing' and that the current form of 'Confucianism, as now practised, is inadequate to

---

1. Roland Allen's letter to the editor of *East African Standard* (5 January 1943) Oxford, Bodleian Library, USPG X622, Box 7: 52.

2. Ibid.

3. David M. Paton, *Christian Missions and the Judgment of God* (London: SCM Press [1953] Grand Rapids: Eerdmans, second edition 1996) Foreword by Bishop K.H. Ting, x.

4. G.F.S., 'China: The Outbreak and the Outlook', IV. *The Outlook* (April 1901) 271-82.

lift us from the present plight.'[5] Interestingly, the Viceroy earlier praised China's history 'for the past 2,000 years with that of Western lands, and triumphantly claims superiority in respect of generosity, benevolence, loyalty, honesty, freedom, and the happiness of the people.'[6] It appears that he appreciated the objectivity of this appointed leader to make these types of distinctions, and therefore, further highlights a section later on:

> In 1898 there were as many as seventy native newspapers (most of these were suppressed after the *coup d'état*) published and circulated in China, of which several translated the most important news from the foreign daily papers in Shanghai and one of them translated largely from the *Times*.[7]

Allen's choice to underline this section comes as no surprise in terms of his major focus on the principle of liberty, especially when it comes to his desire on an unrestrained, free expression of the press. This article ends with the emphasis on the manifest destiny of the missionary cause, which he does not engage with. What is interesting is his rationale for accepting the presence of Western religion – Christianity – to influence Chinese thought as a historic and global faith in their modern context. His tenacious belief was that missionaries ought to find ways to respectfully contextualize the Christian faith in a positive and constructive manner within the culture of the people without imposing foreign customs and paternalistic expectations upon the converts. This concept was beginning to develop in his mind over the next few years, as is disclosed in a paper he presented which expressed his *apologia* for how missionaries were to approach what they called the 'mission field'.

> The object of this paper is to suggest by what methods certain characteristics of the Chinese may be brought more fully into the service of the Christian Church ... not the forcing upon an unwilling intellect of a certain amount of information, however exact; but the discovery and exercise of the powers of the individual mind and character . . . not the thrusting upon an unwilling soul of certain doctrines, however true, but the enlisting of the capacities of men in the cause of Christ.[8]

5. Ibid., 274–75.
6. Ibid., 274.
7. Ibid., 279.
8. Allen, 'Chinese Character and Missionary Methods', 317, Oxford, Bodleian Library, Roland Allen archives, USPG X622.

Three Chinese Characteristics: Conservative Instinct, Love of Propriety, and Union

Allen's cross-cultural etiquette, which continued to take shape by 1903, discloses an understanding as seen in the expression above. This developed out of his immersion in Chinese language, history, and a genuine love for the people he had been serving. In this paper, Allen unpacks three main characteristics located within the Chinese culture: (1) the characteristic of 'conservative instinct'; (2) the characteristic for the people's 'love of propriety'; and, (3) the characteristic of 'union' among the people.[1] Firstly, in a similar tone to that which Paul the missionary used as a defender of the gospel of Christ with the Athenian philosophers,[2] and also how certain patristic apologists, in the early Church, attempted to defend the Christian faith by finding areas of 'commonality' with Greek philosophers,[3] so Allen found common ground with the Chinese religious mindset and their 'conservative instinct' to hold to the 'peculiar tenacity to the tried, the ancient, the historical' because he said 'it would seem to be far better to begin by reinforcing the germs of truth they contain than to proceed to wholesale denunciation'.[4] Of course, this apologetic methodology was even used by Pope Gregory the Great, in a somewhat different way, as he wrote to Abbot Mellitus to send Augustine to Britain in AD 596 to revive the Church in England, asserting:

> that he should by no means destroy the temples of the gods but rather the idols within those temples . . . if those temples are well built, they should be converted from the worship of demons to the service to the true God.[5]

---

1. Ibid., 318, 322, 325.

2. Cf. Acts 17:16-34.

3. E.g. Justin Martyr (*The Second Apology of Justin*, 8:3, 10, 13:3) in A. Roberts, J. Donaldson and A.C. Coxe, *The Ante-Nicene Fathers, Vol.I : Translations of the Writings of the Fathers Down to AD 325*, The apostolic fathers with Justin Martyr and Irenaeus (Oak Harbor: Logos Research Systems, 1997) 191.

4. Allen, 'Chinese Character and Missionary Methods', 318, Oxford, Bodleian Library, Roland Allen archives, USPG X622. See D.A. Carson's comment how biblical writers made reference to individuals, even though [these] 'quotations from Cleanthes in Acts 17:28, Menander in 1 Corinthians 15:33, Epimenides in Titus 1:12, or 1 Enoch in Jude 14-15 are not introduced as Scripture,' in D.A. Carson, *Collected Writings on Scripture* (Nottingham: Apollos [IVP], 2010) 29.

5. G.R. Evans and J.R. Wright, *The Anglican Tradition: a handbook of sources*

There are similarities and differences in Allen's approach. Rather than telling the Chinese that they were worshipping demons (even though Allen believed that elements of demonology did exist in the Chinese mindset) yet he chose a different way to challenge them in a constructive and positive style. On this point, he said that it is 'surely a mistake for the missionary to appear to make it his chief business to attack and undermine these'[6] accepted views of their ancient ways, religious systems and educational practices. Herbert Giles, similarly, says:

> In the hour of battle the God of ancient China was as much a participator in the fight as the God of Israel in the Old Testament:– God is on your side! – was the cry which stimulated King Wu to break down the opposing ranks of Shang.[7]

As Giles sought to show areas of similarity between the biblical text and aspects of Chinese religion, so Allen set out 'not to uproot the old system, but to reform it by the inculcation of sound Christian principles'.[8] By doing this, he maintained that instinct of conservatism, which continues to remain within the boundaries that have been set by the previous generations. Chinese culture and Allen's missionary method appear to agree with the ancient proverb 'Do not remove the ancient landmark which your fathers have set' (Proverbs 22:28, NKJV).

Secondly, the rejection of disorder by the Chinese culture presupposes the characteristic of the people's 'love of propriety'.[9] This Chinese characteristic he defines in reference to their belief in an authoritative administration which functions through a hierarchical structure. He summarizes this characteristic: 'One of the first questions which they put to a missionary is, "Who sent you?"'[10] Essentially, this position presupposes distrust towards any well-intentioned person who sets out to evangelize yet operates out of a context of self-promotion by not

---

(London: SPCK, 1991) 78; Gregory the Great, Bishop of Rome (590-604) *Letter to Abbot Mellitus*, Doctrinal Documents, 1102 (Oak Harbor: Logos Research Systems, 1997).

6. Allen, 'Chinese Character and Missionary Methods', 318, Oxford, Bodleian Library, Roland Allen archives, USPG X622.

7. Herbert A. Giles, *Religions of Ancient China* (London: Archibald Constable, 1905) 19-20.

8. Allen, 'Chinese Character and Missionary Methods', 319, Oxford, Bodleian Library, Roland Allen archives, USPG X622.

9. Ibid., 322.

10. Ibid., 323.

being 'formally admitted by the superior authority'.[1] Here is the point at which Allen delineates the importance for missionaries to present an understanding that they are members of the Church, which is one, holy, catholic and apostolic, in order to explain its relevance as a historic faith. He went on to emphasize that missionaries

> must refrain from presenting the doctrine of Christ to them as a purely Western system, or the worship of the Church in a purely Western form, so that to understand it and join in it heartily would imply a large knowledge of Western things, and stamp the worshipper as a follower of Western fashion.[2]

Thirdly, he surmised that the Chinese culture maintained a characteristic of 'union' among the people,[3] which made it easier to naturally accept the historic catholic teaching of 'the Visible Church', in contrast to what some missionaries were imposing, that is, an 'individualistic doctrine' that 'in the past it has succeeded only in weakening and impeding the progress of the Gospel'.[4] What he was stressing here was an aversion to an 'individualistic doctrine', which he thought gave the wrong impression of the gospel call to be only emphasizing a personal conversion to a faith that could somehow be disassociated from the Church. He noticed that many Chinese converts regarded themselves as belonging only to the specific denominational mission that had an influence on their conversion process in which 'each of whom stands or falls by himself',[5] which was a concept foreign to their cultural concept of belonging to a society. From one perspective, his emphasis on the Church's catholicity and apostolicity gave him reason to confront this form, which he described as 'congregationalism',[6] while from another, to argue for an indigenous Chinese Church which could view themselves as being in 'union' with a global Christianity, that is, a local (particular) society – connected *with* not disassociated *from* – the one, holy, catholic and apostolic Church. This was his main point which he argued at the beginning of this paper when pointing out that the 'object of this paper is to suggest by what methods certain characteristics of the Chinese may be brought more fully into

---

1. Ibid.
2. Ibid.
3. Ibid., 318, 322, 325.
4. Ibid, 325.
5. Ibid., 326.
6. Ibid., 327.

the service of the Christian Church'.[7] For Allen, these three Chinese characteristics – conservative instinct, love of propriety, and union – were inherent culturally and would enhance and provide a contribution to the universal Church. This stance, in 1903, is also echoed later by another Anglo-Catholic at the World Missionary Conference in Edinburgh, in 1910, when Charles Gore argued that:

> all Churches hold the same faith, use the same Scriptures, celebrate the same sacraments, and inhere in the same universal religion, each local Church should from the first have the opportunity of developing a local character and colour. . . . In this way can 'the glory and honour of all nations' – that is, their own distinctive genius and its products – best be brought within the circle of the Holy City.[8]

In summary, Allen's cross-cultural missiology sought to contextualize gospel ministry, firstly, by proclaiming that Christianity is a historic faith which incorporates its converts into a global Church. This did *not* mean that the Chinese converts were to be culturally semi-Europeanized. His missionary ecclesiological method sought to find areas of common ground between Chinese religious thought and world Christianity, such as, aspects of Confucian teaching which he believed to be compatible with Christian theology. On one hand, when Allen's analysis disclosed continuity between these faiths his *apologia* was to show how there exists transcendent principles that provide a basis for unity. On the other hand, when he found deficiencies within Chinese religious thought, he took a counter-cultural position by confronting what he believed to be erroneous and instead advanced biblical principles. Secondly, he confronted Chang Chih Tung's assumption that Western learning was only practical and not morally based. Allen's *apologia* asserted how the Christian faith and its morals were foundational to Western civilization's ethos and that this 'is the lesson which the East needs to learn'.[9] We saw that his prediction currently is taking shape today after some of China's communist leaders and the Chinese Academy of the Social Sciences willingly admitted how

---

7. Ibid., 317.
8. Bishop Charles Gore & his colleagues, 'Education in relation to the Christianisation of National Life,' Report of Commission III, 244; Brian Stanley, 'From "the poor heathen" to "the glory and honour of all nations": Vocabularies of Race and Custom in Protestant Missions, 1844-1928,' *International Bulletin of Missionary Research*, 34 (1) (2010) 8.
9. Allen, 'The Progress of Education in China', 665.

the Christian faith sparked the West's advancements, in general, and its form of capitalism and democratic politics, in particular. Thirdly, he perceived that the only way to evangelize China effectively was through the establishment of the indigenous Church throughout its culture by its own people. Again, his perception was accurate as is now evidenced today through the underground house-church movement, which has spread throughout China. Although it is difficult to accurately assess the growth of Christianity in China, as some estimates range between 20-50 million, the U.S. State Department's survey of the International Religious Freedom (towards the end of the twentieth century) estimated that Christians made up about 100 million of China's population.[1] That said, Allen's belief in the spontaneous expansion of the Church hinged on the indigenous Church principle which is well-established in China today. And, fourthly, Allen's *apologia* for the Church's unity, as expressed through its apostolicity and catholicity, provided a basis for common ground engagement with China's cultural affinity with things harmonious and ancient.

---

1. Philip Jenkins, *The Next Christendom: The Coming of Global Christianity* (Oxford: Oxford University Press, 2002) 70.

3. From Systems to Principles

How Allen's Missionary Experiences in China Shaped his Missiology (1895-1947)

The principles of freedom served as a major influence within the Protestant missionary movement. The missionaries' efforts of service from below stemmed from their desire to practise the principle of the golden rule: 'Therefore, whatever you want men to do to you do also to them, for this is the Law and the Prophets' (Matthew 7:12). In the midst of their grassroots involvement with the people, many missionaries were perplexed by the colonial practice of the slave trade. The evangelical emphasis on 'freedom' in Christ seemed disingenuous in light of the practice of slavery. Basically, it was Christian missionaries who helped pioneer the anti-slavery movement:

> The belief in the freedom of the individual went hand in hand with the advocacy of free trade. The evangelical missionary societies, far from being the harbingers of imperialism at this time played a key part in outlawing slavery.[1]

That said, missionary motivation of compassion flowed from an evangelical awareness to spread Christianity throughout the world. This 'world Christianity' impetus began to encourage eighteenth-century Protestant missionary societies to think more globally. The 'voluntary missionary societies', which had begun to emerge at this time, though springing up within a conspicuously colonial context, tended to create a grassroots movement from below which looked to the generosity and compassion of its churches and individual humanitarian efforts.[2] And, as

---

1. Richard Evans, 'Formal and Informal Empire in the 19th Century', Gresham College lecture:
   http://www.youtube.com/watch?v=7di4zMGIZY8&feature=g-vI.
2. See H.P. Thompson, *Into All Lands: The History of the Society for the Propagation of the Gospel in Foreign Parts 1701-1950* (London: SPCK, 1951) 15-18; (eds) Kevin Ward and Brian Stanley, *The Church Mission Society and*

these societies began to minister cross-culturally they were confronted with various problematic issues imposed from above by the colonial powers. To some extent, Robert Young, a contemporary postcolonial theorist, makes this very point: 'Globalization operates from below in a way that contests the forces of domination and globalization from above with increasing effect.'[1] Although Young's main focus here concerned later issues of injustice and inequality, yet in similar ways during the eighteenth century, various 'voluntary' mission societies recognized the need to address issues of injustice and inequality that stemmed from colonial hegemony. How did these voluntary missionary societies originate and what type of people comprised the organizations?

The Church Missionary Society (CMS)

The Church Missionary Society (CMS) originated on 12 April 1799, when a group of evangelical clergymen and laymen:

> resolved that, it "being a duty highly incumbent upon every Christian to endeavor to propagate the knowledge of the Gospel among the Heathen," a society to achieve that end be constituted: the Society for Missions to Africa and the East.[2]

At the helm of the CMS was the evangelical rector of Clapham, John Venn, who presided as the chair for this new organization. The eighteenth-century evangelical revival had already permeated the English countryside through the preaching ministries of John Wesley and George Whitefield.[3] Now there existed a call for mission beyond the revival's earlier vision. In time, this evangelical renewal produced a dynamic group referred to as the 'Clapham Sect' – members of which included William Wilberforce, Charles Grant, Lord Teignmouth, James Stephen, Granville Sharp, Henry Thornton, Macaulay and Venn. It was Venn who believed that this call to extensive missionary activity

World Christianity 1799-1999, Studies in the History of Christian Missions (Grand Rapids: Eerdmans, 2000) 15-42; Daniel O'Connor *et al.*, *Three Centuries of Mission: The United Society for the Propagation of the Gospel 1701-2000* (London: Continuum, 2000) 7-44; Stephen Neill, *A History of Christian Missions* (London: Penguin Books, 1986) 222-72.

1. Young, *Postcolonialism*, 108.
2. Ward and Stanley, *Church Mission Society*, 'Introduction', 1.
3. See Henry D. Rack, *Reasonable Enthusiast: John Wesley and the Rise of Methodism* (London: Epworth Press, 1989).

by the CMS could address the need with this newer vision. Even so, he recognized the need to be connected to the established Church of England, and yet with this distinctive, that it is 'founded upon the Church principle, not the High Church principle'.[4] Shenk comments that by 'one phrase he staked out a position' which clearly distinguished the CMS from the earlier established societies, 'the Society for the Propagation of Christian Knowledge/Society for the Propagation of the Gospel (SPCK/ SPG) and the London Missionary Society (LMS).'[5] It would be inaccurate to think that the CMS was a reactionary society against a High Anglican ethos. In actuality, it became noted for its engagement with confronting the slave trade, extending the missionary enterprise to India, founding the British and Foreign Bible Society and the eventual establishment of a 'model colony' in Sierra Leone.[6]

Society for the Propagation of the Gospel (SPG)

In terms of current analysis that highlights the missiological history of High Church Anglicanism, Daniel O'Connor's *Three Centuries of Mission* is a major contribution towards understanding this missionary movement's history since its inception in 1701, when it was formerly called the Society for the Propagation of the Gospel in Foreign Parts.[7] The Society's origination stemmed through William III's Charter on 16 June 1701.[8] This Charter mirrored all the earlier English charters dating back to 1482, which sought to 'conquer, occupy and possess' all the lands inhabited by 'heathens and infidels'.[9] A message of Christian mission is portrayed in the Society's seal, which bears the inscription from the Book of Acts, 'Come over and help us'.[10] In response to this missionary call, O'Connor says that the first two SPG missionaries who left for North

4. Wilbert R. Shenk, *Henry Venn: Missionary Statesman* (Maryknoll: Orbis Books, 1983) 2.

5. Ibid.

6. See Ernest M. Howse, *Saints in Politics: The 'Clapham Sect' and the Growth of Freedom* (London: George Allen & Unwin, 1971); cf. (eds.) F.L. Cross & E.A. Livingstone, *Dictionary of the Christian Church* (Peabody: Hendrickson Publishers, 1997) 357.

7. O'Connor, *Three Centuries of Mission*; see also, Thompson, *Into All Lands*, 15-18.

8. O'Connor, *Three Centuries of Mission*, 7.

9. Ibid.

10. 'And a vision appeared to Paul in the night. A man of Macedonia stood and pleaded with him, saying, "Come over to Macedonia and help us".' (Acts 16: 9, NKJV).

America – Patrick Gordon and George Keith – when they set sail on the *Centurion*, 24 April 1702, and arriving 43 days later, had an unfortunate turn of events when Gordon, who 'was appointed by the Society to the parish of Jamaica, Long Island', died of a fever.[1] However, Gordon's idea for 'a global vision for the propagation of the Gospel' was undeniably disseminated overseas.[2]

O'Connor explains how the Charter authoritatively specified the need to raise financial support through collections for 'the better Support and Maintenance of an Orthodox Clergy in Foreign Parts' and discloses how 'an Orthodox clergy' descriptively emphasized the 'High Church tradition' of apostolic succession, traditional church order, biblical teaching, liturgical practice, sacrament celebration; rudiments which necessarily function with the assumption that 'no Bibles be sent by the Society into the Plantations without Common Prayer Books bound up with them'.[3] As missionaries were sent to establish mission churches they expected to train their converts by using these copies of Bibles and prayer books not only in North America but also in New Zealand, Australia, Canada, South Africa and the Caribbean.[4] It was this Society's missionary enterprise that significantly influenced Roland Allen in the late nineteenth century.

Allen's Missionary Experience in China

Allen's articulation of his missionary experiences in China and how these informed his missionary ecclesiology is made clear in his letters both during and after his ministry in China,[5] his chronicle of the Boxer Rebellion entitled *The Siege of the Peking Legations* (1901)[6] papers he presented,[7] and subsequent articles he wrote concerning China.[8] All of

---

1. O'Connor, *Three Centuries of Mission*, 5-6.

2. Ibid., 6

3. Ibid., 7; see 'Committee for Receiving Proposals', 31.3 (1702) Oxford, Bodleian Library, USPG X622.

4. O'Connor, *Three Centuries of Mission*, 9.

5. See Oxford, Bodleian Library, USPG X622, Boxes 1-3.

6. Allen, *The Siege of the Peking Legations*, 1901.

7. See 'The Development of Independent Native Churches', Box 3: 1; 'The Work of the Missionary in Preparing the Way for Independent Native Churches' (November 11-12, 1903) Box 2, File J: 4, Rhodes House, Oxford.

8. Allen, 'Of Some of the Causes Which Led to the Preservation of the Foreign Legations in Peking', *The Cornhill Magazine*, Box 2, File J: 1, the Church of England Mission (September 27, 1900) 754-776; Allen, 'Of Some of the

these sources disclose the experiences of cross-cultural mission in China and how this influenced his thought and practice. In fact, it was during his ministry there that his vision and mission for developing indigenous churches began to take shape. Before analyzing his missionary experiences in China from 1895-1903, it is helpful to take note of a summary statement Allen made at the conclusion of his ministry time in China:

> The Chinese are apt to compare the antiquity of their religion with the modern character of ours. . . . If Christianity is to be presented acceptably to the Chinese, surely it ought to be through Chinese teachers who have remained Chinese in thought and education, but whose Chinese thought is permeated with Christian doctrine and belief. So one might find an Apostle.[9]

Causes Which Led to the Preservation of the Foreign Legations in Peking', the Church of England Mission, *The Cornhill Magazine*, no.53/491, Box 2, File J: 1, (November 1900) 669-680; Allen, 'Of Some of the Causes which led to the Preservation of the Foreign Legations in Peking', *The Cornhill Magazine*, no.54 (new series) no.492 (December 1900) 754-76, Box 2, File J; Allen, 'Of some of the Conclusions which may be drawn from the Siege of the Foreign Legations in Peking', *The Cornhill Magazine*, no.56, New Series, no.494 (February 1901) 202-12; Allen, 'The Churches of the Future', *The Guardian* (June 18, 1902); Allen, 'The Churches of the Future', *The Guardian*, (June 25, 1902); Allen, 'The Unceasing Appeal for Men for Foreign Missions,' *The Guardian* (July 23, 1902); Allen, 'Colonial Church & Missionary News: A Church Policy for North China – I,' LIEN (Roland Allen's incognito name while writing from China) *The Guardian* (1902) 879, Box 1, File B; Allen, 'Colonial Church & Missionary News: A Church Policy for North China – II,' in *The Guardian* (July 1902) Box 1, File B; Allen, 'The Anglican Mission at Yung Ch'ing, North China', Yung Ch'ing, article submitted by Rev. W.C. Allen, Exeter College, to Oxford: Sheppard Printer (February 20, 1903) Box 2, File J: 3, Rhodes House, Oxford; Allen, 'The Chinese Character and Missionary Methods', *The East and The West* (July 1903) 317-329, Box 2, File J: 35;Allen, 'The Progress of Education in China,' *Cornhill*, Box 2, File J: 5A (1908) 655-665 & 5B (proof 1-11); Allen, 'Opium Suppression in China', *The Church Times* (May 1, 1908) Box 1, File B; Allen, 'Missionary Policy in China,' *The Church Times* (November 19, 1909) Box 1, File B; Allen, 'The Message of the Christian Church to Confucianists', *The East and The West* (October 1909) 437-452, Box 2, File J: 7; Allen, 'The Imperialism of Missions', *The Living Church* (January 26, 1929) Box 1, File B: 14; Review by Allen of 'A History of Christian Missions in China', K.S. Latourette, *Church Quarterly Review*, (January 1930) Oxford, Bodleian Library, USPG X622, Box 2, File J: 32.

9.   Allen, 'Chinese Character and Missionary Methods', 317-329, Oxford, Bodleian Library, USPG X622, Box 2, File J: 35.

This demonstrates how Allen began to formulate a missiology that anticipated the emergence of an indigenous Christianity, which incorporated the apostolic 'doctrine and belief' and which would eventually influence the thinking of Chinese Christians concerning the development of their own churches, local leaders, theologians, and those who will do the apostolic ministry of Church expansion. For Allen, foreign missionaries had the opportunities to evangelize and plant churches, ordain and equip indigenous leadership and then immediately retire from that region to establish churches in newer areas. He believed that once these new Christians embraced the Christian faith – not necessarily the forms and customs of the foreign missionaries – then a truly Chinese Christianity would develop. He would view that as his mission accomplished! And yet, when he first arrived in China in 1895, he did not naturally think this way. What, then, were the contributing factors which can be attributed to this change? The answer to this question emerges from his cross-cultural analysis and experience, which is currently the focus of this intellectual biography.

Several decades later, while writing his unpublished work, *The Family Rite* (1943), he reflected on his intellectual and spiritual journey:

> when at the first opportunity I went to Peking to join the Mission there, questions soon began to arise. . . . The first question was, "How long will it take us to establish the Church in China, if we proceed as we are now proceeding?"[1]

He quickly began to question a total reliance upon Western missionaries, along with their 'mission station' methodologies to evangelize the Chinese people. Consequently, while teaching young men at a Chinese clergy school, he was appointed to open for the diocesan region of North China, he began to explore different methods.[2] It was during this time of training indigenous leadership in North East China that he recognized the dilemma between supervising a well-intentioned institutional ministry and planting 'the principles of the gospel' among indigenous leadership. Throughout this next section, his ideas for necessary missional adjustments will be discussed within the historical narrative of his time in China.

1. Roland Allen, 'The Family Rite', unpublished work written in a large notebook (1943) Oxford, Bodleian Library, USPG X622, Box 7.
2. Roland Allen later addressed a conference for the Church Missionary Society at Swanwick and explained his experiences at the clergy school, *Church Missionary Review* (June 1927); also, 'First Impressions', *The North China Mission Quarterly* (October 1896) 53-56.

A Closer Look at Allen's Arrival in China

Concerning his arrival in China, it is clear that he set sail from England towards the end of January 1895 and reached Tientsin, 22 March.[3] Bishop Charles Scott reports the following of his arrival in 1895:

> We have been cheered since the ice broke up by the arrival first, of the Rev. Roland Allen and next, of Miss Wollaston and Nurse Sands, all of whom will, I expect, accompany us to Peking. Mr Allen has been hard at work on the language for some five weeks.[4]

From the outset Allen recognized the need for developing a cross-cultural missiology. With his Oxford educational background in the classics, he was well groomed linguistically, and thus prepared to learn Mandarin. As Bishop Scott observed: 'he began to learn Mandarin quickly and well: in only a few years he was already distinguished as a "3,000 – character man" and was preaching in Chinese.'[5] He continued preaching and teaching within these developmental years in China, and in particular his mentoring of young men as catechists, he increasingly became concerned that the expansion of the Church – a concept that saturated his thinking throughout his life – which appeared to be an impossibility based upon the predictable Anglican missionary methodologies currently used in China. This led him to thoroughly analyze these methods through the lens of what he believed to be a transcendent model.

Allen's Analysis of Missionary Methods and Systems

He increasingly began to question various methods of leadership training, which he had been using, whilst serving in Peking. In his various roles, such as, the primary missionary in charge of its Anglican Mission with its English congregation, the chaplain to the British Legation and its chapel, director of a day school for non-Christians, printing press supervisor and the clergy school which he wrote was the 'college of Peking for the training of Chinese youths for the Native Ministry of the Church',[6] he received first-hand knowledge of what was working and what was not.

---

3. Hubert Allen, *Roland Allen*, 22.

4. *Quarterly Paper of the Mission of the Church of England in North China*, vol.III, (1895) 17, 27, 48, USPG X 622, Oxford, Bodleian Library.

5. Hubert Allen, *Roland Allen*, 27; also, Hubert Allen parenthetically stated: 'This fluency was one reason that Bishop Scott was later to put forward his name for preferment as Bishop for the new see at Shantung' (27).

6. Roland Allen's report for the North China Mission, *Annual Report for 1897*, 3, Oxford, Bodleian Library, USPG X622.

In order to understand Allen's missiological journey it is helpful, again, to refer to his comments in *The Family Rite* (1943), in which he reflects back on this time in China:

> I was teaching a few boys in a theological school to become catechists, all supported by Mission funds, with a view to their ordination later. Looking at that, I said, "We cannot get far on this basis". So my thought became concentrated on the Church, and I began to think how it was that St Paul was not hampered and tied up in his work as we are. He established Churches wherever he went, and certainly did not proceed by way of Clergy Schools or Theological Colleges.[1]

What may seem to be a 'radical' statement concerning the benefits and hindrances of theological colleges and clergy schools, as if he sought to suggest some novel approach, is rooted in his reflection on Pauline missiology. For Allen, he was convinced that Paul was the authoritative example for understanding the 'spontaneous expansion' of the mission of the Church according to a New Testament design. It is not that he disliked theological colleges *per se*, but rather that he saw no evidence from the ministry of the Apostle Paul for the establishment of theological colleges. Instead, he concluded that Paul planted and established *local churches* and that the spontaneous growth and extension of these churches had not stemmed from some centralized theological school. Hence, he reasoned that 'the establishment of a Chinese branch of the Church of Christ'[2] should be built upon the leadership and mentoring process that naturally occurs 'from within' the local setting, and then flows 'out from' indigenous churches, which, he contended, should be self-governing, self-supporting and self-propagating.

Allen later argued this very point in *Educational Principles and Missionary Methods* (1919) following an interview with a mission priest who had shown him a dozen of his 'most successful missionaries in the villages', but who had *no* theological training from diocesan colleges, yet had converted many people from within the surrounding villages.[3] Afterwards, the mission priest asked him 'How long do you suppose that these people have been

---

1. Allen, *The Family Rite*, Oxford, Bodleian Library, USPG, Box 7.
2. Roland Allen, 'Chinese Character and Missionary Methods,' 329, Oxford, Bodleian Library, USPG X622, Box 2, File J: 35.
3. Roland Allen, *Educational Principles and Missionary Methods*, Library of Historic Theology (London: Robert Scott Roxburghe House, 1919) 98, Introduction by Bishop Charles Gore.

Christians?' He was shocked to hear that they had only been Christians for one year. 'What!' he responded, 'Do you make teachers in a year?' The priest answered, 'Yes . . . and the best teachers we have got'.[4] Upon further enquiry, he was told how these new converts evangelized the other villages that were influenced not only by the words they conveyed through gospel ministry but because these villagers saw evidence of their transformed lives, and when asked what actually produced the transformation, these men said 'Christ'.[5] Allen's argument concluded that

> There can be no true education without activity. It is the business of the educator to excite, rather than to restrain, activity. . . . It is easy for us at the first to make ourselves the controlling force to arrogate to ourselves the sole right to freedom of action, to teach our converts passively to receive what we are pleased to give. At the end of that path is sterility and impotence, not manhood but perpetual infancy; or else, as powers grow, a great outburst of revolutionary fury against an authority which has abused its powers.[6]

The 'perpetual infancy' of indigenous converts, according to Allen, was the paternalistic 'Nanny State' of the mission station system. He found within Paul's missionary methodology a quite different philosophy of ministry. The statement above highlights two important points in his argument: (1) the validity of a 'foreign' missionary to plant churches and (2) the 'foreign' missionary's opportunity to *empower* and *not control* the first indigenous converts to evangelize their own local villages. He believed that the spontaneous expansion of the Church to produce multiple churches resided in the empowerment of the local clergy and laity *not* by placing any dependence upon the foreign missionaries, be they recently imported, theologically trained graduates from distant colleges who have little or no knowledge of the cultural setting, or, paternalistic missionaries who think they are indispensable. He believed that Paul, as a 'foreign missionary', was divinely called to plant churches within the provinces, but also that he made himself dispensable to these local churches in terms of their local governance and extension. Another example of his developing thought towards indigenous churches, in 1901, which he called 'independent native churches', can be seen in his 'The Development of Independent Native Churches *and their federation in union with the Church of England*. Here, he argues for the independence of indigenous

4. Ibid.
5. Ibid., 98.
6. Ibid., 98-99.

churches from a *welfare dependency mindset*: 'above all things we must avoid any appearance of desire to keep Native Communities in dependence upon us; any appearance of desire to establish a papacy.'[1] He challenged his own Anglican Communion not to look or act in any papal fashion. In other words, it was this time in China that helped him to rethink the normal practice of the Church of England, which exerted paternalistic control over the local converts' development. He argued rather that the Pauline method established 'from the beginning' an empowerment practice set out to equip the locals to take responsibility immediately for their own churches. He believed that Paul was successful in the provinces because he taught and practiced this indigenous principle of self-government.

Allen's Vision for a Chinese Indigenous Church

At the commencement of training leadership for an indigenous Chinese Church, Allen began to structure this training within the 'college at Peking' with these eight local young men mentioned earlier who were prepared to be catechists. The methodology he used at this time remained largely conventional. Even though he began to question how some of the expected criteria for measuring a catechist's theoretical development and other educational methodologies appeared to be an imposition of foreign standards, he did *not* change the Anglican Mission's order:

> I do not think the Mission ought to be satisfied with less than a year's training in theology proper after the preparation before the student can be licensed as a catechist; and again another and longer period before the diaconate. . . .[2]

His devotedness to a classical Anglican training also included commitment to a 'patristic approach' – an emphasis on Church history from the first three centuries. Indeed, he noticed that students expressed:

> a good deal of interest . . . especially in certain translations which I am making of portions of the Apostolic Fathers. My teacher who translates for me got quite excited over the letter of the Smyrnaeans concerning the death of Polycarp.[3]

1. Allen, 'The Development of Independent Native Churches *and their federation in union with the Church of England*', USPG X622, Box 3:1, Oxford, Bodleian Library.
2. Hubert Allen, *Roland Allen*, 29.
3. Ibid.

His excitement about translating into Chinese this part of early Church history arose from his belief in apostolic and global Christianity and its relevance to the Chinese Church. He was especially keen to show how Christianity is a historic, 'global' faith, which began in the East before it moved to the West.

Although he practised the conventional approach to theological training with these Chinese men he began to recognize how the structural system was effective to prepare leadership for local authority such as the diaconate but was *ineffective* to properly prepare trans-local authority. Reflection upon his work in China, especially the overwhelming challenge of Christian mission within this enormous country, caused him to consider the whole educational system for those preparing for ministry within the Church at large, and the Church of England's missions in particular. In 1901, he wrote: 'Our ideas of ordination are borrowed from England. But if so, our present ordination preparation is not a good one. Our theological colleges do not turn out apostles and evangelists, but deacons.'[4] This assessment of the nature of leadership already established sought to produce local church ministries and they essentially focused on the necessary 'maintenance' model of the local diaconate, and yet, actually minimized an organic context where church planting missionaries – evangelists and apostles – could be nurtured and developed for the 'mission' model of *trans-local ministries* or as Murray argues for a proactive focus 'on mission rather than maintenance'.[5] In other words, these colleges were designed to train its future leaders for the Church to be 'maintenance not mission' minded (note: this will be unpacked in *Roland Allen: A Theology of Mission*). Allen began to question a methodology that seemed to be myopic when it came to preparing future leaders who were called to plant churches and extend the Christian faith beyond the existing borders.

Another aspect he used in China as a teaching method was photography.[6] Hubert Allen's collection of many of these photos provides a context for the viewer even though, as he pointed out to me: 'Tantalizingly . . . none of them have any notes to indicate their

---

4. Original draft was worded as 'Our ideas of ordination borrowed [from England]. But if so our present ordination [preparation is] not a good one. Our [Theological Colleges] do not turn out apostles, evangelists <u>but deacons</u>.' Roland Allen, 'The Church in Japan', *Church Missionary Intelligencer* (1901) 6, Oxford, Bodleian Library, USPG X622, Box 2, File J: 2.

5. Stuart Murray, *Church Planting: Laying Foundations* (London: Paternoster Press, 1998) 242.

6. Hubert Allen, *Roland Allen*, 29-30.

subjects.'[1] By and large, Allen attempted to contextualize theological training by using some innovative ways of communication within a conventional context. Thus, he demonstrated his 'orderly' practice of an Anglican ethos early on in his missionary experiences. Nonetheless, it was during this period of training catechists for gospel ministry that he began to differentiate in his thinking, clearly, between the essentials of the Christian faith that needed to permeate Chinese thought and the non-essential Christian forms and customs which ought not to be imposed upon Chinese thought.

By 1902, he wrote two important articles for *The Guardian* entitled 'A Church Policy for North China' due to the Anglican Church's proposal to establish a 'new bishopric in Shantung', which, in principle, he agreed with: 'I value the foundation of the Shantung bishopric.'[2] And yet, he wanted to articulate various points that he believed the Anglican leadership needed to be aware of. Firstly, he believed that the Anglican Church and other denominational Churches would see this as appropriate in four ways: (1) on 'religious grounds' as a fulfillment of Christ's command; (2) on 'moral grounds' since the 'ancient faiths' were being undercut by 'the inrush of new Western learning' in China; (3) on 'philanthropic grounds' to improve social conditions; and 4) on 'social grounds' because the extent of Christianity's influence would naturally tend 'to the progress' of the Chinese population.[3] Conversely, he recognized the greater influence of the 'Roman Catholic and Nonconformist bodies'. This, he believed, ought to cause the Anglican Church to consider what policy to pursue.[4] That said, Allen proposed three points that he believed looked hopeful: (1) in light of the current court reforms, the population would definitely 'seek for a knowledge of Western affairs'; (2) that this 'widespread thirst for Western knowledge' would be hard to suppress even if these reforms eventually reverse back towards the former obstructionist position; and (3) that the 'local magistrates' preferred to appoint Protestant missionaries as teachers for their schools instead of the Roman Catholics who were 'more powerful' and expressed 'political entanglements' due to their 'reputation for interference' within the Chinese culture.[5] He then argued for the reasonableness of the 'middle position', which he believed to be

[handwritten margin note: Not then 'Manchester Guardian' at that time]

---

1. Interview with Hubert Allen on 4 February 2011; also, Hubert Allen, *Roland Allen*, 30.
2. Allen, 'A Church Policy for North China – I', (1902) 879; and also, Allen, 'A Church Policy for North China – II', (July 1) 902.
3. Ibid., 879.
4. Ibid.
5. Ibid.

'the key to the real purpose of the existence of the Anglican Church in the world'.[6] He argued that, by establishing a new bishopric in Shantung, the Anglican Church's commitment to 'historic Christianity' placed them as a body in a better position with Chinese appreciation of ancient history than the 'Protestant Nonconformists' on the one side, and yet on the other, the 'Roman Catholic methods' portrayed themselves as a 'despotic and intriguing body'[7] that many of the Chinese began to resent. His appeal argued for foreign missionaries who were willing to teach and administer the sacraments in this new bishopric until the people 'could offer a suitable man to the Bishop for ordination to the priesthood' and when the local body could do that then the missionary could 'retire to another field' in recognition that the indigenous body 'would be locally complete'.[8]

Here is early evidence of Allen's incipient development towards an indigenous approach to church-planting. And yet, his view of 'local' churches was not of a 'congregational' polity nature, but of an 'episcopal' form of government whereby 'two or three such communities . . . will not act separately, but will be able to meet together either as a whole or by delegates, and can then decide common matters in common council.'[9] This is apostolic order, according to Allen, because it maintains 'local' networking communities which function from 'the principle of mutual responsibility' and the 'principle of mutual support'[10] in union with the pastoral leadership of the diocesan bishop. This 'method' he believed would work well.

Additional Comments on The Siege of the Peking Legations (1901)

Referring back, chapter 2 disclosed specifics of Allen's personal account of the 'Boxer movement' of 1900. It was during this time that he began to recognize certain ideological differences between the East and the West and was challenged to understand these differences. Firstly, within months after the siege, he wrote some consecutive articles for *The Cornhill Magazine* explaining the context of what preceded and followed the siege, including some conclusions that could be extracted from these events.[11] The Chinese

---

6. Ibid.

7. Ibid.

8. Ibid.

9. Ibid.

10. Allen, 'Chinese Character and Missionary Methods', 317-329 (326).

11. Roland Allen, 'Of Some of the Causes' *The Cornhill Magazine* (September 27, 1900) 754-76; Allen, 'Of Some of the Causes', *Cornhill* (November 1900) 669-80; Allen, 'Of Some of the Causes', *Cornhill* (December 1900) 754-76;

Imperial troops 'were openly in favour of supporting the Boxers' and took great pleasure to attack all foreigners – British, French, Spanish, Italian, American, Japanese, German, Austrian, Russian – so much that Allen said:

> In China, to attack the foreigner means to attack everyone connected with him, and the attack extends not merely to the individual servant in foreign employ but to his whole household . . . guilt lies not only at the door of the individual offender – it extends to every member of his family, and vengeance is sought not only upon the individual but upon his kinsfolk.[1]

That said, after the Boxers began burning various customs office buildings and the Austrian Legation, evacuation from the various foreign legations and missions – Roman Catholic and Protestant – caused 'the allies' and 'native Christians' to find safety together at the British Legation and Prince Su's Palace, about which he said: 'Thus protected, there were within the defended area 473 civilians, 350 marines, and nearly 4,000 natives . . . throughout the two months of our siege. . . . '[2] During this siege, he was perplexed by an action taken by the 'religious' Boxers when they burned the 'Hanlin' – a sacred place within Chinese culture – the very place where 'the first library in the kingdom' was stored, and yet, ironically it was the foreigners and Christians who refused to damage this sacred place, for, as Allen said they would see this as an 'act of aggression against the Imperial Majesty such as we shrank from committing'.[3] Nevertheless, the Boxers 'set it on fire', which destroyed the whole library including 'the great dictionary of Yung Lo' and took their chances with this 'act of insurrection' in order to place blame on the foreigners.[4] He questioned the religious motivations of those who would desecrate such an ancient sacred place. Even though he recognized a growing anger on the part of many of the Chinese against foreign presence, especially due to the growth of Chinese Christianity, he was surprised to see how the Boxers' religious character turned to 'frenzy . . . like madmen . . . ' attacking with 'ancient pattern of sword and spear' against the 'foreign weapons' of the Peking Legations, the Boxers expected the 'spirit soldiers' to descend 'from heaven in thousands upon thousands and tens of thousands'.[5] During and after the two-month siege Allen wrote:

Allen, 'Of Some of the Causes' *Cornhill* (February 1901) 202–12, Oxford, Bodleian Library, Roland Allen archives, USPG X622.

1. Allen, 'Of Some of the Causes' (September 27, 1900) 754, 759.
2. Ibid., 760–61.
3. Ibid., 765.
4. Ibid., 765–66.
5. Ibid., 770; Allen, 'Of Some of the Causes' (November 1900) 672–73.

The attack on the north cathedral in the city failed, the attack on Tientsin failed, and men and guns were withdrawn from the city to meet the expected advance of the Allies. The soldiers grew weary, discontented, and dispirited. Boxer magic failed; the Boxers fell before foreign bullets like ordinary mortals; the spirit warriors did not descend from heaven to aid them; the gods were plainly unable or unwilling to help them against the foreigner's arts.[6]

Although Allen and all the foreigners who withstood these attacks were extremely thankful when the allied forces arrived to end the siege, there is little that is triumphalist in his articles. Instead, he reflects upon the Chinese belief and influence of ancient spirits. Indeed, while he was contemplating this belief system, a discussion ensued with 'the head writer in the British Legation'. He wondered how such 'an astute woman like the Empress, and ministers, who for thirty years had been in constant contact with Western thought, could really believe in the Boxer claims'. The response was as follows: 'That is just where you foreigners always have, and always will, go wrong: you cannot understand that all the Chinese, even if they have been Christian for generations, all at the bottom of their hearts believe in devils.'[7] He took that conversation to heart in 1900 and began to immerse himself over the years so to better understand Chinese religion and culture, particularly their belief in spirit possession.

Immediately after the Boxer Uprising, Allen went on furlough back to England for approximately two years (1900-02). During this time, he married Mary 'Beatrice' Tarleton on 17 October 1901. Hubert Allen writes that: at 'the end of 1902, after his very extended furlough . . . the recently married couple set sail together in S.S. *Kiaoutchou*; and, in December, they settled down at the mission station in Yung Ch'ing.'[8] It was also during his furlough that he also began to reflect more on the expansion of the early Church. He also wanted his missionary observations and analysis in China to be scrutinized in light of Pauline practice. Because of his interest in biblical theology and Church history, he turned to the work of various contemporary scholars 'after his second return from China'.[9]

---

6. Allen, 'Of Some of the Causes' (27 September 1900) 770.

7. Allen, 'Of Some of the Causes' (November 1900) 674.

8. Hubert Allen, *Roland Allen*, 70.

9. Ake Talltorp, 'Sacraments for Growth in Mission: Eucharistic Faith and Practice in the Theology of Roland Allen', *Transformation: An International Journal of Holistic Mission Studies*, 29(3) 214-24 (July 2012) endnote 10 (222).

Summary

The phenomenal extension of nineteenth-century Western mission societies throughout the world made it possible for the Church of England to expand its influence beyond its borders, which precipitated the formation of a global Anglican Communion. The Anglican missionary movement created the SPCK, SPG and the CMS to further its missionary undertakings in these new frontiers. Within the context of this expansion into China, Roland Allen emerged as a young, energetic and significant missionary educator. The Anglican missionary ecclesiology of Allen in the early part of his ministry in China reveals him as a rather conventional missionary. His desire to serve the Church in this capacity conveyed his willingness to work within the mission station system and to promote its missiological goals. However, it did not take long for Allen to realize that the only way for Christianity in general, and Anglicanism in particular, to expand throughout China would be if the Chinese converts would evangelize their own people, plant their own churches and reproduce their own churches without foreign intervention. This began the incipient formation of his understanding for the planting of the 'native' or indigenous Church. His argument was that the Anglican model actually possessed the potential to accomplish this task since its ecclesiastical structure was flexible enough to provide room for diocesan reproduction on a smaller scale within its own provincial setting. Though he argued against the Church of England's general criteria for what constitutes proper theological training of its leadership within foreign locations, he still maintained a certain conventional level of determining the theological and characteristic competence required of indigenous leaders.

His experiences within the siege of the Peking Legations were an education in and of itself for helping to shape his missiology. While he remained a British patriot in the midst of the fighting, he attempted to understand the growing anger that had precipitated among the Chinese population due to foreign occupation. This contributed to his developing missionary ecclesiology, which promoted a methodology for sending gospel ministry to establish the Church but refrained from imposing Western culture and customs upon the Chinese. He did make, however, accommodation for those Chinese representatives who desired to implement Western education within their institutions but refused to directly initiate anything which they did not desire.

4. Allen's Analysis of
St Paul's Missionary Principles

*The Influence of Pauline Missionary Ecclesiology
on Allen's Thought (1902-1912)*

An assessment of the contributing scholars who assisted Roland Allen's formation of a *principled* approach rather than a *systems* approach to missiology is scrutinized in the context of nineteenth-century thought. As a former missionary to China with the *Church of England Mission in North China* (1895-1903), his preliminary surveillance of contemporary missionary practices motivated the formulation for his theology of the indigenous Church, articulated through what he believed was a proper hermeneutic for Pauline theology and practice. In order to understand this way of interpretation, it is incumbent to ascertain who were the key authors and missiologists that Allen was reading and conversing with during this time.

He was particularly interested in the Pauline scholarship of William Mitchell Ramsay and Adolf von Harnack. When looking at the influence of these two theologians upon the thought of Allen, one must come to terms with his catholicity, as evidenced in his eclectic style of doing missionary theology. Moreover, it would be wrong to assume that he uncritically embraced all the ideas of these men, who were, as Talltorp states 'both clearly independent of each other'.[1]

The fingerprints of Ramsay's interpretation of Pauline missiology are evident throughout *Missionary Methods: St Paul's or Ours?*[2] Not only is Ramsay's influence implicitly interspersed throughout the book, but no less than fifteen times, Allen makes substantial reference to Ramsay's *St Paul the Traveller and the Roman Citizen*[3] within the text of *Missionary Methods*. What was the nature of this influence?

---

1. Ibid., 217.
2. For sake of brevity this book will be referred to as *Missionary Methods*.
3. William Mitchell Ramsay, *St Paul the Traveller and the Roman Citizen* (London: Hodder and Stoughton, 1895/96. Repr., 1902). Other significant books of Ramsay were *The Church in the Roman Empire before AD 170* (1893) and *The Cities and Bishoprics of Prygia* (1895).

Ramsay's Pauline missiology and Harnack's discussion of the progress of the Church helped Allen to understand how the early Church expanded within an imperial *milieu*. Their ideas about the nature of Paul's missionary travels, the interpretation of charismatic activities which empowered the early Church, apostolic mission and practice, the imperial infrastructure and the socio-religious character of the Roman Empire, contributed and shaped Allen's own missiology. Indeed, their thinking ultimately informed what he believed were the necessary 'missionary principles' designed to: (1) inculcate mutual responsibility for the newer indigenous churches; (2) encourage a reliance upon charismatic faith for Church expansion instead of relying upon 'foreign' organizational strategies; (3) facilitate a willingness to work within existing systems and infrastructures in order to establish relevant churches; and (4) authorize trans-local 'short term' missionaries to plant churches, transfer the apostolic tradition to all members, delegate all responsibilities to indigenous leadership, and then, require the missionaries to leave in order to begin their next mission. He engaged with their ideas and began to formulate his own type of missionary ecclesiology that was rooted upon these basic principles.

Firstly, he engages with Ramsay's 'south Galatian theory'[1] and also his belief that when Paul left Berea on his second missionary journey he left 'with no fixed plan'.[2] Allen is not concerned with the details of the first missionary journey, but he did agree with Ramsay's argument that it was 'perfectly clear' that Paul's second missionary journey 'was not following any predetermined route'.[3] Eckhard Schnabel agrees: 'Paul's missionary work was not controlled by a "grand strategy" that helped him decide in which cities to begin a new missionary initiative.'[4] Schnabel's engagement with Allen's thought here stems from the overall critical analysis he made of Allen's assertions concerning Paul's ministry within the context of provincial, regional and metropolitan areas.[5] On one side, he states that 'Roland Allen is indeed correct when he asserts that concentrated missionary activity in a strategic centre radiates to other areas only if "the centre," that is, the church in the metropolis, is evangelistic and is actively involved in planting "daughter" churches'.[6] Allen's point here

---

1. Allen, *Missionary Methods*, 10.
2. Ramsay, *St Paul the Traveller*, 234, as cited in Allen, *Missionary Methods*, 11 (footnote 2).
3. Allen, *Missionary Methods*, 11.
4. Eckhard J. Schnabel, *Paul the Missionary: Realities, Strategies and Methods* (Downers Grove: InterVarsity Press, 2008) 287.
5. Allen, *Missionary Methods*, 10-17.
6. Schnabel, *Paul the Missionary*, 284; cf. Allen, *Missionary Methods*, 17.

recognizes what potential could emerge from within a city if the church's missional focus is intentional and evangelistic. And yet, Allen identified that Paul's main focus was towards provincial mission, not metropolitan ministry.[7] Conversely, Schnabel disagrees with Allen when he asserted that 'in St Paul's view the unit was the province rather than the city'.[8] Schnabel argues that Allen's belief here 'needs to be abandoned' because there is no proof that Pauline mission was primarily provincial.[9]

Allen, following Ramsay, articulated what he considered to be a pneumatological influence on Paul's missionary journey in contrast to a type of strategic methodology used for pragmatic reasons. For example, he understood in literal terms that, after Paul's travels through Phrygia and Galatia, he was twice 'forbidden by the Holy Ghost' (Acts 16:6-7) to 'preach in Asia' and later in 'Bithynia' and ended up later in Troas where 'he was directed by a vision to Macedonia' (Acts 16:8-10).[10] Likewise, Ramsay also insisted that 'Paul believed himself to be the recipient of direct revelations from God', so much so that he was 'guided and controlled in his plans by direct interposition of the Holy Spirit'.[11] Again, he was aware of Harnack's point that similar beliefs were held by Justin, Dionysius, Cyprian, Eusebius and Augustine's mother, Monica: 'God speaks to the missionaries in visions, dreams . . . controlling their plans, pointing out the roads on which they are to travel . . . the cities where they are to stay. . . . '[12] Whereas Ramsay and Harnack had argued that the early missionaries believed themselves to be Spirit-led (i.e., under pneumatological influence), Allen read this through a 'missiological' lens, believing it trumped any pragmatic methodology for missionary work. This 'charismatic' focus was central in shaping his missionary thinking toward: (1) reliance upon 'principles' not 'systems' so that 'the Holy Spirit in them would show them how to apply the principles;'[13] and (2) reliance upon 'the spirit of faith'[14] at the time at which there is the 'need to subordinate our methods, our systems, ourselves to that faith'.[15] Pneumatology *not* institutional strategies began to shape his missionary ecclesiology.

7. Allen, *Missionary Methods*, 12.
8. Ibid.
9. Schnabel, *Paul the Missionary*, 286.
10. Allen, *Missionary Methods*, 11, 17.
11. Ramsay, *St Paul*, 87; cf. also pages 55, 62 and 67.
12. Adolf von Harnack, *The Mission and Expansion of Christianity in the First Three Centuries*, trans. and ed. James Moffatt (Gloucester: Peter Smith, 1902. Repr. 1972) 199-202.
13. Allen, *Missionary Methods*, 124.
14. Ibid., 148.
15. Ibid., 149.

Secondly, Allen's ideas coincide with Ramsay's belief that the infrastructure of Imperial Rome provided a necessary orderliness for all of life. Although Paul eventually suffered martyrdom under Imperial Rome, he argues that it is not wise to dismiss the friendly side of certain Roman officials towards Paul earlier on in his missionary journeys in contrast to reactions from the Jewish communities. He agrees with Ramsay that: 'in selecting as the sphere of his work the centres of Roman administration, St Paul was led by the desire to obtain for himself and for his people the security afforded by a strong government.'[1] Andrew Walls similarly makes reference that this 'Hellenistic-Roman civilization offered a total system of thought' and that with the growth of Christianity the 'Christian penetration of the system inevitably left it a total system'.[2] Although his missionary thinking gave precedence to *principles* over *systems*, the outworking of his missionary ecclesiology did not seek to disestablish existing systems or order – either statist or ecclesiastical. Rather, he sought to establish the Church within the present order by inculcating principles through 'persuasion . . . never by command', so that the indigenous members would be given the opportunities 'to do things for themselves'[3] and infiltrate the systems on their own terms.

Thirdly, Allen supplements Ramsay's view of imperial Rome. The 'idea' of a 'world-wide empire' is missiologically important; if it supports 'peace' through 'common citizenship of men of many different races . . . [under] one law . . . [and] the breaking down of national exclusiveness'.[4] According to his reasoning, this programmatic idea paved the way for Paul to teach the transcendence of the kingdom of God in contrast to all other political systems. Central to this is his commitment to the establishment of a *lingua franca*. Again, he agrees with Ramsay:

> There is no evidence of any attempt to translate the Scriptures into the provincial dialects of Asia Minor. St Paul preached in Greek and wrote in Greek, and all his converts who read at all were expected to read the Scriptures in Greek. For St Paul, the one language was as important as the one government.[5]

---

1. Ibid., 13.

2. Andrew Walls, *The Missionary Movement in Christian History: Studies in the Transmission of Faith* (Maryknoll: Orbis Books and Edinburgh: T&T Clark, 1996. Repr. 2009) 19.

3. Allen, *Missionary Methods*, 149.

4. Ibid., 14.

5. Ibid., 14; also Ramsay, *St Paul*, 132.

Consequently, he follows Ramsay's understanding that 'there is not even any evidence that evangelization in these languages was ever attempted', because the 'Empire had succeeded in imposing its languages on the central districts of Asia only so far as education spread'.[6] Rome's imposition of both Latin and Greek was thus profoundly significant. Of course, from a postcolonial perspective, we might want to question this imposition of an empire's language upon its subjects as 'linguistic' hegemony.[7] However, undisturbed by the weight of such concerns, both Ramsay and Allen believed that there was much that was good to be gained from the imposition of a *lingua franca*. His missiology endeavored to apply the Pauline principles of (1) submission to 'governing authorities' as those divinely appointed to serve the general public (Rom. 13:1) and (2) becoming 'all things to all people' for the sake of ministry (I Cor. 9:22-23, ESV). The point is that this was aided by an infrastructure united by a common language.

Fourthly, Allen agrees with Harnack's interpretation of the socio-religious sentiments within the Roman Empire. Though he admits that the morality within Greek and Roman life 'was bad', he argued that it 'was even worse' within Asia Minor.[8] He concurs with Harnack: 'No one could be a god any longer unless he was also a saviour.'[9] Agreeing, he argues that Paul's social and soteriological emphases were the solution:

> In the world to which the apostles preached their new message, religion had not been the solace of the weary, the medicine of the sick, the strength of the sin-laden, the enlightenment of the ignorant: it was the privilege of the healthy and the instructed. The sick and the ignorant were excluded. The philosophers addressed themselves only to the well-to-do, the intellectual and the pure . . . It was a constant marvel to the heathen that the Christians called the sick and the sinful.[10]

On the basis of Romans 2:11 – 'there is no respect of persons with God' – Allen argued for the *apostolic principle* of human equality.[11] His examination of the early Church's expansion challenged him to develop a missionary ecclesiology rooted in a socio-spiritual commitment to

6. Ramsay, *St Paul*, 132-33.
7. Young, *Postcolonialism*, 138-39.
8. Allen, *Missionary Methods*, 36.
9. Harnack, *Mission and Expansion*, 107, as cited in Allen, *Missionary Methods*, 47.
10. Allen, *Missionary Methods*, 46.
11. Ibid., 65; cf. Romans 2:11-16 for the context of his thinking.

transform the weak, the disenfranchised and the poor. He began to formulate a 'charismatic' understanding of an empowered ministry – from below – which clearly stemmed from his recent missionary experiences in China.

Allen's archives make evident that Allen held an emphasis on 'Word and Spirit', which specifically began to emerge at the same time he was studying Ramsay and Harnack after his 'return from China'.[1] During this period, when he was also serving as parish priest at Chalfont St Peter's (England), he delivered a four-part Easter sermon series from John 14-15 on 'The Holy Spirit'. Even a cursory perusal of these sermons reveals a substantive shift of interest towards the ministry of the Holy Spirit within the life of the Church. Indeed, this is significantly noticeable in comparison to his other sermons.[2] His incipient ideas about how charismatic ministry effects missionary activity were developed as a result of his study of Harnack's work on Tertullian's pneumatology[3] and missiology[4] and the latter's examination of the influence of *charismata* on the early Church's global expansion.[5]

Allen continued to be the missiological realist when dealing with the issue of how to combat modern ideas relating to the activities of 'spirits'. He quotes Harnack: 'Not merely idolatry, but every phase and form of life was ruled by them, they sat on thrones, they hovered round cradles, the earth was literally a hell.'[6] He agrees with Harnack and then cites the Apostle John's words: 'The whole world lieth in the Evil One.'[7] He carefully identifies that this idea of the demonic was not only embraced by 'Barbarians' and 'Phrygians', but also by the 'Romans, Greeks, and Jews'.[8]

1. Talltorp, 'Sacraments for Growth in Mission', 222.
2. However, other *later* sermons which are also detailed are: 'Gold and Frankincense and Myrrh', no.18-26, Harpenden (1918); 'There Was War in Heaven: Michael and His Angels Fought Against the Dragon', no.29-32, Nairobi, Kenya (1935); 'Thou Shalt Call His Name Jesus', no.52-55, Beaconsfield, (1925); 'Conversion of St Paul', no.67-74, Harpenden (1916); 'Law and Gospel', no.194-205; 'On Prophecy and the Prophetic Word', no.333-343; 'Baptism of Philippian Jailor,' no.347-349 (1920); 'Athanasian Creed: St. John 3:35-36 & Ephesians 2:11-12', no.351-53, Beaconsfield (1921); and 'Repentance in Apostolic Teaching', no.532-53, USPG X622, Box 5, Oxford, Bodleian Library, Roland Allen archives.
3. Allen, *Missionary Methods*, 46; cf. Harnack, *Mission and Expansion*, 140.
4. Harnack, *Mission and Expansion*, 94.
5. A more detailed discussion of this shift will follow.
6. Ibid., 131, as cited in Allen, *Missionary Methods*, 27.
7. 1 John 5:19 (ἐν τῷ πονηρῷ κεῖται).
8. Allen, *Missionary Methods*, 27.

It is obvious that much of Allen's ministry *principle* of deliverance stems from Harnack's understanding of exorcism as 'one very powerful method' of the Church's 'mission and propaganda . . . exorcising and vanquishing the demons that dwelt in individuals, but also of purifying all public life from them . . . '.[9] Firstly, he personally believed that the Church was given supernatural power to confront evil spirits. For example, his commentary notes on Acts discloses the exorcism by Paul of a 'girl' who had the 'power of divination'[10] after she had already been disrupting his 'preaching' ministry. Furthermore, he comments on the 'miracles' that accompanied Paul's preaching in Ephesus, which included the exorcism of evil spirits.[11] Allen's belief in the miraculous – signs and wonders – was comprehensive in that it 'dominates the whole personality, not intellect alone, but will and emotion also'.[12] He believed that the miraculous stemmed from the same charismatic power that spontaneously equipped 'untrained and unpaid native Christians' into being effective evangelists and teachers in Southern Nigeria in 1921; he argued this from a report given by the 'Bishop of Lagos'.[13] Allen's charismatic theology was enhanced by Paul's deliverance ministry which confronted occultism but equally recognized that the same power was demonstrated in the establishment of churches by 'unlearned' evangelists who were ministering by 'the control of a divine power'.[14] Finally, his trust in this charismatic power was firmly centred on and stemmed from a transcendent message of the cross of Christ.[15] He argued that Paul 'would have the Christian faith rest on nothing else than the power of God',[16] and by that he meant, Christianity's focus on the cross enabled the Church to identify with Christ's atonement, as Allen wrote 'an act in [which] he (St Paul) partakes Χριστῷ συνεσταύρωμαι'[17] or what J.D.G. Dunn said: ' . . . what we actually see in Christ's life, death and

---

9. Ibid., 47.

10. Acts 16:16-18 as referred to in Allen's commentary notes on Acts, Oxford, Bodleian Library, USPG X622, Box 3: 29.

11. Ibid., Acts 19:11-20.

12. Allen, *Spontaneous Expansion*, 86.

13. Allen, Church Missionary Society *Gleaner* (April 1921) 69, as cited in *Spontaneous Expansion*, 146.

14. Allen, *Spontaneous Expansion*, 86.

15. Allen cites 1 Corinthians 2:2: 'For I determined not to know anything among you, save Jesus Christ, and him crucified.'

16. Allen, *Spontaneous Expansion*, 86.

17. Allen's commentary notes on Galatians 2:20 (Χριστῷ συνεσταύρωμαι; verb, finite, first person, singular, perfect, indicative, passive, i.e., 'I am crucified with Christ', Oxford, Bodleian Library, USPG X622, Box 3: 9 (Galatians notes).

resurrection is the very power by which God created and sustains the world.[1] Thus, his hermeneutic of Paul's theology of the cross shaped his charismatic understanding of exorcism and miraculous phenomena.

As Allen continued to engage with Pauline missiology, his thinking shifted away from the 'long term' paternalistic mission-station system and towards 'short term' trans-local mission. He says that 'Ramsay's calculation'[2] of how Paul 'laboured for only five months' in Thessalonica would have been enough time to establish the Thessalonian Christians in the 'fundamental truths', which Paul saw as necessitating the essentials of 'first importance'.[3] For Allen, this limited time for ministry reinforces the *apostolic principle*, by which missionary church planters establish their converts with a basic creed before retiring from the region.[4] What did he consider to be the basic truths of 'first importance'? Paul's 'simple' message was, he argues:

> That Gospel involves a doctrine of God the Father, the Creator, a doctrine of Jesus, the Son, the Redeemer, the Saviour; a doctrine of the Holy Spirit, the indwelling source of strength; but these in the simplest and most practical form. Besides this St Paul left a tradition to which he constantly refers . . . the teaching on the Holy Communion . . . the teaching of the resurrection included an account of the appearances of the Lord to the disciples after His death, beginning with the appearance to St Peter and ending with the appearance to St Paul on the Damascus road.[5]

As to Paul's methodology for conveying the 'teaching. . . received' (2 Thess. 3:6) in the newer churches, Allen observed that it 'is unfortunate that we cannot determine whether this tradition was written down'.[6] He then refers to Harnack's comment about how, in the synagogues, 'the Jews had already drawn up a catechism for proselytes'.[7] He recognizes that this method was typical in Judaism and early Christianity, especially later when observing the mission societies' approach. However, after further reflection,

---

1. James D.G. Dunn, *Unity and Diversity in the New Testament: An Inquiry into the Character of Earliest Christianity* (London: SCM Press, 1980. Repr. 1989) 195.

2. Allen, *Missionary Methods*, 68.

3. Ibid. Allen cites Ramsay's *St Paul the Traveller* (p. 146) however, Ramsay makes *no* reference of the Epistle to the Thessalonians.

4. Allen, *Missionary Methods*, 111.

5. Ibid., 87.

6. Ibid., 88.

7. Harnack, *Mission and Expansion*, 391-92, as cited in Allen, *Missionary Methods*, 88.

he appears to come to the conclusion that this was *not* Paul's method: '. . . there is no sure ground for arguing that in these early years such a book existed'.[8] He thus reinforces the need for missionaries to follow Paul's example of passing on 'an oral teaching of those fundamental facts'.[9] He argues that 'the Apostle's success' for church-planting centres around 'the observance of principles', and that the *primary principle* is that 'all teaching to be permanent must be intelligible', it must be 'grasped and understood' and 'once received' it must be retained and passed on.[10] This concept of a basic 'oral' creed for new converts shaped his missionary thinking and led to a simpler approach to Christian discipleship. He concluded that all new converts needed to know was what Paul called the 'tradition' (2 Thessalonians 2:15; 3:6).[11]

That said, Ramsay's and Harnack's influence provides a backdrop for disclosing how their ideas prompted a response from Allen to critically analyze the methodologies used by missionary societies of his day. This gave birth to *Missionary Methods*. A further analysis of the rest of this book will uncover how his thinking promoted a 'radical' challenge to certain missionary practices that he believed had nothing to do with Pauline missiology.

Allen's *Magnum Opus:*
Missionary Methods: St Paul's or Ours? (1912)

Eckhard Schnabel's *Paul the Missionary* (2008) reinforces Allen's contemporary significance by reiterating what he and other missiologists regard as the quintessential definition of 'mission':[12]

> In little more than ten years St Paul established the Church in four provinces of the Empire, Galatia, Macedonia, Achaia and Asia. Before AD 47 there were no churches in these provinces; in AD 57 St Paul could speak as if his work there was done, and could plan extensive tours into the far west without anxiety lest the churches which he had founded might perish in his absence for want of his guidance and support.[13]

---

8. Allen, *Missionary Methods*, 88.

9. Ibid.

10. Ibid., 151.

11. 2 Thessalonians 2:15 παραδόσεις; 3:6, παράδοσιν.

12. Schnabel, *Paul the Missionary*, 21.

13. Allen, *Missionary Methods*, 3; as cited in Schnabel, *Paul the Missionary*, 21.

The paragraph above concisely summarizes Allen's compelling argument for understanding the Pauline church-planting principle. He unpacks his understanding of Pauline missionary practice throughout *Missionary Methods* in five parts: '(1) Antecedent Conditions; (2) The Presentation of the Gospel; (3) The Training of Converts; (4) St Paul's Method of Dealing with Organized Churches; and (5) Conclusions.'[1]

Firstly, in Part One, Allen discloses the backdrop of Paul's work within the Roman provincial districts in which Greek civilization's educational focus had previously prepared the groundwork for the coming of the Christian faith which 'from the very first was a religion of education'.[2] He believed Paul 'naturally turned'[3] to plant churches in 'the provinces rather than the cities'[4] because of the 'strategic value' of establishing 'centres of Christian life in two or three important places'.[5] As stated earlier, Schnabel disagreed with Allen and argued that Paul valued the cities rather than the provinces and, moreover, the 'Jews lived in the cities of the Roman provinces'.[6] Although Schnabel's interpretation of Paul might be correct, nevertheless, Allen was committed to the view that a few centres at which churches were planted within a province would have a tendency to multiply more naturally than if they were only planted within the cosmopolitan setting. His missionary ecclesiology incorporated *both* rural districts and metropolitan areas for planting churches because of his interpretation of Paul's charismatic principle (Acts 16:6-10) of going where he 'was led as God opened the door'. Furthermore, the place at which Paul 'was led he always found a centre, and seizing upon that centre he made it the centre of Christian life'.[7] This charismatic principle, Allen says, was 'the key to his success'.[8]

Secondly, he addressed financial issues of the foreign missionary societies and their desire to practice devolution. He assesses the willingness of the missionaries to turn over the patronage to the local Christians but then states that this action would cause a disruption amongst the foreign 'subscribers' and 'trustees at home' who might not be willing to trust the 'native bishops' to maintain 'those peculiar views

---

1. Allen, *Missionary Methods*, Contents list.

2. Ibid., 14.

3. Ibid., 14.

4. Ibid., 12.

5. Ibid., 12.

6. Schnabel, *Paul the Missionary*, 287.

7. Allen, *Missionary Methods*, 17.

8. Ibid., 9.

whether of doctrine or ritual' which were held by the foreign supporters.[9] According to Allen, herein lies the problem of benevolent paternalism: 'Of all sources of strife, material possessions are the most prolific.'[10] He engaged with the issue of 'benevolent paternalism' and began to identify this as a hegemonic problem of control and *not* a Pauline principle. This missionary practice challenged his thinking to radically change in a different direction by arguing for the *rights* of the indigenous church to 'administer its own funds'[11] without any interference from local foreign missionaries or any organizations overseas.

Thirdly, he deals with the 'substance' of Paul's preaching ministry in the synagogues and among the Gentiles.[12] He attempts to clarify how some could misrepresent his advocacy for a basic creed for new converts as suggesting, 'No creed but Christ'. He responds to this misrepresentation as follows:

> Though I think it unwise to *begin* our teaching to new converts by translating and teaching by heart the creeds as we have them in their present form, yet I am not one of those who hold that we can, or should go 'behind the creeds' and try to preach a 'Christ of the gospels' as opposed to 'the Christ of the creeds'. We may teach simply to simple people, as the Church Catechism teaches an abbreviated explanation of the Apostles' Creed to little children, but behind all our teaching, as behind that abbreviated explanation, there must be the catholic creeds. The catholic creeds contain the only answer possible for us.[13]

Allen's advocacy for a creedal faith clearly reveals his Anglo-Catholic bias. On the surface, his missiology attempts to simplify the essentials of the Christian faith for younger converts so that they can personally embrace the faith concisely for themselves. On a deeper level, his ecclesiology also includes a didactic approach to train the converts over time so as to articulate this 'simple' faith as one that is rooted in the *catholic* creeds. His missionary experiences in China (1895-1903) and India (1910-11), along with his parish ministry in England (1904-07), helped shape his flexible – yet traditional – way of doing theology among new converts. His desire to maintain both a *traditional* creedalism and

9. Ibid., 58-59.
10. Ibid., 59.
11. Ibid., 59.
12. Ibid., 62-77.
13. Ibid., 91 (footnote 1).

also a *contextualized* creedal flexibility made him appear to be, from one perspective, a missionary with an oxymoronic methodology, and, from another, a 'pioneer' cross-cultural missionary who was more devoted to the principle of 'learning by doing' instead of imposing a foreign 'rote' methodology.

The centrality of Paul's missionary ecclesiology, according to Allen, was this adherence to *apostolic principles* and *methods*. Throughout the whole of *Missionary Methods*, he articulates his understanding of Paul's methods in contradistinction with current missionary methods that undergirded an ongoing paternalistic system of control. More than twenty-five times he describes Paul's principles and how they are relevant as follows:

(1) they relied *not* on 'elaborate systems of religious' ceremony but 'grasped fundamental principles with an unhesitating faith in the power of the Holy Ghost to apply them to his hearers;'[1]

(2) mission was made more effective by sending Timothy, Silas and Titus on short-term visits to Berea and Corinth with orders to confirm the younger churches without managing the churches autocratically;[2]

(3) converts were baptized immediately after conversion;[3]

(4) mission functioned on the 'great principle of mutual responsibility' with a reliance on local Christians, not foreign mission societies;[4]

(5) 'a general principle' should be established 'that converts should be presented by members of the church to the church'[5] in order to reinforce local accountability;

(6) churches ought to be 'fully equipped' with ordained indigenous elders authorized with 'the orders of ministry both permanent and charismatic' and 'no longer' dependent on Paul's ministry presence;[6]

(7) missionaries should resist teaching converts 'the habit of unreasoning obedience', but appeal 'to principles' which inculcate them towards 'the labour of thinking them out and applying them'[7] on their own; and

---

1. Ibid., 6.
2. Ibid., 86.
3. Ibid., 95.
4. Ibid., 98, 123 (this principle is also called 'doctrine' and is located in part four).
5. Ibid., 99.
6. Ibid., 111; this principle is located in part four.
7. Ibid., 118; this principle is located in part four.

(8) these principles 'seem to underlie all the Apostle's practice:
    (a) that he was a preacher of Gospel, not of law, and
    (b) that he must retire from his converts to give place for Christ.'[8]

These provide an overview of some of the apostolic principles and methods which Allen highlights throughout *Missionary Methods*.[9]

Part Four of the book consists of two chapters that, firstly, address 'authority and discipline', and, secondly, focus on 'unity' and assesses whether Paul was actually successful in establishing it. Allen weaves Paul's *apostolic principles* into the framework of these topics. (1) He argues against foreign missionaries regulating indigenous churches. Such an approach, he insists, 'is Judaism not Christianity; it is papal not Pauline'.[10] (2) By appealing to the conscience of the Corinthian Church when confronting discipline problems, he argued that Paul's method remained the same and 'that the Holy Spirit in them would show them how to apply the principles'. So, 'he showed them the right way, but left them to discover how to walk in it'.[11] (3) Finally, by refusing 'to set up any central administrative authority from which the whole Church was to receive directions',[12] Allen's missiology clearly rejected any centralized administrative system. This was contentious, but, as Hubert Allen argues, his grandfather would not 'have worried at all about a divided Anglicanism'.[13]

In the remaining section of Part Four, Allen meanders through the ideologies of what substantiates the 'principles' for Christian unity. He said that Paul 'declined to establish *a priori* tests of orthodoxy', but rather 'handed on the tradition and the Scriptures, how he established the orders of the Ministry, how he insisted upon the due administration of the Sacraments'.[14] Allen argues that the newer churches ought to be 'fully equipped' communities of faith with what F.D. Maurice called the 'Signs of the Kingdom'[15] – Apostolic tradition, the Scriptures, Ministry

---

8. Ibid., 148; this principle is located in part five where the chapter is entitled 'Principles and Spirit'.

9. Allen further discloses these 'apostolic principles and methods' in *Missionary Methods*, 121-125, 131, 145, 149, 151, 152, 154, 156, 157, 161, and 173.

10. Allen, *Missionary Methods*, 118.

11. Ibid., 124-25.

12. Ibid., 131.

13. Hubert Allen, 'Would Roland Allen still have anything to say to us today?', *Transformation*, 29(3) 183 (July 2012).

14. Allen, *Missionary Methods*, 132.

15. Frederick Denison Maurice, *The Kingdom of Christ: Or Hints to a Quaker: Respecting the Principles, Constitution and Ordinances of the Catholic Church* (second edn) 2 vols (London: SCM Press, 1842).

orders, and the Sacraments. Two important items stand out when examining the overlapping conclusions of both Maurice and Allen: the first, both men recognized the significance of these four criteria which they believed make up the catholic Church; and the second, both men repetitively contrasted principles[1] from systems[2] and explained how apostolic principles – not systems – truly established unity within the Church.

No archival evidence exists to confirm that Allen engaged with Maurice's *Kingdom of Christ* or any of his other works. However, it is highly likely that he was influenced by Maurice's ideas, since the latter was 'probably the greatest Anglican theologian of the Victorian age'.[3] What specific evidence is there to suggest that Maurice's ideas played a part in Allen's ecclesiology? H.H. Kelly (1860-1950), one of Allen's most trusted friends, rejoiced in being 'an F.D. Maurician'.[4] Kelly and Allen frequently made reference to each other in their writings. It is possible that, in their joint communication, Maurice's ideas were discussed. But what is clear remains that when it comes to understanding 'unity' as perceived through the lens of catholic Christianity, these men – Maurice, Kelly, Allen – were like-minded in terms of what defines the Church as one holy catholic and apostolic.

Part Five presents Allen's concluding thoughts about principles, pneumatology, and application.[5] Chapter 12 isolates 'three very disquieting symptoms' of foreign missions:

(1) Instances of Western missionary efforts that have failed in planting indigenous churches;[6]
(2) cases of the mission stations' dependence on foreign support and the people 'look[ing] to us for leaders, for instructors, for rulers;'[7] and

---

1. Maurice, interestingly, uses the word 'principle' throughout these two volumes more than 150 times in Maurice, *The Kingdom of Christ.*
2. Maurice frequently identifies how a denomination or some movement develops a 'system' which differs from the original founders' ministry 'principles,' in Maurice, *The Kingdom of Christ*, Vol. 2, 320-347.
3. Alistair Mason, *History of the Society of the Sacred Mission* (Norwich: The Canterbury Press, 1994) 78.
4. Letter 14: 2, 1934 (cited in *No Pious Person*, 133) as cited in Mason, *Sacred Mission*, 85.
5. Allen, *Missionary Methods*, 139.
6. Ibid., 141.
7. Ibid.

(3) even though the missions in different countries tend to 'bear a most astonishing resemblance one to [one] another. . . . There has been no new discovery of new aspects of the Gospel, no new unfolding of new forms of Christian life.'[8]

He was deeply disturbed with the 'racial and religious pride' towards those whom they were evangelizing.[9] He was sharp in his criticisms: 'we have treated them as "dear children", but not as "brethren".'[10] This comment by Allen is similar to what his friend, Vedanayagam Samuel Azariah (1874-1945), the first indigenous Anglican bishop from India, declared at the Edinburgh 1910 conference. 'In many respects', Immanuel David observes, 'Allen and Azariah shared a deep affinity. Azariah's plea at the Edinburgh 1910 conference, in which he asked western missions to 'give us friends' resembled Allen's condemnation of missionary paternalism.[11] Paul's 'multiethnic' missionary ecclesiology, so Allen believed, embodied a practice of servant leadership − called to empower − the newest converts of any nationality and 'not that they may be stupidly obedient to the voice of authority'.[12] Azariah had a desire for the churches of India to be treated not only as Christians from a distance, but 'as friends' within the Church, was a necessary emphasis that was well overdue. Similarly, there was a resounding call from Edward Blyden for expatriate Africans in the Western world to return back to Africa in order to: 'build up negro states; we must establish and maintain the various institutions; we must make and administer laws, erect and preserve churches . . . we must have governments . . . instruct the schools . . . thus aid in shaping mankind.'[13] This type of indigenization in India and Africa encouraged local empowerment and challenged the *status quo* to eventually engage with the Church as 'partners' not followers.

---

8. Ibid., 142.

9. Ibid., 142.

10. Ibid., 143.

11. S. Immanuel David, 'The Development of the Concept of Indigenization among Protestant Christians in India from the Time of Henry Venn,' M.Th. thesis, United Theological College, Bangalore, 1975, 21-23, as cited in Susan Billington Harper, *In the Shadow of the Mahatma: Bishop V.S. Azariah and the Travails of Christianity in British India, Studies in the History of Christian Missions* (Grand Rapids: Eerdmans, 2000) 209-210.

12. Allen, *Missionary Methods*, 145.

13. Edward Wilmot Blyden, 'The Call of Providence to the Descendants of Africa in America' (New York, 1862) 69, 75, 76, as cited in Hollis R. Lynch, *Edward Wilmot Blyden: Pan-Negro Patriot 1832-1912*, West African History Series (London: Oxford University Press, 1967) 29, 30.

Chapter 13, entitled 'Application', commences with five essential Pauline *principles*, which he believed could be reduced to 'rules of practice':

(1) '[A]ll teaching' must be 'permanent' and 'intelligible' whereby everyone can practically grasp, understand, retain, use and pass it on;

(2) 'all organization' ought not to be so elaborate but 'understood and maintained' and only necessary if they agree to support it;

(3) 'all financial arrangements' are given to the people so they can 'control and manage their own business' and without any dependency on 'foreign' financial subsistence;

(4) 'the whole community' is mutually responsible for one another and ought to responsibly administrate their church's baptisms, discipline and ordination services; and

(5) all 'authority to exercise spiritual gifts' ought to be 'given freely and at once' without any reservation from the foreign missionaries and understood that the 'test of preparedness to receive the authority is the capacity to receive the grace.'[1]

All of these *interlinked* principles provided the groundwork for Allen's missionary ecclesiology for this time and for the rest of his life. He presents a *principled* example after experiencing Azariah's ministry: 'I have seen converts of the lowest castes in India after one year's teaching capable of reading and understanding the Gospels and doing the work of lay evangelists most efficiently.'[2]

The concluding chapter in Part Five, 'Epilogue: A Present-day Contrast',[3] consists of two stories – one imaginary and one actual – designed to 'add point and reality to the argument'.[4] The first story represents the paternalistic methodologies of the mission station approach and their style of devolution.[5] The second story relates the application of the five principles previously mentioned with an emphasis on how a smaller diocesan region with a bishop can function more effectively when 'the church as a body' not only supports its own business but also establishes a 'representative council' to govern the diocesan churches. When Allen argues for the 'local church' what he means is *not* one autonomous congregation but rather churches

1. Allen, *Missionary Methods*, 151-57.
2. Ibid., 161 (footnote 1).
3. Ibid., 164-73.
4. Ibid., 164.
5. Ibid., 164-68.

that are networked together and led by a bishop who lives nearby. His missionary ecclesiology, therefore, articulated a form of church government in which the indigenous representative council – *not* the foreign missionaries – addressed the needs of the local memberships. He said: 'For no one can expect a committee directed by foreigners to act on Pauline principles.'[6]

Summary

Reflecting upon the Pauline scholars who influenced Allen's thinking at the turn of the twentieth century, substantial evidence was given to explain how both Ramsay and Harnack helped to shape his missiological thought in terms of the Church's expansion. Both authors argued how many benefits existed under Roman imperialism due to its ability to keep the peace in travel against piracy. The authors also disclosed how Paul's gospel ministry flowed from within an infrastructure of empire that was united by a common language. Allen recognized these overarching benefits to have provided a better context for Paul's missionary journeys and it *may* be the reason that he did not react wholeheartedly against Britain's imperialism in his day. He appreciated Ramsay's experiential knowledge, which stemmed from his archaeological research, for it reinforced his own observational methodology. He appreciated Harnack's extensive historical research into the first three centuries of the early Church and how it provided a foundational understanding of the indigenous nature of the Church's expansion by planting small Christian communities everywhere gospel ministry had infused a message of salvation for the disenfranchised, hope for the aimless and deliverance from demonic influences. He, also, admired Harnack's research that substantiated how the Church expanded without all the unnecessary supports of a highly organized system but rather that 'the faith' and reliance upon the charismatic dynamic within the Church causes spontaneous expansion. Allen received from these scholars their suppositions about how the 'concept' of empire paved the way for Paul to communicate Jesus' words concerning a 'greater' kingdom which transcends all empires.

Allen's *Missionary Methods* put his missiological thought within the context of missionary academics and practitioners from its arrival, even until now. Whether it is the missionary martyr Jim Elliot (1927-1956), the missiologist David Bosch (1929-1992), the missionary bishop Leslie Newbigin, (1909-1998), or the indigenous bishop V.S. Azariah,

6. Ibid., 158.

the practical missiology of Allen is still held in high esteem due to the influence that this seminal book has had for the past century. His clarion call for an apostolic application of indigenous Church principles confronted the paternalistic mission station methodology and hegemonic tendencies. His belief in the simplicity of Pauline missiology compelled him to argue for a better way to do mission. What eventually emerged from his thought was a missionary ecclesiology which was rooted in *apostolic principles* and *methods* in contrast to *paternalistic systems.*

5. The World Dominion Movement and its Evangelical Mission

Theologian for the World Dominion Movement and its Publications (1917-1931)[1]

Roland Allen's influence as a missionary theorist moved beyond the Anglican Communion and began to draw the attention of missionaries and mission societies from various branches of Christ's international Church. Due to his prophetic insight into the nature of indigenous church -planting and what this meant for conventional missionary practice in his day, he became the primary writer and the major voice for a cutting-edge missionary journal entitled *World Dominion*. This journal was dedicated to assessing global mission work by conducting surveys throughout the world. Allen advanced his understanding of how apostolic principles enhanced missionary practice and clearly articulated a 'better way' for missionaries to empower the indigenous leadership entrusted to their care. For the sake of clarity, it is necessary to preface this section with an explanation as to why this missionary journal was entitled *World Dominion*. After many years of publication, various criticisms emerged globally 'from people who only saw *World Dominion* on the cover and who did not trouble to read the explanatory Scripture reference, and thought that it was an imperialistic production.'[2] The journal representatives explained that they chose the biblical references from Psalm 72:8 and Zechariah 9:10: 'His [God's] dominion shall be "from sea to sea".' The editors meant for it 'to be a provocative title' primarily because of its doctrinal belief: 'the supreme place for our Lord and Saviour Jesus Christ and His final supremacy as the world's only hope.'[3] From the onset

---

1. Allen made other contributions to *World Dominion* and World Dominion Press after 1931: Allen, 'The Application of Pauline Principles to Modern Missions', *World Dominion* 11 (1933) 352-57; Allen, *Sidney James Wells Clark: A Vision of Foreign Missions* (London: World Dominion Press, 1937).

2. 'London', *World Dominion*, London: World Dominion Press, vol.XIV, no.1 (January 1936) 3.

3. Ibid.

of the journal's existence, the editors made sure that the publications maintained a 'belief in the Deity and Atoning Death of the Lord Jesus Christ, the World's Only Saviour, and in the Final Authority of Holy Scripture.'[1] This backdrop implicitly affirmed the spirit of 'evangelical' fundamentalism in contrast to a 'social gospel' emphasis. In terms of the journal's 'fundamental principles and policies',[2] the following can shed light on the missional impetus:

(1) The journal underscored its commitment to global evangelism;
(2) propagated a consistent goal to plant indigenous churches;
(3) encouraged empirical survey work on 'unreached and needy fields' along with 'meeting the need revealed';
(4) discouraged against any imposition of hegemonic institutions which were 'not likely to become indigenous' within the 'rising spirit of nationalism' and 'which might use resources' for projects that were not oriented to 'evangelistic' purposes; and
(5) publicized 'the value of non-professional missionaries.'[3]

The story of the origin of the World Dominion Movement centres on 'a wealthy Christian philanthropist, one S.J.W. Clark, whom Roland met in 1914'.[4] Sidney Clark was a successful clothing businessman,[5] a profession that allowed him to travel overseas. It was in 'Japan, Korea and China in 1905', while on business, that he noticed the 'lack of systematic planning and co-ordination' among missionary societies and also something of their 'gross inefficiency and wastage of resources'.[6] This concerned Clark. Eventually, he decided to resign from business and devote himself to full-time 'work of overseas missions'.[7] Clark, a Congregational layman, 'not a clergyman or professional missionary',[8] sought to make good use of his finances and initiated a ministry devoted to advancing global mission work. Hubert Allen believes that it was probably during Clark's visit to China in 1905 that he met up with the 'Presbyterian Scotsman' missionary doctor, Thomas Cochrane, who had served earlier (1897) in Chaoyang, eastern Mongolia, and later, after the Boxer Rising, began to

1. 'Mission Statement,' Contents list, *World Dominion*, XVII, no.4 (London: World Dominion Press, October 1939).
2. 'London', *World Dominion* (January 1936) 3.
3. Ibid.
4. Hubert Allen, *Roland Allen*, 90.
5. Ibid.
6. Ibid.
7. Ibid.
8. Ibid.

'build up the Peking Union Medical College'.[9] Cochrane, like Clark, was
equally 'shocked and concerned' by his analysis of 'grossly unsystematic
missionary effort in China' and ended up compiling an extensive 'detailed
Survey of the Missionary Occupation of China, with an accompanying
atlas'.[10] These two men – Clark and Cochrane – placed much value in the
function of 'surveys and quantitative research'.[11]

Both men were also influenced by Allen's *Missionary Methods* and, in
1917, Clark, Cochrane and Allen had agreed to meet and set up the World
Dominion Movement in London's East End.[12] This diversified giftedness
and theologically cohesive ministry team made use of 'Clark's business
acumen . . . Cochrane's charm and sensitivity . . . and Roland with his
trained analytic mind and wide learning;'[13] the result was that each man
had a function within the movement which was well-suited to their
particular skill: management fell to Clark, diplomacy and communications
to Cochrane and Allen – naturally – kept to theological analysis.[14] World
Dominion's journals maintained an evangelical posture over the years.
Cochrane's biographer outlines three foundational beliefs that Clark,
Cochrane and Allen referred to as 'the Three Supreme Loyalties: (1) To
the Lord Jesus Christ and the centrality of His Cross. (2) To the Bible
as the final authority on Faith and Practice. (3) To the Lord's command
to world-wide witness.'[15] This concise foundational statement clearly
articulates their philosophy of ministry.

The next year, 1918, these three men became the trustees of 'the
precursor of the Survey Application Trust, with its publishing branch,
the World Dominion Press'.[16] However, for Allen, being a trustee was
'too restrictive' and 'excessively irksome', so he was released from
these responsibilities and the trusteeship position was filled instead by
Cochrane's son.[17] Allen was then able to serve the Survey Trust in a more

9. Ibid., 91; Hubert Allen states that this medical college was eventually 'taken
   over by the Rockefeller Health Foundation', 91 (footnote 1).
10. Ibid., 92; Hubert Allen says 'The Survey' and *Atlas of China in Provinces
    showing Missionary Occupation* were both published in 1913 by the Christian
    Literature Society for China' (footnote 2).
11. Ibid.
12. Ibid., 93.
13. Ibid.
14. Ibid.
15. Francesca French, *Thomas Cochrane: Pioneer & Missionary Statesman* (London:
    Hodder & Stoughton, 1956) 89f.; as cited in Hubert Allen, *Roland Allen*, 93.
16. Ibid.
17. Ibid., 94.

effective way by focusing primarily on his task of missiological writing, and secondly, on his missionary survey analysis.

Clark, Cochrane, and Allen set out to assess the opportunities that lay before the Church to take on the mission challenges set before them. Over the next decade, Clark devoted continuous efforts of leadership to assure that his and Allen's writings found their way into the expansion of what they believed was a Pauline approach to world mission. It was years later that Kenneth Grubb and Alexander McLeish commented that: 'the greatest single service of the World Dominion Press has been to keep the study of [Allen's] writings alive, and emphasize their still essential and contemporary relevance.'[1]

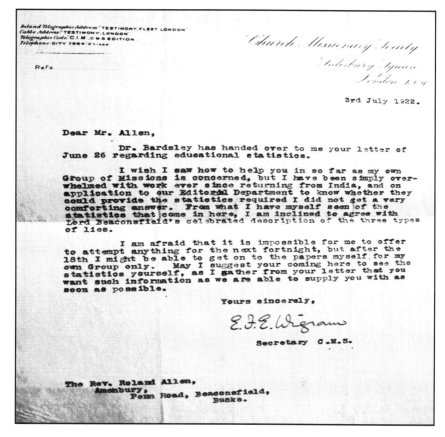

Figure 6. A Letter from the secretary of the Church Missionary Society.

---

1. David Paton, *The Ministry of the Spirit: Selected Writings of Roland Allen*, Biographical Memoir by Alexander McLeish (Grand Rapids: Eerdmans, 1970) ix–xvi; also Paton, *Reform of the Ministry: A Study in the Work of Roland Allen* (London: The Lutterworth Press, 1968) 67.

MISSION COLLEGES IN INDIA.

The Question of Christian Influence.

By

THE REV. ROLAND ALLEN, M.A.

(Author of *Missionary Methods, Educational Principles, etc.*)

If I had been hunting for an illustration of the character of the Christian education given in Mission schools, which I described in my article published in the *Record* on January 19, I could scarcely have found a better than that which the Editor of the *Church Missionary Outlook* has provided for his readers in the number for this month. It is an article worthy of most careful attention. It contains a very pathetic and illuminating letter from a pupil in a C.M.S. college in North India, with comments either by the Editor or the Principal himself. The article is called "The Working of an Indian Student's Mind," but it might better have been called "The Character of the Christian Teaching in a Mission College." For there is nothing peculiarly Indian in this letter except the local vocabulary. If we eliminate a few expressions which are peculiar to India the letter might have been written by a student anywhere in the world. For by no means only Indians are capable of self-sacrifice for a cause which they think worthy. What is really instructive in the letter is the revelation of the teaching which this young man has received in the Mission college.

It so happens that this letter has appeared in a C.M.S. paper and is concerned with a C.M.S. college, but what I have to say about it is not peculiar to C.M.S. What I say might apply equally well to almost any Mission college in India. I am not concerned particularly with the action of any one society. I am anxious to reveal as well as I can what is implied in the idea that Christian colleges exist to permeate educated society with Christian ideals, and I have taken this example because it came to hand and is fresh in the minds of many of my readers.

I wish that I could print in full the whole letter; but in brief it tells how this young man sacrificed what men call his prospects in order to fulfil a duty, as he conceived it, to his country by joining the non-co-operation party. The writer expresses with admirable simplicity and sincerity the struggle through which he went before he ultimately gained his victory, and was prepared to sacrifice himself for what he deemed the truth.

Now here, of course, it is completely beside my point to consider whether this young man did right or wrong in sacrificing himself to this particular ideal

of Swaraj. Whether Swaraj is, or is not, an object for which Indians ought to make great sacrifices is a question with which I have nothing whatever to do in this paper, for I am not writing about the political condition of India, but of the teaching in missionary schools; and it is only as his letter reveals the character of that teaching that I call attention to it now.

After expressing the sense of joy and relief which came to him when he had finally made up his mind this young man says: "To you, sir, I am indebted also for this success, for it is, no doubt, to a little extent, due to the timely help of your teachings, of the teachings of your co-operate professors, of the teachings of the Bible, and of the teachings of Socrates, that I have won this great victory."

From this passage and from other references in the letter it is perfectly clear that this young man has studied the Bible; but it is equally clear that he has studied it as a man who is not, and has no intention of becoming, a Christian; in a Mission college where the object set before us in the editorial note to which I referred in my last paper of bringing the pupils "into vital touch with the Divine Personality of Christ" is not being attained; and where that other object, which Canon Davies and those like-minded with him set before us, of pouring " a Christian influence into the life of educated India" is being pursued. And if we want to know what is meant by pouring a Christian influence into the life of educated India, we can have no more illuminating example. The writer of the article in his preface to the letter says that "it is clear that the writer believes that in following his vision he has the support of the religion of Christ . . . that he has chosen the highest way, and can claim to be following Christ." That is, I suppose, what those who talk about bringing Christian influence to bear upon educated India mean. They wish their pupils to follow Christ. But in what sense has this young man learnt to follow Christ? He says that he has been inspired by the example of Christ and Socrates, and by the teaching of the Bible, of Oliver Goldsmith and Dr. X. concerning honesty and steadfastness of purpose. Honesty and obedience to the dictates of conscience are certainly Christian virtues. Self-sacrifice is certainly a Christian ideal, and when pupils from Mission colleges practise those virtues and follow such ideals it is quite possible to say that they are following Christ. But the man himself realises quite clearly that these are not peculiarly Christian virtues or Christian ideals. Anything that is peculiarly Christian he has not accepted : only what is common to all the great moral teachers has been accepted by him. His editor says he is following Christ : he says he is following Christ and Socrates. This is what he has learnt in the Christian college.

Figure 7. Allen's argument for the pre-eminence of Christ within the 'Mission Colleges in India'.

There was no one any closer to his thought and mission than Clark. Before Clark's death in 1930, he wrote a tribute concerning his work in World Dominion:

A man of this type of mind must find some object of devotion, and if such men do not find the supreme object of devotion in Christ, they will find it in something lower than Christ. This man has found it in Swaraj; and therefore into the service of Swaraj he pours all his devotion and all his self-sacrifice. To do that is what he has learned in a Christian college. And that is the true meaning of pouring Christian influence into the life of educated India. Christian education in missionary colleges in this sense means setting before men ideals of truth and sacrifice, and leaving them to find as best they may some other object of devotion than Christ on which to expend their lives.

As I tried to set forth in my last paper, I cannot call this Christian education. Not any self-sacrifice for any object is Christian, because Christ taught us self-sacrifice; but only self-sacrifice in Christ and for Christ. And therefore I said that Christian education is impossible when the pupils are not ready to become Christians, and that all this talk about giving Christian education to Hindus is a contradiction in terms. The editor of this letter says: "When this splendid idealism and this readiness for sacrifice can be won for the Kingdom of God the day will not be far distant when India will acclaim Christ as Saviour and Lord." If we read "Christ" for that very ambiguous expression, "The Kingdom of God," the saying may be true; but it is at the same time a confession that it is not being done in Mission colleges as they are at present constituted.

I said in my last paper that the proposal to enforce a conscience clause in India had its importance for us simply because it calls attention to the character of the Christian education given in our schools now. Whether a conscience clause is enforced or not, so long as the Christian education given in missionary colleges is of the character revealed by this letter, and given under conditions which make it inevitable that it should be of that character (seeing that a very large majority of the pupils and of the masters are non-Christians), such enforcement or the absence of it will, as Canon Davies justly argues, make comparatively little difference. If the pupils have not the example of Christ, they may still have the example of Socrates and the teaching of Goldsmith and Dr. X. on honesty, and consistency in thoughts, words, and deeds.

I said in my last article that I could at any rate to some extent sympathise with those men, those really learned and devout Christian men, who believe that it is the part of Christian men, and a right course for Christian Missions, to carry to heathen countries Western enlightenment and high ethical principles; but I also said that I could not now accept that position because I was convinced that only Christ and Faith in Christ could enable those whom we taught to find a true object and use for those gifts which we

impart. Only when devoted to the service of Christ can they be put to their proper use. Now in this case before us this young man might quite conceivably have made the same sacrifice which he has now made externally, but if he had made it in the Name of Christ, and for Christ, it would have been a very different thing, and he would have spoken of it in a very different way, and it would have had a very different effect. There is all the difference in the world between sacrifice of self in Christ and for Christ, and sacrifice of self for Swaraj, however laudable an object that may be. In the letter of this young man Swaraj is the object of devotion, and Swaraj, however high an object that may be, is not the right object for a man's devotion. Looking at his action from a purely human standpoint we can all admire it; but looking at it from a Christian standpoint we cannot but realise how this devotion has missed its true mark. And when we think that this young man has come out of a Christian college, having learned so much that was morally good but apparently without any conception whatever of the Person of Christ, of the claim of Christ, of the true object of life and its true end as directed towards Christ, so that he writes to his Principal as though he expected him to admit that he is fully obeying the teaching which he has received, I confess that my mind is overwhelmed with a sense of disaster. The boy has been taught everything, except the one thing which gives everything else direction for Christian men. He has learned much; he has received much: what he has not learnt is for whom, and for what he has learned and received all the rest. And that I cannot call Christian education.

If we all know perfectly well, as we now ought to know, that the whole environment and atmosphere of these schools, the whole tradition, the whole attitude of these Hindu pupils and their parents, put an almost insuperable difficulty in the way of the conversion and therefore of the Christian teaching, of these young men, even where there is no conscience clause, how can we possibly imagine that we ought to spend our thought upon the possibility of adapting ourselves to the imposition of a conscience clause, and not rather to the much more serious question what we mean by Christian education, and whether the colleges we have, under their present conditions, can really be called Christian colleges at all? And if we find that they are not, to consider what steps ought to be taken. To continue to teach boys and young men the way of honesty, obedience to conscience, and self-sacrifice, without ensuring that they are in a position to come with equal readiness of mind to learn, and with equal opportunity to surrender themselves to, the one object for which, or rather the one Person at whose Feet, they may pour out all the treasures of their devotion, is surely not to put Christ first.

Figure 7. 'Mission Colleges in India' *(continued).*

Of Mr Sidney Clark's missionary enthusiasms and ideas since I first met him in 1914 it is easy to write . . . He always took a large view of missions . . . "Self-support from the very beginning" was a favourite cry with him; and by self-support he meant something very much more than contributions of money. He meant spiritual as well as material self-support. He meant . . . Christian Churches, in every village . . . able to stand on their own feet. . . . [1]

Allen explained what the indigenous principle of self-supporting churches actually entailed due to Clark's ideas about this issue. This is evidenced in his *The Spontaneous Expansion of the Church* (1927) and later in his 'The "Nevius Method" in Korea' (1930) in which his missionary theology became more sharply defined to articulate a philosophy of ministry concerning the application of apostolic principles for self-governing, self-supporting and self-extending churches. For example, Allen challenged a 'weakness', which he identified in Uganda's Bishop Alfred R. Tucker and 'his followers all over the world who quote his formula'[2] for independent support, government and extension. Allen disagreed with Tucker because he believed that these three functions could be seen as three separate expressions, whereas Allen said that 'the three are intimately united'.[3] Allen acknowledges that he came to this conclusion after engaging with Clark as they discussed that 'self-support' was to occur 'from the very beginning'.[4] Allen was convinced that Tucker's practice thwarted indigenous ministry in Uganda by putting into effect 'the formula separately at different times, and by different means'.[5] Clark and Allen believed that Tucker's methodology was anaemic because it still kept the Ugandan indigenous leadership dependent on foreign finances. That said, Allen also argued that 'self-support' applied not only to finances, but to the ability of indigenous churches to supply and propagate its own internal leadership. Again, his thinking here stemmed from Clark's definition which 'meant spiritual as well as material self-support'.[6]

After the death of Clark in 1930, new trustees served on the Survey Application Trust. It became apparent that the new trustees did not adhere to Allen's viewpoint on voluntary clergy. Therefore, he chose to withdraw, largely because of an apparent personality conflict with Thomas Cochrane. After Clark's death, the annual honorarium of £200.00 (GBP), which he had previously 'arranged that the Trust should continue to pay Roland', was, says Hubert Allen, discontinued. 'Roland and Beatrice were much too

---

1. Roland Allen, 'Business Man and Missionary Statesman: Sidney James Wells Clark: An Appreciation' *World Dominion* (London: World Dominion Press, December 1928) 3, 7.

2. Allen, *Spontaneous Expansion*, 27.

3. Ibid.

4. Allen, 'Business Man and Missionary Statesman', 7.

5. Allen, *Spontaneous Expansion*, 27.

6. Allen, 'Business Man and Missionary Statesman', 7.

proud to protest.'[1] However, years later, Cochrane wrote these words for Allen's obituary in *World Dominion*: 'I recall with a glow of gratitude the many hours we spent together. I often tried to find a flaw in his logic or a weak spot in his arguments, but I was beaten every time.'[2]

World Dominion eventually merged with the Mildmay Movement publication, *The World Today*. Andrew Porter describes The Mildmay Movement's evangelical emphasis as 'revivalism, a pronounced piety, foreign missions and concern for the Second Coming'.[3] In 1936, the editor of *The World Today*, Wilkinson Riddle, along with World Dominion's editor, decided to form a 'greatly improved' and 'absorbingly interesting' journal, with the expressed purpose that 'its principles be unchanged' and 'its theological outlook' remain the same.[4] The journal 'was published regularly until 1958, when it merged with *The Christian Newsletter*, under the title, *Frontier.*[5]

Missionary Survey as an Aid to Intelligent Co-operation in Foreign Missions (1920)

The book, *Missionary Survey as an Aid to Intelligent Co-operation in Foreign Missions* (hereafter referred to as *Missionary Survey*) was co-authored by Roland Allen and Thomas Cochrane in 1920 and published by World Dominion Press. In his Preface, Cochrane begins by crediting Allen with writing the book. That said, it is clear that they 'studied the material together . . . discussed and disputed, and finally found [themselves] in complete agreement . . . ' and so 'decided to issue the book in our joint names'.[6] The title of the book is entirely appropriate as the authors argue for the legitimacy of missionary survey work, which asks the proper questions for developing closer co-operation between mission societies, such as:

(1) What purpose governs the policy of the societies who send out evangelistic missionaries?;

(2) When assessing foreign missions can we even understand how the parts relate to the whole if their purpose is not clearly defined?;

1. Hubert Allen, *Roland Allen*, 118.

2. Thomas Cochrane, *World Dominion* (1948) 66.

3. Andrew Porter, *Religion versus empire?: British Protestant missionaries and overseas expansion, 1700-1914* (Manchester and New York: Manchester University Press, 2004) 198.

4. 'London', *World Dominion* (1948) 66.

5. Hubert Allen, *Roland Allen*, 117 (footnote 1).

6. Roland Allen and Thomas Cochrane, *Missionary Survey as an Aid to Intelligent Co-operation in Foreign Missions*, London: World Dominion Press, 1920, Preface.

(3) On what principles are decisions made to send missionaries to various locations?;

(4) Which type of information is necessary to determine what location is more urgent than another?; and

(5) How can 'a survey of the missionary situation' assist in the gathering of the facts?[7]

Allen's questions provide a framework for examining whether the mission societies' system is based upon principles of purposeful government and extension or arbitrary policy making. His enquiries have obviously been influenced by Clark's and Cochrane's thinking in these matters. In defence of the methods established by Allen, Clark and Cochrane, Allen addressed the missionary situation, arguing that firstly, 'scientific survey' is concerned with the 'facts' and that the inferences that stem from the facts gleaned from the surveys, which generally direct the foreign missionary societies' policies.[8] Cochrane and Allen state that even if there is a 'manipulation of facts' within the survey, this does not necessarily 'discredit' the *purpose* of the survey, but rather challenges 'the moral character of the man who made the survey'.[9] He argues that the 'missionary survey must justify itself' by dealing with the needs of the communities to be addressed and concluded what specifically is 'our purpose' for doing anything in a certain region.[10] If a community suffers 'changing circumstances', the survey has to take this into consideration by 'not simply a single act but a continual process' because the reality is that 'mission work is not a task which can be undertaken and finished on a predetermined plan, like the construction of a railway'.[11] When attempting to justify the methodology for the way that World Dominion administered their missionary surveys, anyone who is familiar with Allen's belief in the benefits of the 'small' or 'cell' church concept will basically recognize his pivotal understanding of how the apostolic principle of planting small – but fully equipped – churches provides the basis for his missionary ecclesiology. He said:

> The main difference between our tables and those of others is that we make them very small and express in each a relation. The figures supplied by the societies in their reports are seldom related to anything; they are mere bundles of sticks; we suggest

---

7. Ibid., 13-20.

8. Ibid., 21-22. This will also be addressed later.

9. Ibid., 22.

10. Ibid., 24-25.

11. Ibid., 25.

the introduction of a relation into every table which gives to each figure a significance which by itself it does not possess. In our tables every figure is set to work. Our idea of missionary statistics demands that they should be a basis for action.[1]

Allen's comment here concurs with his overall belief that smaller is better, or 'less is more'. That is to say, 'small'[2] churches within a 'reduced' diocesan district can enhance relational involvement with its members. And yet, a symphonic blend of Clark's church-planting methodology of 'small village churches' – although 'congregational' and different from Allen's – combined with his diocesan 'local church' ideal carved out a proactive missionary ecclesiology that applied the apostolic principle for establishing the Church 'in places where it might have been least expected, among the most down-trodden and degraded tribes and races'[3] because both Allen and Clark understood that 'the poor of this world' have been called 'to be rich in faith' (James 2:5). This was Bishop V.S. Azariah's vision, also.

Allen admits that Clark's idea for Church growth in China was a radical shift in which 'the idea of an indigenous Church was not the idea of something which might emerge after a century or two of training' because he believed, and Allen agreed, that Clark 'pictured to himself the establishment of little Churches of Christians all self-supporting . . . without any direction from foreigners'.[4] This concept functions better with Cochrane and Allen's methodology of scientific survey work because the 'smaller' survey, according to Allen, tended to augment a more realistic way to measure the data. What he calls the 'mere bundles of sticks'[5] of the mission societies' reports and theoretical surveys do a disservice to the overall perception of the missionary situation.

As a published author, Allen learned how to strive for clarity and reasonable arguments whenever critics periodically reacted against his writings, whether by unintentional misunderstandings or by intentional misrepresentations. When addressing the philosophy of mission, his critics argued that he was sometimes too abstract. This *cannot* be said of his contribution to *Missionary Survey* (1920) because this book's quantitative approach reasonably responds to the contrary opinion. Between chapters 3 and 11, Allen and Cochrane developed no less than 75 survey tables which specifically detailed everything from: how many villages, towns

---

1. Ibid., 27-28.
2. Cf. Allen's use of 'little Christian congregations'; Ibid., 43.
3. Allen, 'Business Man and Missionary Statesman', 8.
4. Ibid.
5. Allen and Cochrane, *Missionary Survey*, 27-28.

and cities are within a district that has a 'mission station'[6] and the amount of work to be accomplished there; the 'proportion of Christians to non-Christians';[7] the proportion to population of women;[8] communicants;[9] paid and unpaid workers in missions;[10] enquirers brought in by indigenous Christians and 'congregations evangelizing their neighbours';[11] proportion of 'literates';[12] Christians given to 'higher education';[13] number of medical doctors, assistants, nurses, hospitals, and beds for patients,[14] as examples of the factual data surveyed. This type of quantitative research[15] demonstrates his concern for a comprehensive approach to missionary analysis, which provided an organized arrangement of the data to properly direct the mission societies to be more purposeful in their vision and mission.

The World Dominion Movement questioned the 'popular' way that many missionaries tabulated and compared the criteria of their converts 'zeal' on the basis of them 'putting money into a box', which Allen argued was 'most dangerous' and 'a most delusive and deluding test'.[16] He and Cochrane agreed that a better way to measure the devotion of indigenous converts was to evaluate the 'Christian Constituency' as a whole; then to calculate the number of 'Inquirers [sic] brought in by Native Christians'; furthermore, to see how this related to the way congregations were choosing to evangelize their neighbors; and then to assess the 'Amount Subscribed for Missionary Purposes'.[17] Immediately after the fifteenth survey table, Allen shifts gears and articulates what appears to be an evangelical missionary theology that he believed was indicative of 'nearly all those for whom we write'.[18] He said:

> We stand for the open Bible; we believe that the Christian Church in every country will progress and develop strongly if it is based on a widespread knowledge of Holy Writ, and we are prepared to

---

6. Ibid., 33.
7. Ibid., 35.
8. Ibid., 38.
9. Ibid., 40.
10. Ibid., 40-43.
11. Ibid., 44-45.
12. Ibid.
13. Ibid.
14. Ibid., 56-57.
15. Ibid., 38, 63.
16. Ibid., 43.
17. Ibid., 44.
18. Ibid.

believe that a capacity to read the Bible is a sure sign of health in any Christian Church. The test of literacy commonly adopted in our missions is the capacity to read the Holy Gospels: we accept that gladly and confidently.[1]

Allen's emphasis here on 'the open Bible' for all to read the Gospels – the mission's literacy test – reaffirms the Church's historical practice. As Andrew Walls states: 'The Church's Scriptures are those read in church, and it was this public reading of Scripture, a natural continuation of synagogue practice, which must have been normative for most members of the early Christian communities.'[2] The Church's historic practice of publicly reading the Bible for all to hear, retain and assimilate, also incited the illiterate to pursue literacy. The ancient practice, Walls affirms, merges with Allen's attention paid to another survey that examines the proportion of 'literates' within the non-Christian population and the proportion of 'literates' within the entire Christian community, in light of the proportion of 'Christians of Higher Education'.[3] To suggest an analogy, Elliott-Binns highlights the need for literacy and 'training in moral and religious principles' to the people living in Lancashire and Yorkshire as they displayed the 'brutish ignorance of the lower classes'[4] during times of great conflict. Elliott-Binns's reference to the illiterate condition of many in Northern England at that time makes the point that, until these conflicts emerged, there seemed to be a lack of awareness of the problems. An argument could be made that, if there had been educational surveys done in Lancashire and Yorkshire, such as Allen and Cochrane's, then the problems possibly could have been identified and a plan of action for educational development enacted sooner. That said, Allen and Cochrane did survey analysis to identify areas in which mission societies could implement more effective educational approaches to address the problems of illiteracy. This did not negate his belief in the primary focus of apostolic mission but rather he recognized the place for educational influence through missionary involvement provided it was *an extension of* the indigenous Church's ministry to their people. These surveys were rooted in a framework of indigenous principles

---

1. Ibid.
2. Andrew F. Walls, *The Missionary Movement in Christian History: Studies in the Transmission of Faith*, (Maryknoll: Orbis Books and Edinburgh: T&T Clark, 2009 [1996]) 36.
3. Allen and Cochrane, *Missionary Survey*, 45.
4. L.E. Elliott-Binns, *Religion in the Victorian Era* (Cambridge: James Clarke & Co., 1936) 90.

that germinated from his missionary thinking. At the end of this table analysis is a category, 'Remarks and Conclusions', which formed the end of each of the survey tables and disclosed their desire to objectively and democratically solve mission station problems rather than to force their own agenda.

Furthermore, in the chapter that addresses 'Medical Work in the Station District', there is evidence for how Allen incorporated a 'holistic' approach to medical mission by examining his survey investigation into the 'medical work as an evangelistic agency'.[5] Firstly, he explains how the survey examines the 'relative extent' that those who administer the medical work actually attempt to use 'evangelistic workers' through this table does *not* disclose any 'evangelistic influence of the hospital' directly.[6] Secondly, he comments on those 'medical workers' who recognize their 'medical work in the Spirit' because they tend to pray with their patients as having a 'wider and deeper' level of evangelistic outreach even if there were not any appointed 'evangelistic workers' within the context of the hospital administration.[7] He explains how the next three survey tables (27-29) help to differentiate whether or not evangelistic workers are employed within the hospitals; whether these 'medicals assist in evangelistic tours' by 'healing the sick . . . preaching' or 'by sending them to hospitals'; or, whether they implement 'all these ways'.[8] He concludes by stating that these three tables could work in conjunction to 'contribute to our study' and possibly allow for them 'to justify medical missions as an evangelistic agency'.[9] That said, over the years, he did appreciate the humanitarian efforts of medical missions but has been misunderstood because he often confronted the mission station focus on 'medical mission' in contrast to his primary emphasis on 'apostolic' gospel evangelization from village to village.

Right after Allen shows the relationship between evangelistic and medical work, he addresses the institutional side of educational work and what happens when the presence of missionary 'evangelistic' educators appears to create a context in which other educators 'consider themselves absolved from personal effort by the occasional presence of an evangelist', thus making a bifurcation between 'religious teaching' and 'secular teaching'.[10] He saw this as a 'danger' but not one that is 'unavoidable'.[11] Survey

---

5. Ibid., 58.
6. Ibid.
7. Ibid.
8. Ibid., 59-60.
9. Ibid., 60.
10. Ibid., 68.
11. Ibid.

table 36 is broken down into the following categories: schools, quantity
of schools, which are regularly visited by evangelists, and ratio of schools
visited by evangelists.[1] He acknowledges that the nature of evangelistic
work is definitely 'educational to the core' and that the end result leads
to education.[2] That said, his next table (37) makes distinctions between
evangelistic tours, the number of evangelistic workers and educators who
assist, and the length of time for these tours.[3] This last survey highlights
one of his *key principles*, which shapes the basis for his proactive 'trans-local'
missionary ecclesiology where 'apostolic evangelists' not only plant but also
equip indigenous churches by teaching and empowering the laity to develop
their vocations for local church ministry.[4]

He recognized that the 'relation between the medical and educational
work' presents a certain tension, which he believed 'has not been carefully
thought out in the past' and therefore, due to uncertain policies shows
evidence of 'that confusion of purpose'.[5] Later in this volume, Allen sets
out to address this confusion and proposes the need for both the medical
and educational branches to work towards 'one common dominant
purpose', and yet, acknowledges the difficulty to develop a survey table
with proper details. He suggests three types of tables (41-43) to cover
this proposal and take the evangelistic, medical and educational branches
to assess the following categories: 'foreign missionaries, natives assisting
in evangelistic tours, assisting in hospitals and assisting in schools.[6]
Allen's 'holistic principle approach' for hospital care and education is
evangelistic to the core and incorporates within its methodology one of
his *key principles* by which 'all Christians are missionaries – the Church is
a missionary body'.[7] His missionary thinking encapsulates the indigenous
faith communities to be the fountains of holistic outreach within the
medical field and educational institutions.

The last four chapters of this volume addresses the following: the
'native' or indigenous Church; surveying of defined and undefined
districts where more than one mission society is working; surveying
the provincial work; and the final chapter of surveying the mission

---

1. Ibid.
2. Ibid., 69.
3. Ibid.
4. Roland Allen, 'The Ministry of Expansion: the Priesthood of the Laity',
   Oxford, Bodleian Library, USPG X622, Box 3, Number 27, chapter 4:5.
5. Allen and Cochrane, *Missionary Survey*, 72-73.
6. Ibid., 74-75.
7. Roland Allen, 'The Work of the Missionary in Preparing the Way for
   Independent Native Churches', 40, 61, 67, 75, 77-80, 165.

station and how it relates to the world.[8] These chapters propose survey tables 44-75 and cover issues such as self-supporting churches (44-47),[9] patriarchal, monarchical and constitutional episcopacy (48),[10] 'the creation of an independent native Church',[11] competing mission societies who claim ownership of the same district,[12] incipient expressions of ecumenical co-operation whereby 'one mission must complement another' and attempts to work together to comprehensively address the evangelistic, medical, and educational influence on all of society where their work is accepted.[13] And, in typical Allen-style, his focus emphasizes the application of principles and methods on the 'vision of the whole' so that 'our eyes are fixed on the final goal', in which 'our policy in every part should be part of a policy designed for the whole'.[14] Towards the conclusion of this book, he took the contents of the quantitative categories and moved from the 'micro' to the 'macro' with these words:

> We should not send hasty missions here and there because some interesting political event attracts the eyes of men to this or that particular country, but on definite missionary principles, acting on a clear and reasonable understanding of the missionary situation in the world. The commission of Christ is world-wide, the claim of Christ is world-wide, the work of Christ is world-wide, the Spirit of Christ are all-embracing; and the work which missionaries do in His name should be all-embracing too.[15]

The significance of Allen's work – without wanting to underestimate Cochrane's and Clark's influence – relates to his painstaking analysis of many of the issues that were apparently bypassed within the policies of several prominent mission societies. This book provides a basis for his work as a methods-analyst as he surveyed mission work in different countries and gives a glimpse into his way of analyzing the missionary situation within the Anglican Communion for the forthcoming decades. His closing comments expressed his (and Cochrane's) deprecating posture by saying: 'we admit, rather a hasty and tentative expression of the way in which we might satisfy the present need . . . and we can think

---

8. Allen and Cochrane, *Missionary Survey*, 76-116.
9. Ibid., 76-83.
10. Ibid., 83-84.
11. Ibid., 87.
12. Ibid., 88-93.
13. Ibid., 94-112.
14. Ibid., 114.
15. Ibid.

of no better plan than to propose tables, and then leave to others to criticize and amend them.'[1] Here stands 'the quantitative methodology' of a man who is generally noted for primarily writing in philosophical and theological terms.

Significant events in 1926-27

During 1927, Allen published *The Spontaneous Expansion of the Church and the Causes Which Hinder It*,[2] wrote an important article entitled 'Devolution and its Real Significance'; assessed missionary strategies from the 1926 Conference: 'Le Zoute – a Critical Review of "The Christian Mission in Africa"' (discussed below); published a 'revised' edition of *Missionary Methods* (World Dominion Press); and, visited Bishop V.S. Azariah and his Dornakal diocesan work in India. Another event that took place in 1927 was the 'Revised Trust Deed' of the Survey Application Trust. The original trustees of the World Dominion Movement (1917) – Clark, Cochrane and Allen – formed a trust called the Survey Trust (1918), later called the Survey Application Trust (formed 3 November 1924).[3] Then, it was called the 'new Deed' (4 February 1927)[4] until Clark's health really began to deteriorate and he was unable to 'play even an advisory part' that 'a further Deed was executed' (4 July 1927).[5] Some of the contents of what Hubert Allen called 'the revised deed' emphasized that the:

> trust and the press were set up with the specific task . . . of helping to apply, anywhere in the world, the principles asserted by Clark in his pamphlets and by Roland in his two best known books to that date, namely *Missionary Methods,* and *The Spontaneous Expansion of the Church.*[6]

It was during this time (while Allen was in his late fifties) that his argument against 'professional clericalism' within the Church of England's missionary methods, especially 'professional missionaries' that received government funding for their missions, had abandoned, he argued, their apostolic calling. This *apologia* for a 'voluntary' approach to mission is disclosed within his review of the Le Zoute Conference.

---

1. Ibid., 116.
2. Roland and his family referred to this book as 'Sponx' as is later reiterated by Hubert Allen, *Roland Allen*, 107-108.
3. Paton, *Reform of the Ministry*, 67-68.
4. Ibid.
5. Ibid., 68.
6. Hubert Allen, *Roland Allen*, 94.

MISSION COLLEGES AND SCHOOLS.
II.— THE MEANING OF CHRISTIAN EDUCATION.
By the REV. ROLAND ALLEN, M.A.

LATELY missionary societies have been sending out commissions to India to enquire, and have been seriously discussing at home, under what circumstances they can admit the application of a conscience clause in their mission schools and colleges.

It is commonly supposed that this is a question for experts, and that without considerable local and practical experience no one should speak on the subject. I want to argue that this is an immense mistake, and that there never was a missionary question on which it was more important that the supporters of missions at home should exercise their own proper judgment. It needs no local knowledge to judge whether a college or school in which 80 per cent. of the masters and 90 per cent. of the scholars are non-Christian can be properly called a Christian college or school ; we could speedily decide that question in the case of our own children. The question is not one of local circumstances but of our conception of Christian education : it is not one of local conditions but of our object and intention in supporting Christian missions at all.

What do we mean by Christian education ? The other day Sir Michael Sadler presented us with this admirable climax :—(1) " Initiation into a way of life is a desirable, if not an indispensable, element in a liberal education " ; (2) " Religion assigns their relative values to the various good things which a man may enjoy but must learn how to use ;" (3) " We believe that the Christian Faith and the Christian experience teach, reveal, communicate the Way, the Truth and the Life. This is the priceless treasure of a Christian education." A liberal education, then, involves initiation into a way of life : a religious education involves initiation into a religious way of life : a Christian education involves initiation into the Way. Now when Sir Michael speaks of " The Way, the Truth and the Life " we may be certain that he is thinking of the " I am," which explains them in St. John's Gospel. Christian education on those terms must be no less than initiation into Christ.

Christ First.

If this conception of Christian education is accepted, three consequences follow :— (1) Certainly Christ, and faith in Christ, assume the first place in thought. All else in life, all else in education, derives its value and place and use from its relation to Christ. *Si Christum noscis, nihil est si cetera nescis, si Christum nescis nihil est si cetera noscis*, is the true rule of a Christian education. All human knowledge imparted on any other foundation is worthless, misunderstood, liable to abuse. Worthless in the sense that it is nothing worth in regard to the true issue of life : misunderstood in the sense that it is divorced from that which alone gives it meaning for true life : liable to abuse because it is not directed to the only true end.

From the point of view of the Christian teacher this relation is the essential thing. He cannot teach any subject except in this relation. Consequently he can no more teach a pupil who does not bring a ready mind and heart to this teaching than a secular teacher can teach mathematics or science to a pupil who refuses to give him attention. No teacher of mathematics would go on teaching a pupil who deliberately declined to accept and practise his teaching, who flatly refused to believe what he was taught. Under such circumstances the teacher would decline to teach. Similarly, a Christian teacher cannot teach a pupil who obstinately refuses to accept his religious teaching of the relation of his subject to the Christian life. If he attempts to do so, if he allows such an attitude, he wrongs himself, he wrongs the pupil, he wrongs the Truth. He wrongs himself : he abrogates

his position as a Christian teacher : as teacher he has a right to attention, and to that moral attention which issues in obedience ; and if he teaches without receiving that moral attention, he ceases to be worthy of the name of teacher. He wrongs the pupil : the pupil comes to learn ; and if he comes to a religious teacher, he ought to find the religion first ; and if he is allowed to approach the religious teaching without giving it that moral attention which issues in obedience to the truth, he is allowed to learn an immoral attitude to all learning and to all life. He wrongs the Truth : the Truth demands moral attention and obedience. If the teacher allows the pupil to refuse moral obedience to the Truth, he wrongs the Truth : he places the Truth below his subject in importance.

Non-Christians Cannot Receive Christian Education.

(2) Christian education can only be given to baptized Christians, or to pupils who are preparing to become such. If religious education can only be given to pupils who are capable of, and willing to take, a religious view of life, Christian education can only be given to pupils who are capable of, and willing to take, a Christian view of life. Christian education cannot possibly be given to pupils who deliberately refuse to accept and to act upon the teaching given to them. If they, and their parents, deliberately intend that they shall not become Christians, and be baptized ; so long as they maintain that attitude they are not receiving a Christian education. How can they learn to relate themselves and all that they learn to Christ whilst they are deliberately refusing to recognise the claim of Christ to their reasonable service ? They may, indeed, accept a certain amount of the moral teaching of Christ ; but if they are not learning to relate themselves and their gifts to Christ, in active obedience ; if they do not become Christians, they are not receiving that moral teaching Christianly ; they are not receiving Christian education. They are not being educated in Christ ; but as non-Christians they are being taught certain teachings of a master of the moral life.

Religious pupils can receive instruction at the hands of irreligious men ; Christian pupils can receive instruction from non-Christian masters in Government schools ; because they can transmute a teaching given on an irreligious or non-Christian basis into religious and Christian education. What they learn they learn as religious and Christian persons, and they can absorb it and grow upon it as Christians. But Christian teaching cannot be given by Christian men to heathen pupils ; because without the co-operation of the pupil it is not received as Christian. The heathen pupil learns something from a Christian master : of that teaching some part he can assimilate as a heathen, and he absorbs it and grows upon it as a heathen ; some part, and that the most vital part, he cannot receive as a heathen, and he therefore rejects it, that he may remain a heathen. But that is not receiving Christian education.

A Christian Teacher does not make a School Christian.

Hence we make a serious mistake when we imagine that the education is Christian because it is given by Christian men ; or when we imagine that a school attended by heathen is a Christian school because it has some Christian masters ; or when we think that a pupil has received a Christian education, because he has been taught by Christian men. Just as there must be co-operation on the part of the pupil and willingness to receive instruction in order that any intellectual education may be given him ; so there must be co-operation on his part and willingness to receive Christian teaching

in order that any Christian education may be given him.

The Divided Life.

(3) Christian education declines the common distinction between secular and religious education. That distinction is familiar to us and acceptable because we are an irreligious people, but it is quite unjustifiable. We divide life into compartments, religious and secular ; and therefore we divide education into the like compartments. " Governments which give grants in support of education, the parents of our pupils, and our pupils themselves, all alike recognise that we acknowledge the distinction. They all alike think that they can support or partake of the secular without supporting or partaking of the religious element. They think that they can enforce the distinction by means of a conscience clause. And we agree, and talk of a conscience clause just as they talk. We have in fact done ourselves before the conscience clause is applied what the conscience clause presupposes. We have accepted the idea that the Christian Faith is one subject in a school curriculum, like mathematics, or science, or music. Viewed simply as a historical, philosophical or ethical subject it can obviously be so treated. As a subject of human knowledge it can be excluded : a boy can learn mathematics or science without learning the life of Christ or the Creeds or the Ten Commandments. But in our saner moments we refuse to admit that the Christian Faith is one subject among others, or can properly be so treated ; we refuse to acknowledge that division of life into religious and secular compartments which is the bane of our modern Western thought and activity ; we know that Christ claims to direct and govern all life, not merely fragments of it, and that to do anything whatsoever except in relation to Him is to go astray. We know that a man cannot relate some of his acts to Christ on one day in the week and act all the rest of the week without relating his acts to Christ, and yet be living the Christian life. But that is exactly what the distinction between religious and secular subjects in schools presupposes can be done. We say, " there is nothing peculiarly Christian or religious in arithmetic or science." We might as well have said, there is nothing peculiarly Christian in eating or in drinking, or in marriage. The body is common to all human beings, marriage is common to all organised human life. We might as well have said, Christ has nothing to do with business or trade : these things are common to civilised life whatever the religion may be. There is nothing, indeed, peculiarly Christian in any of these things except for Christians ; and we were not sufficiently Christian to see that as marriage is for Christians quite peculiarly Christian, as trade is for Christians quite peculiarly Christian, so arithmetic or science is for Christians quite peculiarly Christian. All learning is, for Christians, Christian learning, unless they cease to act as Christians when they learn, and then they divide their lives.

Bible Lessons do not Make a School Christian.

In schools where this distinction is recognised the pupils learn to make that fatal error. They learn the Bible, and that is a religious lesson ; they learn mathematics and that is a secular lesson. But Christian education should be initiation into a Christian way of life ; and it is impossible to learn to live a Christian life except by learning to relate every act of life to Christ. If a boy does not learn mathematics, or science, religiously, he is not learning to direct his life religiously ; if he does not learn these things Christianly, he is not learning to direct his life Christianly. He is not being initiated into the Christian Way, even if he attend Bible classes every day. Thus the distinction between the religious and secular teaching in schools is not merely a mistake of method, it is a practical negation of Christian education.

Now it is unquestionable that in our mission schools and colleges all these viola-

---

Figure 8. Allen's apologetic for an integrated Christian worldview within the educational process is articulated within this article, *The Challenge*, 2 June 1922.

Le Zoute – A Critical Review of
"The Christian Mission in Africa" (1926)

Allen prefaces this review by explaining how: (1) he gathered and examined a few of the 'statements made' and 'arguments used' at this conference at Le Zoute; (2) he closely examined one of the papers read at the conference which clearly stated the 'purpose and intention' that the conference was called in the first place; and (3) he added an article that he previously wrote 'before' this conference commenced, which was included with this pamphlet.[1] He began by explaining how the conference's title was 'also the purposely chosen title of the book, "The Christian Mission in Africa"'.[2] And yet, he immediately critiqued the placement of this title as being strangely placed 'in the middle of the chapter' in the midst of information dealing with 'personnel' and conference 'arrangements'.[3] That said, he specifically describes the type of people who attended and the agenda before them: (1) that it consisted of 'professional missionaries' who had 'proposals' set in front of them that 'concerned co-operation with governments composed of Christians and non-Christians; and (2) these missionaries were 'invited to co-operate with governments and settlers' to engage with 'every form of philanthropic, social, and political activity'.[4] He was upset that the 'title' of the conference 'begged the whole question and begged it in a misleading form', because, on one hand, although it advocated a 'Christian' approach to mission, it became apparent that the governing body that had set the agenda and direction of the conference were advocates of 'a social gospel' message.[5] On the other hand, he was already suspicious of i ow various missionary societies had embraced the 'social gospel' idea, which he obviously opposed:

> I recall that the missionary societies began to speak of preaching a Social Gospel, a Gospel of Health, a Gospel of Sex Equality, and all the rest, only after they had accepted the money which was given by people who would give nothing for evangelistic work. When they accepted money which was given by people who would give nothing for evangelistic work, then they began to find these terms to express their Gospel, and then they began to preach what the terms expressed.[6]

---

1. Roland Allen, *Le Zoute: A Critical Review of 'The Christian Mission in Africa*
   (London: World Dominion Press, February 1927).
2. Ibid., 3.
3. Ibid.
4. Ibid., 3-4.
5. Ibid., 4, 15.
6. Ibid., 15.

Earlier in 1926, the evidence indicates that Allen became more convinced that evangelism was compromised whenever the Church received finances from government agencies or humanitarian sources, which had their own 'special interest' agenda to implement. He argued that the Church need not receive money from these sources: 'for to build upon money is to build on a foundation that is not of the Gospel; it is to bind the Church to the chariot wheels of Mammon.'[7] He writes against this tendency and this plays a major part of his missionary ecclesiology for, he believed, and that *if* the Church is compromised due to: (1) receiving government funding; or (2) when the Church makes the 'stipendiary system' a necessity for the Church's expansion, then the Church has compromised, what he calls, the basic apostolic principle of self-support. This was also shown later in life (1943), while he was living in Africa, he wrote in a letter to the editor of the *East Anglican Standard* that the stipendiary system 'ties the church to the chariot wheels of mammon and men see it and know what that means'.[8] All in all, he believed that the mission societies were 'and have been, and are being led far from their true objective' – evangelism – and were tending to place more emphasis on education,[9] even though, as he observes, the 'Conference refused to face the plain truth that Christian education can only be given to men who want to be Christians'.[10]

In terms of the effect of the conference upon the African situation, Allen concludes by clarifying that both the conference and the subsequent book that articulated the contents expressed how 'the African Church is indeed mentioned, but is practically ignored'.[11] The addendum consists of Allen's preliminary article (1926) in which he critiques a paper by J.H. Oldham, challenging Oldham's view that, for the African Church, 'the best guarantee will be the presence of men of exceptional training as *educators*'.[12] He disagrees with Oldham and states that 'some of us doubt' whether that is the case because there is no guarantee 'that men will be full of the evangelistic spirit'.[13] He continues to argue against Oldham's claims because it 'distracted attention' from the missionary

---

7. Roland Allen, 'Money: the Foundation of the Church', *Pilgrim* (July 1926) 428, Oxford, Bodleian Library, USPG X622, Box 2, File 2: 20.

8. Roland Allen, 'Church Reform', letter to the editor, *East Anglican Standard* (27 January 1943) 53, Oxford, Bodleian Library, USPG X622, Box 8: 53.

9. Allen, *Le Zoute*, 6-7.

10. Ibid., 12.

11. Ibid., 23.

12. Ibid., 25.

13. Ibid.

societies' primary vocation for 'propagating the Gospel in the regions beyond, where the Church does not exist'.[1] He thought that Oldham's desire for the missionary to take on the vocation of becoming a 'scientific anthropologist . . . [and to] engage in secular education. . . . Christian statesman busy about social questions' was becoming a major distraction and was only 'typical of modern thought about Missions and Missionary Societies.[2] Hendrik Kraemer disagrees with Allen:

> Many missionaries are not good revolutionaries, but blind ones, because their minds are closed to the inestimable advantage they can derive from the labours of the anthropologists, and to the grievous damage they cause by their blindness to the healthy development of those peoples. At the present time one of the great needs of the missionary task is that the missionary agencies demand from their missionaries a serious and intelligent appreciation of the significance of anthropological insight for the right execution of the missionary task.[3]

Kraemer generally agreed with Allen's missiological emphasis on the indigenous Church's instrumental[4] involvement for Christianity's expansion,[5] but yet here he disagrees with Allen's criticism of Oldham's concern. That said, Kraemer had his own doubts concerning 'the background of Le Zoute',[6] especially the 'romanticism' focus evident in the Conference and through Gutmann's 'kind of romanticism',[7] which he believed 'is no good and lasting foundation to build strong and lasting Christian Churches upon'.[8] Timothy Yates also agrees concerning 'the sharply critical eye of a thinker like Roland Allen', whose 1928 'carping little piece on [the] Jerusalem [Conference] indicated'[9] a progressively

1. Ibid., 27.
2. Ibid., 28.
3. Henrick Kraemer, *The Christian Message in a Non-Christian World* (Grand Rapids: Kregel Publications, 1969 [1938]) 343.
4. Ibid., 413.
5. Henrik Kraemer, *A Theology of the Laity* (London: The Lutterworth Press, 1960 [1958]) 20.
6. Kraemer, *Christian Message*, 340-43.
7. Ibid., 340.
8. Ibid.
9. Timothy Yates, *Christian Mission in the Twentieth Century* (Cambridge: Cambridge University Press, 1999) 70; cf. Roland Allen, *Jerusalem: a Critical Review of the World Mission of Christianity* (London, 1928) 1-38.

social 'understanding of the kingdom' which stems from Le Zoute (1926) to Jerusalem (1928). David Bosch concurs with this change in attention as he argues that by the 'third decade' of the twentieth century mission societies' had experienced 'a distinct evolution' from charitable benevolence – disaster aid, care for orphans, the provision of rudimentary health care' – that is, a shift from providing an 'ambulance service' to more of a 'comprehensive approach'[10] of involvement in 'rural reconstruction' due to 'industrial problems', which was also popularized during the Jerusalem Conference of the International Missionary Council (1928)'.[11] Lamin Sanneh called this 'a revisionist understanding of the mission of the Church' being promoted at a conference, which, in addition, presented a 'revisionist view . . . that the Christian claim about the uniqueness and finality of Christ was no longer tenable in view of the reality of other faiths'.[12] Allen *rejected* this missional direction. Bosch, also, states that later this shift continued to escalate after World War II, during which both 'Roman Catholics and Protestants' began to revamp the 'comprehensive approach' and 'replaced' it 'with the notion of "development"'.[13] That said, Oldham's view that missionaries ought to engage in the social forces – education, social science, medical training, economic –[14] stemmed from his earlier thinking expressed through his work *The World and the Gospel* (1916) in which he clearly stated that it 'is *not* to be expected that every missionary should be a statesman, familiar with questions of government policy and administration . . . if costly mistakes are to be avoided, some missionaries must have a competent knowledge of these matters'[15] (emphasis added). In Allen's thinking, he did *not* overstate his concerns about this shift in emphasis for himself and others[16] within the network of the World Dominion Press readership, including advocates of 'faith missions',[17] expressed disfavour with the changes in missional tone and direction.

---

10. Bosch, *Transforming Mission*, 356.

11. Ibid.

12. Sanneh, *Disciples of All Nations*, 273.

13. Bosch, *Transforming Mission*, 356.

14. J.H. Oldham, *The World and the Gospel* (London: United Council for Missionary Education [UCME], 1917 [1916]) 175.

15. Ibid., 175-76.

16. Allen, *Le Zoute*, 25.

17. Robert B. Dann, *The Primitivist Missiology of Anthony Norris Groves: A Radical Influence on Nineteenth-Century ProtestantMmission* (Chester: Tamarisk Books, 2007) 192-93; cf. Bosch, *Transforming Mission*, 332-33; and Stanley, *The Bible and the Flag*, 76.

Not only that but his concern with Oldham's *progressive* view dates back to his earlier concerns with the emphasis on 'manifest destiny' and, what Stanley describes as, Alfred Hogg's 'Ritschlian theological framework',[1] which was echoed by some of the leaders within the World Missionary Conference in Edinburgh, 1910. Bosch would agree with Allen's concern as he defined 'manifest destiny' as the 'product of nationalism'[2] which views the Western nations to be providentially called 'Christians of a specific nation would develop the conviction that they had an exceptional role to play in the advancement of the kingdom of God through the missionary enterprise'.[3] Bosch expressed concern that this 'nationalistic spirit' had the tendency to 'be absorbed into missionary ideology' and implied 'an organic link between Western colonial expansion and the notion of manifest destiny'.[4] Stanley calls this approach a 'liberalized postmillennialism', which promotes 'the spread of Christian civilization and idealism . . . without the cutting edge of Puritan theology' as a 'degenerated' and 'facile creed of liberal imperialism'.[5] He clarifies that the 'Puritan' missionaries whose mission focus was on spiritual conversion had a *different* focus on what is called 'manifest destiny' in that their version was a 'postmillennial eschatology' that was based upon a 'Christian hope . . . on the promises apparently given in the Bible', which 'constituted an ideology of exceptional self-confidence and power' while doing missionary 'work with very little visible fruit in terms of conversions' and under the most extreme 'difficulties'.[6] That said, Allen maintained an optimistic view for the advancement of the Kingdom of God without the trappings of imperialistic overtones. For Allen, he believed that the Kingdom of God was extended by the Holy Spirit's spontaneous empowerment of newly planted churches that were nurtured by means of apostolic faith and mission.

1. Brian Stanley, *The World Missionary Conference, Edinburgh 1910*, Studies in the History of Christian Missions (Grand Rapids: Eerdmans, 2009) 224.

2. Bosch, *Transforming Mission*, 298.

3. Ibid., 298-99.

4. Ibid., 298.

5. Brian Stanley, *The Bible and the Flag*, 75-76.

6. Ibid., 74-75.

6. Field Work in Various Countries

Field Work Analysis: India (1910-11; 1927-28); Canada (1924); South Africa (1926)

During Roland Allen's first visit to India, he was accompanied by his wife Beatrice. They spent 'a couple of months' and visited 'Delhi, Calcutta and Madras' where he was 'invited to preach in these and several smaller places'.[1] Hubert Allen's family have preserved 'letters to their two children' while the Allen's were visiting 'from Barisal in the Ganges delta, and from Ramnad, far to the south near the great temples of Madurai'.[2] It was during this visit that Allen was able to meet Vedanayagam Samuel (V.S.) Azariah and more than likely met Bishop Henry Whitehead of Madras who wrote the Introduction to his first edition of 'the wryly entitled'[3] *Missionary Methods: St Paul's or Ours?* (1912).[4] This visit provided the embryonic friendships with Whitehead and especially Azariah which would last for years to come.

In 1927, he was invited back by Azariah to minister within his diocese (Dornakal), and also, by Bishop George C. Hubback to minister within his diocese (Assam). This visit took place between 2 December 1927 and 8 March 1928. As he travelled within Dornakal and Assam, he spent most of this time answering questions and arguing in defense of ways to apply the *principle of voluntary clergy* within their village churches (see *Figure 12* below).[5]

Canada (1924)

Later in life, while living in Africa, he wrote an article for the *East Anglican Standard*, wherein he reflected back to 1924 when he was constructing survey analysis for the Survey Application Trust for a project called 'the

---

1. Hubert Allen, *Roland Allen*, 86.

2. Ibid.

3. Ibid.

4. Ibid.

5. A detailed case-study on this application of apostolic principles to the dioceses of Dornakal and Assam is addressed within *Roland Allen: A Theology of Mission.*

12A, LOWER GROSVENOR PLACE,
S.W.

June 11th, 1912.

My dear Allen.

Your letter to the Church Times hits the right nail on the head. The only point in it which an opponent might take hold of is that most of the converts in the Dornakal Mission were made before Mr. Azariah actually went there as head of the Mission. The Mission was first established about seven years ago, and Mr. Azariah went there three years ago. But you are substantially right: the establishment of the Indian Missionary Society of Tinnevelly was almost entirely due to the faith, zeal and energy of Azariah. He was secretary of the Mission from the first, and the whole success of the work is really due to him; so that, even though he did not actually make the converts himself, they are ~~entirely~~ due to his faith, wisdom and enthusiasm.

I did not see the statement in the Church Times. I gather from your letter that the protest in question is said to have been made by communicants of Tinnevelly. Apparently, it was not stated that a counter-petition, far more weighty and far more numerously signed, was also sent to the Metropolitan, in favour of Mr. Azariah's appointment, in addition to ~~the~~ numerous letters

Figure 9. Bishop Henry Whitehead's letter to Roland Allen
(11 June 1912).

2.

from people of standing and influence. A petition against his
appointment was also sent from the Telugu country: but it was
not signed by the people in any of the districts which are to
be assigned to the new bishop. Petitions were sent to them, but
the people tore them up, and refused to have anything to do with
them.   The objection that Mr. Azariah has not got a university
degree is not quite ingenuous; it is well known that he read
for the B.A. degree in the University of Madras, and would certainly have taken his degree, but that he fell ill the week
before the examination, and was unable to appear for it.   He
took up some form of Christian work next year, and so did not
sit for the examination ~~again~~ *in the following year*.

You are quite right in your conjecture as to the real reasons for *the* petition.   It has been openly stated: (1) that the
appointment has caused heart-burning among the senior Indian
clergy; (2) that some of the Indian Christians objected to
Azariah because they think he is not of sufficiently high caste, *(3)*
and others because he worked with Nonconformists in connection
with the Student Volunteer Movement.   Jealousy, caste feeling
and party spirit are the real causes of the opposition.

These facts may be useful to you in case you get involved

Figure 9. Bishop Henry Whitehead's letter (*continued*).

3.

12ᴬ, LOWER GROSVENOR PLACE,
                                        S.W.

in a controversy as a result of your letters, after I have left
England. But the most important points to emphasise are just
those which you have brought forward in your two letters, namely:
(1) that the appointment of the head of the first purely Indian
mission to be the bishop of the district which he is evangelising
is eminently suitable and right, and strictly in accordance with
the best precedents of the Christian Church; (2) that no other
Indian priest has done work of such unique value as Mr. Azariah.
The fact that a good deal of the work was done while he was still
a layman does not in any way affect its value. (3) that the only
people who have constitutionally any right to a voice in the
appointment are the clergy and laity of the district over which
he is to be appointed as the bishop. The Indian Christians of
Tinnevelly or Madras, or any other of the Telugu districts, can
no more claim a voice in the appointment than the clergy and
laity of the diocese of London.

I hope there will be no more controversy in England on the
subject; but, if there is, you will do good service to the Church
by emphasising these points, and exposing the true character of
the opposition.
                    With many thanks,
                       Believe me,
                          Yours sincerely,

                          Henry Madras.

Figure 9. Bishop Henry Whitehead's letter (*continued*).

Archbishop's Western Canada Fund', to which both the Archbishops of Canterbury and York subscribed by sending 138 missioners to Canada, where they purchased '168 sites' and built 70 churches.[1]

> In 1924 I went to Canada and made a long and very careful enquiry into the result of this work. I found that where the missioner had really settled and had remained as priest of one congregation, and his place supplied on his death, or retirement, there the work still continued; but that where the missioner had tried to serve a large district and had several churches in his care, it was not so. I was strongly advised not to attempt to discover the 168 sites: I was told that it would be impossible. Of the 70 churches built, more than half were derelict or lost. In one diocese, for instance, out of 42 mentioned in the synod journal, 25 did not appear in the Church Year Book.[2]

Once again, this missionary methods-analyst attempts to gather information about whether or not well-intentioned projects such as these were any better than sending missionary bishops and priests to plant indigenous churches. Hubert Allen refers to his grandfather's comments concerning the 'several months making diligent enquiry in 1924'[3] in Canada:

> I had to interview men who had been on the spot throughout the whole period; I had to sift conflicting and sometimes contradictory statements; I had to study masses of local magazines, and to trace carefully the history of individual parishes, and the movements of individual members of the Mission. I travelled to the Pacific and back by different routes . . . I gave myself wholly to this one thing.[4]

In addition to survey work in Canada, Allen continued his normal policy of writing letters to bishops, canons, archdeacons and lay people, as he had previously conducted surveys. During the months of his travels in Canada in 1924, the archives disclose eleven letters and draft letters to leadership in Saskatchewan, British Columbia, Manitoba, Alberta and Ontario.[5] Although

1. Roland Allen, 'The Church in Kenya' in the *East Anglican Standard,* letter to the editor 28 July 1939, 44, Oxford, Bodleian Library, USPG X622, Box 8: 44.
2. Ibid.
3. Hubert Allen, *Roland Allen,* 119.
4. Ibid.
5. Roland Allen's letters to Canadian leadership: USPG X622, Box 6: 13, 14,

his criticisms sometimes give the impression that he was cantankerous, the archives reveal the opposite, as the letters display respect towards the leadership of the existing churches and their positive feedback to Allen.

South Africa and Southern Rhodesia (Zimbabwe, 1926)

Later on, during the 1920s, Roland Allen's missionary journeys included survey work in South Africa and Rhodesia (Zimbabwe) 'from May to November 1926'.[1] One might wonder if he had any previous influence within South Africa? It seems clear that he did. For example, H.H. Kelly notes that: 'It appears that SA [South Africa] has been Roland-Allenising and is hankering after the possibilities of a "lay" priesthood – i.e. unpaid . . . I do not think [bishop] Carey (certainly not Roland Allen) quite realizes the complexity of the conditions involved.'[2] By the time he set foot in South Africa, his writings had *already* created an atmosphere of debate. He was invited to address Pretoria's diocesan synod and, according to Hubert Allen, he 'read from a prepared text', which he only did if 'he was anxious to use no word that he had not meditated on and prayed over'.[3] The topic he addressed was 'voluntary clergy' but he argued it by saying: 'My real subject is therefore not Voluntary Clergy, but the Establishment of the Church.'[4] He went on to assert that: 'application of principles may change as years pass, but principles do not change, and I am going to confine myself closely to principles tonight.'[5] His address called the synod to repentance and amendment of their subordination of 'Christ's commands, Christ's sacraments, to money, in that you say "We must have money before we can constitute the Church" '.[6] The responses and reactions to this address are located in Allen's archives.[7]

19, 21, 22, 23, 24, 25, 26, 27, and 28; see also, his letters in the first half of 1925 to Canadian leadership, USPG X622, Box 6: 30, 31, 32, and 33, Oxford, Bodleian Library.

1. Hubert Allen, *Roland Allen*, 119.
2. Alistair Mason, *History of the Society of the Sacred Mission* (Norwich: The Canterbury Press, 1994) 212, footnote: 89; Society of the Sacred Mission/ H.H. Kelly/NL (February 1929).
3. Hubert Allen, *Roland Allen*, 134.
4. Ibid.
5. Ibid.
6. Roland Allen: Beginning and close of paper read to Synod of Pretoria (26 October 1926); Box 3: 30; also, the rest of this was printed in *The East and the West* (1927) entitled 'Itinerant Clergy and the Church', Oxford, Bodleian Library, USPG X622, Box 3: 30.
7. Oxford, Bodleian Library, Roland Allen archives, USPG X622, Box 6.

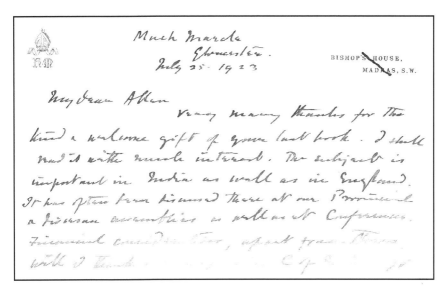

Figure 10. A letter from Bishop Henry Whitehead to Roland Allen
eleven years later (25 July 1923).

His survey work also took him to Johannesburg to discuss the
'voluntary clergy' concept. While there, he was impressed with the
critical thinking of various laymen on this topic and made reference to a
certain manager of a mine:

> In 1926, I was talking to a mine manager at Johannesburg of
> voluntary clergy, and he began at once to warn me, not that men
> would not be found to serve, but that we should have to be careful
> to guard against the danger of men using undue influence to
> secure the position. He did not argue that men would not be found
> to serve.[8]

Whenever he felt compelled to speak so forcefully, he believed it was
necessary, especially if the institutional side of the Church was more
concerned with maintenance than mission. Allen's biographer said: 'We
can only be sure that Beatrice was with him in Rhodesia, for example,
because he used for some of his notes an envelope addressed to her in
that country'.[9] There is also a letter he received from Southern Rhodesia

8. Roland Allen, *Voluntary Clergy Overseas: An Answer to the Fifth World Call*
   (privately printed at Beaconsfield, England, 1928) Oxford, Bodleian Library,
   USPG X622, Box 2, File J: 89-90.
9. Hubert Allen, *Roland Allen*, 133.

Dornakal,

Singareni Collieries, Deccan.

December 29th, 1923.

RAILWAY STATION: DORNAKAL JN., N.G.S.R.
TELEGRAMS: BISHOP, DORNAKAL N.

The Rev.Rolland Allen,

    Amenbury, Beaconsfield,

       Bucks, England.

Dear Mr.Rolland Allen,

       I am sorry not to have acknowledged your letter of
July 15th earlier. The book is welcome and is in time.

       You say in your letter that you fear "that a Bishop
who accepted the arguments of the book and acted on it will be
more or less martyred!". I am afraid there is very little chance
for a martyr's crown in India under this head. For the Bishops
have already expressed themselves in favour of an order of
permanent Deacons and Voluntary Permanent Deacons too.

       The Voluntary Priest is not yet accepted, but it will
come. Meanwhile you will be interested to see movement of
thought in that direction in our own Diocese. I know this is
not what you ask for. But once the principle is accepted, prog-
gress along the line indicated by all the implications of the
principle is only a matter of time. The Church which is accus-
tomed to the rule of "University graduates", "Latin learning"
and "a Title to a living" will not change in a day! Give us the
liberty- see what we can do.

       I am sending you under separate cover the papers con-
nected with these and allied matters. I know you will rejoice
with us in the growth of these ideas.

       My wife and family join me in sending their warmest
greetings and New Year wishes to Mrs.Rolland Allan and yourself,

                    Yours very sincerely,

                    V.S. Dornakal

Figure 11. Bishop V.S. Azariah's letter to Roland Allen
(29 December 1923).

VOLUNTARY
CLERGY

By
ROLAND ALLEN

Shows the divergence between the qualifications for priests required to-day and those found in the Pastoral Epistles.   Advocates the ordination of devout elderly men who have made their mark in other walks of life, and do not require to be supported by the faithful.

Figure 12. Allen's original publication of *Voluntary Clergy* (London: SPCK, 1923) provided the theological basis for Allen's missionary ecclesiology. This publication was in wide circulation within the Dioceses of Dornakal and Assam, India.

NEW TESTAMENT MISSIONARY METHODS

BY ROLAND ALLEN, Amenbury, Beaconsfield, Bucks, England

Author of "Missionary Methods: St. Paul's or Ours," Etc.

The word "ideals" is one which is ever on our lips in these days, and sometimes seems to lead us astray. We too often appear to think that we have done our duty by them when we have talked about ideals. In the New Testament we do not hear so much about ideals as about springs of activity, controlling principles, prophetic visions of the glory to be. There is a great gulf between these and our "ideals." Contrast for instance, "the ideal missionary is a man of strong Christian personality, of winning Christ-like character," the talk which we hear at missionary conferences about the ideal minister, with the direction: "Look ye out men of honest report, full of the Holy Ghost and wisdom" (Acts 6: 3), or "The Bishop must be blameless, the husband of one wife, vigilant, sober" (1 Tim. 3: 2, seq.). The one may be remote from the facts, the other is an earnest, vigorous, demand which keeps close to the facts. Contrast the Christian "ideals" by which some missionary educationalists hope to permeate heathen society with Christ's words, "Ye are the salt of the earth." Too often when the word "ideals" is the subject of our missionary speech, the strong, salutary, sober, force of "the obedience of Christ" seems to disappear, and a weak and nebulous "Christianity" takes its place. In place of "ideals" let us consider some of the principles and directions of the New Testament in relation to: (1) The missionary and his work, and (2) The society and its rites.—*R. A.*

The Missionary and His Work

THE first sending out of missionaries by Christ Himself, as told in the Gospels, reveals some important facts.

(1) Christ prepared His first Apostles by taking them about with Him and showing them by word and example what they were to do. He did not train evangelists theoretically in a school apart from the work. He trained them *in* the work, not outside it; in the world, not in a hothouse.

(2) He sent them forth with the charge: "Go not into the way of the Gentiles and into any city of the Samaritans enter ye not: but go rather to the lost sheep of the house of Israel." And He told them (Matthew 10: 5-15; Mark 6: 7-11; and Luke 9: 1-5): (a) to preach, (b) to heal (including raising the dead and casting out devils), (c) to go without provision, (d) to accept hospitality, (e) to turn away openly from those who refused to receive them and to hear them. We must observe that the direction not to go to Gentiles or Samaritans was obviously only for that time; the direction to heal was not to use the art of a physician but the faith of an exorcist; the direction to go without provision was only for that time, because it was later definitely withdrawn (Luke 22: 35); the direction to accept hospitality is connected closely with the acceptance of their peace, as the direction to turn away from those who refused hospitality is connected with the refusal to hear them. Where the message of Christ is refused a moral hearing, there it is a moral duty to refuse to continue to repeat it. We see this in the practice of St. Paul (Acts 18: 6).

(3) Christ sent out the Seventy in like manner as His personal forerunners (Luke 10: 1-12) with very nearly the same directions. In this passage the saying ocurs, "The laborer is worthy of his hire." That applies to wandering messengers, bidding them accept hospitality, and is quite different from a direction that missionaries

21

Figure 13. Allen's article for *The Missionary Review of the World* (January 1929).

dated 21 October 1928[1] but that was two years after he and his wife had left the country. Hubert Allen states that they used St Faith's, Rusapi, as a base of ministry and assisted 'Canon Edgar Lloyd'[2] and that, during October, he was in Umtata.[3] When contrasting 'his reports and diaries' with his visit to India,[4] there is no comparison with this visit in Southern Rhodesia (Zimbabwe) where 'these travels tend to be singularly uninformative on everyday topics'.[5]

Summary

Chapters 5 and 6 reveal the effects of his writings through the World Dominion Press and his survey work under the Survey Application Trust, as well as the way in which this enabled his missiological thought to infuse, not only the Anglican Communion, but also the Church universal. There are many other significant published works by Allen, not previously mentioned, which tend to be forgotten that he wrote from 1903 to 1947. Some of these are: *Foundation Principles of Foreign Missions* (1910); *Pentecost & the World: the Revelation of the Holy Spirit in the Acts of the Apostles* (1917); *Educational Principles & Missionary Methods* (1919); 'The Case for Voluntary Clergy: An Anglican Problem' (July 1922); *Voluntary Clergy* (1923); *Voluntary Clergy Overseas* (1928); *Non-Professional Missionaries* (self-published in 1929, see figure below); *The Case for Voluntary Clergy* (1930); and, *Sidney James Wells Clark – A Vision of Foreign Missions* (1937).[6] It is important to see his unique blend of speaking into the missionary situation through his writings and missionary work in China, India, Canada, South Africa, Zimbabwe, and Kenya, and how this gave him a first-hand understanding of world mission.

---

1. Oxford, Bodleian Library, Roland Allen archives, USPG X622, Box 6: 122.

2. Hubert Allen, *Roland Allen*, 133.

3. Ibid.

4. To be explained further in *Roland Allen: A Theology of Mission*.

5. Ibid.

6. The names of all of these books, pamphlets, and articles are documented within the bibliographies of this book and its companion volume, *Roland Allen: A Theology of Mission* and it will suffice at this time to mention only a few of them briefly. I will address these works within the context of the companion volume and unpack how Allen's missional thought developed over time.

NON-PROFESSIONAL
MISSIONARIES

By

ROLAND ALLEN

AMENBURY, BEACONSFIELD, BUCKS

Price 6d.

Figure 14. Roland Allen, *Non-Professional Missionaries*, 1929. This book was privately printed at Beaconsfield, England.

7. Friends, Family and African Ministry

Friends of the Allen family

Besides the previous colleagues mentioned, Allen had other friends who influenced his thought. Those most significant were Sidney J.W. Clark (discussed in chapter 5) and Herbert Hamilton Kelly. Clark[1] and Kelly[2] were perceptive missiologists and advocates of the indigenous Church. Also, 'Cosmo Gordon Lang (1864-1945), then Archbishop of York, and Canon W.H. Temple Gairdner of Cairo and his family' (1873-1928), were, according to Hubert Allen, close theological friends.[3] Firstly, in terms of Archbishop Lang, the archives contain no evidence of correspondence between himself and Roland Allen. However, Allen's Anglo-Catholic understanding of 'apostolic succession' was modified and suggests that Lang's thought on this issue possibly influenced him. J.G. Lockhart's biography, *Cosmo Gordon Lang*, 1949, unpacks how Lang's ecclesiology 'remained nearer to them [Liberal Catholicism] than to any other body in the Church' but found Bishop Charles Gore's 'strict Apostolic Succession very difficult to accept'.[4] Allen agreed. He also had difficulty with Gore's (and Professor Robert Moberly's) understanding and challenged their 'legal, formal, and strained theory',[5] which he believed resulted in an exclusiveness that denied any 'lay expression' of sacramental grace.[6] That said, both Lang and Allen, it is important to point out that, as High Anglicans, believed in the legitimacy of apostolic succession as

---

1. Roland Allen, *Sidney James Wells Clark: A Vision of Foreign Missions* (London: The World Dominion Press, 1937).

2. Alistair F. Mason, *History of the Society of the Sacred Mission* (Norwich: The Canterbury Press, 1993). Father H.H. Kelly was the founder of the Society of the Sacred Mission.

3. Hubert Allen, *Roland Allen*, 110.

4. J.G. Lockhart, *Cosmo Gordon Lang* (London: Hodder and Stoughton, 1949) 74-75.

5. Discussed in *Roland Allen: A Theology of Mission*.

6. Unpublished work by Roland Allen: 'The Ministry of Expansion: the Priesthood of the Laity' (1930) Oxford, Bodleian Library, USPG X622, Box 3, Number 27, Preface, 3.

a historic order within the Church, and yet, they also recognized the validity of other 'independent' churches to exist outside of established episcopacy.[1] As High Anglicans (of the Oxford persuasion) they were still able to refrain from ecclesiastical exclusiveness, as demonstrated by how both men worked towards greater co-operation between Protestant denominations.[2]

Secondly, in Allen's publications he sometimes made reference to Temple Gairdner[3] as 'Canon Gairdner of Cairo', an Anglican missionary of the Church Missionary Society and the one authorized to write the history of The World Missionary Conference, Edinburgh 1910.[4] During an interview with Bridget Davidson, the granddaughter of W.H. Temple Gairdner, she loaned me no less than fifteen copies of his published books and out-of-print pamphlets (with 'artistic' drawings) – designed dramas – that he developed and that were based upon various biblical stories. These dramas were designed to engage with local Muslims in Cairo by giving them the opportunity to participate in these performances (playing the parts of biblical characters) and then they would perform these dramas for the public.[5] Temple Gairdner's missionary method was

1. Lockhart, *Cosmo Gordon Lang*, 264-84.

2. Ibid., 264-84; Roland Allen, *Foundation Principles of Foreign Missions* (May 1910) Box 2, File J (Repr. as *Essential Missionary Principles*, Cambridge: The Lutterworth Press, 1913. Repr. entitled *Missionary Principles – and Practice*, Grand Rapids: Eerdmans, 1964; *Missionary Principles – and Practice*, London: World Dominion Press, 1964); *Missionary Principles – and Practice* (Cambridge: The Lutterworth Press, 2006) 81-84.

3. Hubert Allen told me that: 'Temple Gairdner always used the double surname, though without a hyphen.' Interview with Hubert Allen, 4 February 2011.

4. W.H.T. Gairdner, *Edinburgh 1910: An Account and Interpretation of the World Misionary Conference* (Edinburgh and London: Oliphant, Anderson & Ferrier, 1910). See Brian Stanley, *The World Missionary Conference, Edinburgh 1910*, Studies in the History of Christian Missions (Grand Rapids/Cambridge: Eerdmans, 2009) 99; Roland Allen, *The Spontaneous Expansion of the Church: and the Causes which Hinder It* (London: World Dominion Press, 1927. Repr. Grand Rapids: Eerdmans, 1960; repr. Cambridge: The Lutterworth Press, 2006) 112, 115; also Paton, *The Ministry of the Spirit: Selected Writings of Roland Allen*, 77-80.

5. Interviews with Bridget Davidson on 7 and 10 April 2011 (Oxford); Some of his works are: W.H.T. Gairdner, *Edinburgh 1910: An Account and Interpretation of the World Misionary Conference* (Edinburgh and London: Oliphant, Anderson & Ferrier, 1910); Gairdner, *The Good Samaritan: A New Testament Morality Play in Four Scenes* (London: Society for Promoting Christian Knowledge, 1923); Gairdner, *D.M. Thornton: a Study in Missionary Ideals and Methods*; Gairdner, *The Reproach of Islam* (1909); Gairdner, *The Rebuke of Islam*; J.O.H. Gairdner, 'Twenty Years: A Study of Temple Gairdner in His Home 1908-1928'.

very effective as a contextualization of gospel ministry. Both the Temple Gairdner family and the Allen family remain closely associated even today.[6] Hubert Allen said 'She [Bridget Davidson] and I are godparents to one another's children, and so very old friends'.[7] These families became friends decades ago in Africa. Although, after enquiring about any letters between Temple Gairdner and Roland Allen, both Bridget Davidson and Hubert Allen stated that no copies exist today.[8] Also, there are no extant letters in the archives.[9]

Roland Allen was impressed by Temple Gairdner's work among Muslims in Egypt, especially the practical methods that he used for gospel ministry and church-planting methods. He began quoting from Temple Gairdner's ideas in 1923 and found commonality in his thought concerning 'the danger of "Foreign Missions by proxy" [warning] if we do not amend "we shall beget native communities in our own likeness who will also insist before long in doing this work by proxy"'.[10] This resonated with Allen's own concerns about how missionary societies and mission stations had taken priority over indigenous church-planting. Another major point that Temple Gairdner had raised highlighted the significance of lay ministry as delineated in his assertion that every Christian is a missionary.[11] Allen agreed and was an advocate for 'more unofficial missionaries'[12] as revealed throughout his missiological writings. Temple Gairdner's applied missionary principles and practices among the Muslims in Cairo shaped Allen's missiology for years, especially later as he moved to Kenya and began to work among Muslims.[13]

---

6. The interview I had with Temple Gairdner's granddaughter in Oxford, 10 April 2011, was arranged by Hubert Allen.

7. Email correspondence from Hubert Allen, 8 September 2010.

8. Interviews: Hubert Allen (4 February 2011) and Bridget Davidson (10 April 2011). See also the collection of letters arranged by Temple Gairdner's wife for publication: M.D.G., *W.H.T.G. to His Friends: Some Letters and Informal Writings of Canon W.H. Temple Gairdner of Cairo 1873-1928* (London: Society for Promoting Christian Knowledge, 1930).

9. Oxford, Bodleian Library, Roland Allen archives, USPG X622.

10. W.H.T. Gairdner, *Brotherhood – Islam's and Christ's* (Edinburgh: Edinburgh House Press, 1923) as cited from Allen's 'Non-Professional Missionaries' in Paton, *The Ministry of the Spirit*, 77-80. See also Allen, *Spontaneous Expansion*, 112-13.

11. Temple Gairdner, *Brotherhood*, 1923, as cited from Paton, *The Ministry of the Spirit*, 78; also Allen, *Spontaneous Expansion*, 116.

12. Allen in Paton's, *The Ministry of the Spirit*, 78.

13. Roland Allen's translations of Muslim texts from the Swahili: 'The Story of Mbega' (part 1) by Abdullah bin Hemedi 'lAjjemy, *Tanganyika Notes & Records*, 1936-37; 'Inkishafi – A Translation from the Swahili' *African Studies*, December

Thirdly, Hubert Allen describes his grandparents in the following way:

The Allens, relatively elderly and set in their ways when they married, did not find it easy to "socialize" outside their own family, though they kept up in particular with a few of the friends [of Beatrice's] . . . such as the well-known authoress of Bible stories for children – C.P.S. Warren (Mrs Watkin Williams) – whose son and daughter were among the two children's [Priscilla and Iohn, i.e., John] closest friends.[1]

Fourthly, Hubert Allen also affirms that the friendship that his grandfather and grandmother had with the David Seth-Smith family. While Roland's and Beatrice's son, Iohn, was attending the 'sixth and seventh forms at Westminster School as a day-boarder' he was permitted 'to live with the Seth-Smith family at the London Zoo in Regent's Park'.[2] The distinguished David Seth-Smith, also known as 'The Zoo Man'[3] of the BBC was the Director of the London Zoo at the time that Iohn lived with his family. I digress by drawing attention to the previously mentioned Warren family, and in particular their son, Max, because of his ongoing friendship with Iohn. This is significant because both Iohn and Max were highly devoted to missionary work. Max Warren worked within the institutional side of the CMS.[4] Warren was 'later to become

1946, USPG X622, Box 4; 'Utenzi wa Kiyama (Siku ya Hukumu)', an appendage to *Tanganyika Notes & Records*, c.1946, USPG X622, Box 4, Oxford, Bodleian Library; 'Utenzi wa Kutawafu Naby' (author unknown), an appendage to *Journal of the East African Swahili Committee*, June 1956; re-edited as 'Utendi wa Kutawafu Nabii', Edward Mellen Press, 1991. 'Utenzi wa Abdirrahmani na Sufiyani' by Hemed Abdalla el Buhry, *Johari za Kiswahili*, no.2, 1961.

1. Hubert Allen, *Roland Allen*, 109.

2. Ibid., 113.

3. David Seth-Smith, *The Zoo Man Talks about The Wild Birds of Our Country* (Worcester: Littlebury & Company, 1946); also, David Seth-Smith, *The Zoo Man Talks about the Wild Animals of Our Country* (Worcester: Littlebury & Company, no date). Hubert Allen, *Roland Allen*, 109.

4. M.A.C. Warren, *Caesar the Beloved Enemy: Three Studies in the Relation of Church and State*, Reinecker Lectures at the Virginia Theological Seminary, Alexandria, Virginia, February 1955 (London: SCM Press, 1955); see also, Max Warren, *Problems and Promises in Africa Today* (Hodder, 1964); Warren, *The Christian Mission* (London: SCM Press, 1951); Max Warren, *The Missionary Movement from Britain in Modern History* (London: SCM Press, 1965); Max Warren, ed., *To Apply the Gospel: Selections from the Writings of Henry Venn* (Grand Rapids: Eerdmans, 1971).

the long-serving General Secretary of the Church Missionary Society.[5] Iohn served as 'a colonial officer for most of his career'[6] in the Sudan, Tanganyika, the Western Aden Protectorate (southern Yemen) and later left colonial service to do extensive Swahili work.

> Leaving the Colonial Service in 1958, he [Iohn] moved to Makerere University in Uganda, as both secretary of the East African Swahili Committee, and warden of a new student hall of residence. Thence, with funds from the Rockefeller Foundation and other sources, he and his wife [were] undertaking research and the collection of Swahili documents. . . . From 1968-1970 he became Director of the University of Dar-es-Salaam's Institute of Swahili Research.[7]

During Iohn Allen's teenage years, he recalled one of their 'near neighbors in Beaconsfield' who was viewed as a 'distinguished friend' of his father, Roland, that being, G.K. Chesterton (1874-1936). Hubert Allen stated that his grandfather 'enjoyed Chesterton's Father Brown stories: but he and his neighbor found their theological views were so divergent that it was better to refrain from discussions that would have been only acrimonious' [Chesterton, at that time, was Roman Catholic].[8]

Missionary in Kenya: Allen family moves to East Africa (1931-1947)

When Allen took a tour of Kenya in 1931, Paton pointed out that 'unexpectedly, this tour lasted for the rest of his life'.[9] Due to the relocation of their son and daughter to East Africa, Roland and Beatrice moved there and spent most of his retirement years in Bible study and exposition, learning and translating books in Swahili, attempting to understand Islamic thought, and ever broadening his missiological *influence*.[10] Hubert Allen admits that their move to Africa was influenced by their desire to: (1) live 'reasonably close' to their daughter, Priscilla, and their son, Iohn and his growing family; (2) establish roots and enjoy

---

5. Max Warren in Hubert Allen, *Roland Allen*, 112.
6. Correspondence from Hubert Allen, 31 May 2012.
7. Hubert Allen, *Roland Allen*, 180-81.
8. Ibid., 110.
9. Paton, *Reform of the Ministry*, 23.
10. John K. Branner, 'Roland Allen, Donald McGavran and Church Growth,' Th.M. thesis, Fuller Theological Seminary (1975) 8.

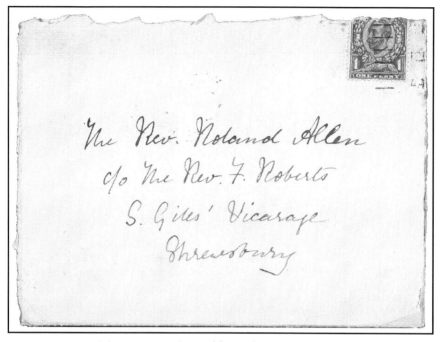

Figure 15. Envelope addressed to Roland Allen.

the 'healthy climate'; and (3) transition into the 'inexpensive environment of Nairobi'.[1] During interviews with Hubert Allen concerning his early childhood growing up in Africa – where his parents served as teachers within the colonial educational service – he reminisced concerning various fond memories that he had of his grandparents and of his visits to their home.[2] With this move to Africa, did Roland Allen continue to function as a priest while living in Africa? Yes!

During the war years, Allen made himself available to preach for Anglican churches in Kenya and he was invited on different occasions to preach for Nairobi's All Saints Cathedral. Hubert Allen wrote:

> When Roland first arrived in East Africa he used sometimes to be invited to preach. On 1st May 1932, in particular, he preached a notable sermon in Nairobi's All Saints Cathedral, and again on Palm Sunday in 1937. But his unorthodox views were disturbing in a very conventional missionary environment.[3]

1. Hubert Allen, *Roland Allen*, 154.
2. Interviews with Hubert Allen and email correspondence (7 September 2010; 4 February 2011; 31 May 2012).
3. Hubert Allen, *Roland Allen*, 155.

Allen's archives disclose the Palm Sunday sermon (1937) which addressed Luke 19:41: 'He beheld the city and wept over it.'[4] On another occasion, he had preached a Michaelmas sermon in which he challenged the congregation to imagine that, if in years to come, they had decided to relocate, where there was no existent church, he went on to ask them:

> Well then, what are you going to do? . . . Will you say . . . the Church is here where I am, and if there is no Chaplain here, I am here a King and Priest unto God, for myself, for my household, for my neighbours . . . You have the secret. You know what is the Christian fight, and that you are fighting it, and that Michael and all his angels are on your side.[5]

The *apostolic principle* that, Allen believed, authorizes the laity as part of 'the priesthood of the Church'[6] to sacramentally act for themselves, even if ordained clergy are *not* within close proximity to the community of faith, actually became a fundamental principle he debated.[7] His unique missionary ecclesiology argued for the practice of ordaining non-degreed university men to serve the Church as priests but this did not always gain western episcopal acceptance. An example of this very point is seen as Bishop Whitehead argued in a letter to Allen after proposing V.S. Azariah to be consecrated to the episcopate, even though Azariah had not yet completed his BA from the University of Madras.[8] He agreed with the principle on the grounds that Azariah's effective evangelistic ministry had already proven his 'spiritual' qualifications since 'the establishment of the Indian Missionary Society of Tinnevelly was almost entirely due to the faith, zeal and energy of Azariah'.[9]

---

4. Sermon for Palm Sunday (1937) All Saints Cathedral, Nairobi. The archives do not specify whether or not this was Matins or Evensong. However, since the text is Luke 19:41, according to 'An Alternative Table of Lessons' in the Book of Common Prayer (1662) it has Luke 19:29-end, as the appointed Gospel lesson for Evensong. Oxford, Bodleian Library, USPG X622, Box 5.

5. Allen's sermon notes: 'There Was War in Heaven: Michael and His Angels Fought Against the Dragon', Michaelmas, 1st lesson- Rev. 12:7, The Cathedral Church, Nairobi, Kenya (29 September 1935) Oxford, Bodleian Library, USPG X622, Box 5: 29; see also Hubert Allen, *Roland Allen*, 155.

6. Roland Allen, 'The Priesthood of the Church', *Church Quarterly Review*, art. IV (January 1933) 234-44, Oxford, Bodleian Library, USPG X622.

7. This is discussed extensively in *Roland Allen: A Theology of Mission*.

8. Letter from Bishop Whitehead to Roland Allen, 11 June 1912, Roland Allen archives, Oxford, Bodleian Library, USPG X622, Box 6, File M: 110.

9. Ibid.

Allen's Swahili: Knowledge and Translations[1]

Allen's interpretation of the Pauline principle of 'becoming all things
to all people' for the sake of gospel ministry (I Cor. 9:19-23) was the
missionary code that compelled him to engage with African culture.
Hubert Allen says of his grandfather that 'in his old age he translated
Muslim epics from Swahili into English, in Nairobi, where he lies
buried'.[2] His desire to learn Swahili all began in his mid-sixties, according
to Hubert Allen, and he 'never spoke it well, but he rapidly learned
to read the very difficult literary Swahili of the East African coast'.[3]
Roland's son, John (Iohn) W.T. Allen, became a 'notable Swahili scholar'
and assisted his father when dealing 'with complexities of language:
but the bulk of the translation work was Roland's own'.[4] All five of
Allen's translations were eventually published but 'only three of them
during his lifetime'.[5] The translations are: (1) 'The Story of Mbega'
[part 1] by Abdullah bin Hemedi 'lAjjemy; (2) 'Utenzi wa Kiyama (Siku
ya Hukuma)'; (3) 'Inkishafi'; (4) 'Utenzi wa Kutawafu Naby' (author
unknown); and (5) 'Utenzi wa Abdirrahmani na Sufiyani' by Hemed
Abdalla el Buhry.[6] In 1920, he had previously written a significant article
(discussed later) entitled 'Islam and Christianity in the Sudan'[7] and it
was obvious that 'Roland had long been sensitive to Islamic thought and
doctrine'.[8] This interest is also shown by a friendship he developed with
Mohamed Hasan, a professor from the University of Dacca, who had
stayed in the Allen home on a visit and, likewise in 1928, when Allen
visited him and 'had long discussions' with Hasan.[9] His son's linguistic

1. This case study derives from a paper I presented at the *Yale-Edinburgh Group*
    on the History of the Missionary Movement and World Christianity –
    'Religious Movements of Renewal, Revival, and Revitalization in the History
    of Missions and World Christianity' (28-30 June 2012) New College,
    Edinburgh, Scotland.

2. Hubert Allen, 'Would Roland Allen still have anything to say to us today?',
    Transformation: An International Journal of Holistic Mission Studies, 29 (3)
    (July 2012) 179-185 (184).

3. Hubert Allen, *Roland Allen*, 161-62.

4. Ibid., 162.

5. Ibid.

6. Ibid., 219.

7. Roland Allen, 'Islam and Christianity in the Sudan', *International Review of
    Mission*, IX/36 (October 1920) 531-43.

8. Hubert Allen, *Roland Allen*, 162.

9. Ibid.

abilities and colonial work in the Sudan and 'on the coast of Tanganyika, made him even more aware of the worth of other cultures' symbolism, and the danger of brushing it aside contemptuously in the name of a westernized Christianity'.[10]

Further Ministry in Africa

Roland's missionary ecclesiology was not 'nationalistic' but rather was cross-cultural and sought to engage with other religions and cultures through service and interpersonal dialogue. This is one of the great strengths of his as a Christian missionary for he learned how to be, what Andrew Walls identifies as, a 'representative of the total Christian community who has in principle exactly the same faith, testimony, and responsibility as all other Christians, but who exercises these in a cross-cultural situation'.[11]

Two main Pauline principles transcended Allen's dedication to the British Empire and these are: (1) the principle of ongoing *unity* in the one, holy, catholic and apostolic Church (Eph. 4:3-16);[12] and (2) the principle of *love* demonstrated through prayers for 'everyone' (I Tim. 2:1-7). As a *priestly-missionary*, Allen's words and deeds were permeated by these principles. This can be seen especially in the ways he 'acted as an up-country locum during his retirement in Kenya, where during the War [World War II] he ministered to Germans interned in prison camps'.[13] He 'hated jingoistic nationalism'[14] and was always willing to serve as a priest to any race, colour or creed. Hubert Allen states that 'Roland frequently visited the internment camp at Kabete, where Germans, Hungarians, and other "enemy aliens" were being held'.[15] This is consistent with his frequent personal adage 'Once a Priest always a Priest' and highlights what kind of pastoral heart he carried all throughout his life.[16] He took time to 'sometimes read Shakespeare with some of the inmates' as well as serving as an advocate to the 'British authorities' when various issues developed.[17] In fact, Roland and Beatrice took into their home a

---

10. Ibid., 162-63.

11. Walls, *Missionary Movement* (2009) 255.

12. Allen, *Missionary Methods*, 7, 107.

13. Hubert Allen, 'Would Roland Allen still have anything to say to us today?', 184.

14. Hubert Allen, *Roland Allen*, 166.

15. Ibid., 167.

16. Ibid., 15, 20.

17. Ibid., 167.

motherless 12-year-old Jewish girl, Valerie Fliess, when Roland found out that her father from Hamburg 'had been appointed camp leader, to represent all its inmates, even the Nazis'.[1] The Allen family also made sure that Valerie's brother, Ralph, was cared for by their neighbour 'an eminent architect'.[2] These examples of Christian charity in the midst of international conflict illustrates the caring nature and servant-leadership of both Roland and Beatrice Allen.

Hubert Allen provides further information by writing: 'Later in the 1930s, Granfer often took services, especially at St Mark's Church in Nairobi's Parklands suburb.'[3] He did this for a while until he noticed that the members were happy for him to continue to 'fill gaps' and because they had decided *not* to contact the bishop to 'appoint "voluntary clergy" that he advocated'.[4] In response to this inaction, he eventually wrote a resignation letter to 'the Communicants at St Mark's Church'[5] and based his decision upon principle, that being, for their need to apply the principle of indigenous voluntary clergy for their parish, which he believed transcended their need for his services as a priest.

The impact of the Allen family's life and ministry in Africa remained for years to come. Forty years after Roland Allen's death, a special service was held for his daughter at All Saints Cathedral, Nairobi, 30 October 1987, as 'A Service of Praise and Thanksgiving for the life of Priscilla Mary Allen (1903-87).'[6] This is evidence of the Allen family's lasting influence on this parish.

---

1. Ibid.
2. Ibid.
3. Ibid., 157.
4. Ibid.
5. Ibid. and Appendix 6.
6. Interview with Hubert Allen (5 February 2011); copy of an Order of Service for Priscilla Mary Allen's funeral (30 October 1987).

8. Select Sermons and Teachings on the Old Testament[1]

Overview of Allen's Sermons

Those who are relatively familiar with Allen's parish ministry at Chalfont St Peter, Buckinghamshire, from 1904 to 1907, may assume that he basically resigned from serving any other parish until his move to Kenya in 1931. Nothing could be further from the truth. Exhaustive and detailed research of the primary sources in the archive, reveal, for the first time, a treasure of *unexamined* information concerning Allen's sermons, teachings and notes; everything from Confirmation classes he taught in various churches in England between Good Friday, 1901,[2] (3 years before parish ministry at Chalfont St Peter) until he delivered a sermon entitled 'God' (Psalm 45:1) in February, 1930.[3] After his parish ministry at Chalfont St Peter (1904-07), the archives provide evidence of Allen's preaching in various churches in England approximately 194 times.[4] Also, there is evidence of

---

1. The archival collection of Roland Allen's sermon and teaching notes is not in chronological order and were generally written on small pieces of paper. The numbering system within the archives ranges from 1 to 553 and it should be understood that many of these sermons consisted of more than 2 or 3 pages. The lengthiest sermon is 14 pages ('Repentance in Apostolic Teaching', no. 532-545) and was handwritten by Roland's wife, Beatrice. Another interesting point is that whenever Allen preached the same sermon to another congregation, he made a note of what parish it was and the date of the sermon.

2. Sermon no. 433; see also, Sermon no. 288 'The private use of Holy Scripture' Deuteronomy 6:6-9; I Timothy 1:5-7 (12 May 1901); Sermon no. 345 'The Order of Angels' (Michaelmas Day 1901). Oxford, Bodleian Library, USPG X622, Box 5.

3. Sermon no. 444, Beaconsfield, February 1930. Oxford, Bodleian Library, USPG X622, Box 5.

4. These mainly consist of sermon notes, along with some complete sermons and teaching notes from 1908-31. One can only assume that Roland Allen preached and taught more than what is reserved in the archives. That said, my research is based on archival evidence from the Bodleian Library (Oxford) and information received from Hubert Allen, Roland Allen's grandson.

various sermons he preached later in Africa.[1] For instance, he preached at St John's Church, Harpenden, Hertfordshire, in 1908 and again in 1912, and yet later during World War I, there is evidence that between 1914 and 1919, he served as Curate-in-charge for this congregation and preached for this parish no less than 52 times.[2]

After careful examination of all that remains of Roland Allen's sermons, teaching notes and catechetical lessons, I concluded that it was important to disclose how his evangelical commitment to the authority of the Bible shaped his interpretation. This must also be seen within the context of an 'orderly' commitment to the historic Church of England's tradition of preaching through the liturgical calendar. The sermons that Allen prepared for Anglican parishes were carefully structured according to the appointed lessons from the Old Testament, the Psalms, the Epistles and the Gospels, as outlined within the daily lectionary readings for Morning Prayer, Evening Prayer, Feast Days and Holy Communion services. While scrutinizing these sermons, it was encouraging to see how Allen's commitment to the lectionary readings of Scripture appointed for each day actually shaped the direction of his exposition of the Biblical texts.

The primary purpose of this chapter is designed to engage with Allen's theology of the Old Testament, as disclosed through his preaching and teaching ministry. Firstly, some aspects of Allen's theology can be seen as extensions of selected sermons that he had written. This selection process was carefully advanced so as to inform the reader of his engagement with the Old Testament scriptures, especially the points at which there might be some misunderstanding of his view of the Law, the Prophets and Wisdom literature. Secondly, for those familiar with Allen's most famous books – *Missionary Methods: St Paul's or Ours?* and *The Spontaneous Expansion of the Church* – one might assume that his

---

1. E.g. sermon no. 29 'There Was War in Heaven: Michael and His Angels Fought Against the Dragon', St Michael and All Angels (Cathedral Church) Nairobi, Kenya (29 September 1935). Hubert Allen mentions that Roland also preached at The Cathedral Church (Nairobi: 1 May 1932; Palm Sunday 1937) and St Mark's Church (Nairobi) Allen: 155. Even though he spent time ministering in China, India, South Africa, Rhodesia and Canada, none of these sermons can be found in the archives. It is more than likely that there are additional sermons he delivered in England that are not in the USPG archives, Oxford, Bodleian Library.

2. These sermons are: no. 13, 14, 18, 65, 66, 80, 81, 83-87, 89, 92, 94-96, 98, 100, 101, 103, 104, 207, 209, 212, 213, 216, 217, 243, 249, 297, 298, 302, 308, 311, 358, 359, 362, 369, 374, 383, 388, 389, 401, 405, 407, 408, 413, 415, 456, 463, 515, Box 5, Oxford, Bodleian Library, Roland Allen archives, USPG X622.

theology was shaped *only* by the New Testament.[3] Within the Allen archives, there are sermons and teaching notes that disclose that his theology was *also* shaped from an understanding of the Old Testament. That said, this chapter advances evidence that his faith was significantly informed by the Old Testament and that there is covenantal continuity, he believed, within the *whole Bible* – both the Old and New Testaments.

Select Sermons on the Old Testament

The first word of [the] Bible proclaims [the] supremacy of God. He made. He governs . . . The ungodly is slave of forces, chance happenings. The godly see God's will and are in God's hands (statement from Roland Allen's sermon on Genesis 1:1 during a pre-Lenten service [Septuagesima], 1923).[4]

The Spirit of God for the Psalmist [is] immanent in the world. All-pervading. Everywhere the H. [Holy] Sp. [Spirit is] at hand. No escape. (Statement from Roland Allen's sermon on Psalm 139:6, during an Evensong service on Whitsunday [Pentecost], 1915).[5]

The focus that Roland Allen placed on teaching from the Old Testament is clearly evidenced by his sermons, especially by those in which he addressed each of the *Ten Commandments* for both his parish of Chalfont St Peter's, 1906, and also, later, when he ministered as Curate-in-charge of St John's Harpenden, Hertfordshire, 1915. Within the context of these series of sermons for both parishes, it is interesting to note that Allen believed in the abiding validity of God's law, that being, he believed that these commandments were *timeless*. For example, in sermons for both parishes during the Second Sunday in Lent (1906 and 1915) – while explaining the second commandment – he reminded the people that in Jesus' Sermon on the Mount, he emphasized Jesus' *timeless* words: 'Think not that I am come to destroy [the Law and the Prophets]' (Matthew 5:17). In fact, he further drew their attention to St Paul's assertion that 'the law is holy, and the commandment holy, and just, and good' (Romans 7:9-13). The next point that Allen made in his exposition was that even the early Church's adherence to God's law was articulated within a second-century document commonly called

---

3. The *Index of Scripture* at the end of both of these books disclose biblical passages only from the New Testament.

4. Sermon no. 441 at the parish church of Beaconsfield (small market town west of London).

5. Sermon no. 362 at the parish church of St John's Harpenden, Hertfordshire.

The Didachē[1] with a comment it made on Deuteronomy 6: 'Be not prone to anger for anger leads to murder . . . Be not lustful for lust leads to fornication.'[2] Next, he put forth four principles of God's law as 'positive not negative, universal not limited, internal not external, the Law is a unity'.[3] It is important to point out that as Allen conducted this series of sermons on the Ten Commandments that he specifically reminded his parishioners *how* the Church of England's process for those preparing for Confirmation precisely emphasized these commandments within the Catechism, as articulated within the Book of Common Prayer.[4]

A momentarily digression is needed to point out that these sermons were given *before* 1906 and *after* 1915, when Allen's famous book *Missionary Methods: St Paul's or Ours?* (1912) was first published. The reason for this digression is purposely directed towards those who have read *Missionary Methods* and may have concluded that his arguments against 'a rule' or 'a code of law' somehow suggests that he diminished the purpose of God's law as a standard for sanctification.[5] This is not the case. A careful examination of how he used these phrases will reveal that what he opposed were any 'customs' and 'precedents' that were externally applied and imposed by foreign missionaries upon their converts.[6] No matter how effective these customs and precedents were in a missionary's homeland, Allen argued, it was *not* a Pauline practice to impose these rules upon indigenous churches. Thus, Allen definitively said: 'Precedents are not of universal application.'[7] To summarize, Allen is making a distinction here between 'human' laws (culturally time-based) and God's laws (timeless; abiding).

The Ten Commandments

Firstly, within this sermon series, Allen continued to preach from Deuteronomy 6:4-5 and argued that within the Decalogue (the Ten Commandments of Exodus 20:1-17) that the first Commandment clearly

---

1. Thomas O'Loughlin, *The Didachē: A Window on the Earliest Christians* (Grand Rapids: Baker Academic/SPCK, 2010) 163 (3.2-3.3).
2. Sermon notes on Deuteronomy 6:4-5, no. 210-11, Box 5, Oxford, Bodleian Library, Roland Allen archives, USPG X622. See *The Didachē* (3.2-3.3).
3. Ibid.
4. The Book of Common Prayer's chapter is entitled *A Catechism, that is to say an Instruction to be Learned of Every Person before he be brought to be Confirmed by the Bishop.*
5. Allen, *Missionary Methods*, 119, 161.
6. Ibid., 137, 144.
7. Ibid., 133.

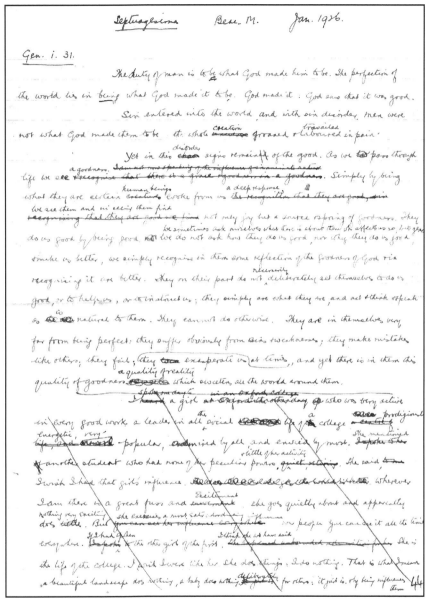

Figure 16. Portion of a sermon on Genesis 1:31.

establishes a covenantal relationship with 'a Father' within a 'covenant rite' (as affirmed in the Catechism). He argued that this showed his personhood to be 'from Love', and also expressed 'all because He is what He declares Himself to be [that is] a Person to be Believed in, to be feared, to be Loved'[1] (original emphasis). Secondly, he continued to describe how the Catechism directs a covenant member towards understanding what the second commandment teaches about one's duty to love, worship, trust and to call upon the God who has unilaterally established a covenant with his people. Allen's theology of this covenant relationship embraces 'a practical way' to understand how believers are 'to pray privately and publicly' because 'one of the marks of the Ch. [Church is] The prayers [Acts 2:42]'.[2] Objectively, he does express concern about cultural idolatry and quoted from Augustine's *City of God* (8:23), which dealt with such idolatry, in order to emphasize his point.

Thirdly, he gave a 'practical sermon' to address the emphasis of the third commandment, which is about not taking God's name in vain. He addressed:

> perjury, profanity, mockery of religion, mockery of religion in others, treating divine things as mere subjects for arguments, neglecting the Bible, offering meaningless prayers (without intention) by following the 'Rules to keep this Commandment: 1) Bow at Name of H. [Holy] Trinity or Name of Jesus; 2) Never let a day pass without reading [the] Bible; 3) Never open [the] Bible without prayer; 4) Never speak in Church; 5) Never sit at Confession of sins or H.C. [Holy Communion].[3]

The five Anglican customs mentioned above (which Allen personally respected) are contrasted with the ethical intention of the third commandment. This reveals his theology for the *inward* function of God's law which addresses the issues of the *heart* in contrast to external customs. Fourthly, his interpretation of the focus of the fourth commandment is defined by the Sabbath, which teaches 'perfect service' (i.e., true Sabbath – perfect service).[4] Also, he described the Sabbath rest within the context of the Epistle to the Hebrews; not in order to demonstrate the shift from the Jewish Sabbath to the Lord's Day, but rather as that which is 'fulfilled in the eternal Sabbath of God's rest into wh [which] Xts [Christians] enter'.[5] He then addressed how this commandment has influenced society by saying that to 'break up Sunday . . . [it] is a <u>social</u> crime'[6] (original

---

1. Sermon notes for First Sunday in Lent (no. 207).
2. Ibid., no. 209.
3. Ibid., no. 212.
4. Ibid., no. 216.
5. Ibid.
6. Ibid.

emphasis). He stressed the importance of Sunday worship: 'The Lord's Day [is] a day of worship, devotion, consecration. To work on Sun [Sunday] is not to break the commandments. To forget God is to break it'.[7] Fifthly, Allen made the connection between Sunday worship and the direction of the fifth commandment's to honour one's father and mother: 'For parents, to bring their children, to sit with them, to help them to learn the art of worship' in church disclosed how his theology saw no divide between loving and honouring God (commandments 1-4) with honouring parents and loving one's neighbour (commandments 5-10).[8] Allen's sacramental theology put forward the understanding that all of life is *sacred*; that being, nothing is secular since all of life, for the Christian, is sacred.

Sixthly, Allen made use of the structure of the Catechism to teach Commandments 6-9. In reference to murder (the sixth commandment) he stressed the need to suppress the internal issue of 'hatred' within one's heart in order to avoid the sin of murder.[9] Again, he taught from the statement of the Catechism on how to suppress the sin of adultery (seventh commandment) by reminding each Christian to 'keep my body in temperance, soberness, and chastity'.[10] When dealing with the instruction of the eighth commandment against stealing, he reminded his parishioners to look closely at the New Testament teaching 'in regard to property'[11] and the legitimacy of owning what one works for. Towards the end of this sermon, he made this important statement about one's spiritual life:

> Insistence upon 'mine', callousness in relation to others, trust in the material. Those three errors or vices destroy the spiritual life. The love which is the law of liberty . . . refers to see [seeing] a brother in need. . . . The love which is the law of liberty: seeketh not her own.[12]

Seventhly, the sin of lying – bearing false witness (ninth commandment) – according to Allen is a major violation of 'the spirit' of all of these commandments. He taught that this sin could be suppressed if parents seriously taught their children the *spiritual meaning* behind this law, and the other commandments. He said:

---

7. Ibid., no. 218.
8. Ibid., no. 217.
9. Ibid., no. 223.
10. Ibid., no. 225.
11. Ibid., no. 227.
12. Ibid., no. 228.

At family prayers this supremacy of the spirit is known. This is a parable: the supremacy of the spirit is before us in all our dealing with the commandments. . . . In the N.T. I find this spirit. I choose here to call your attention to three passages: 1) St Matthew 5:44-45; 2) Eph. 4:15-25; 3) Col. 3:8sqq. Here is revealed the spirit which fulfills this commandment (and the rest).[1]

Allen's understanding of God's law was rooted in the supremacy of the 'spirit of the law'. As seen in the quote above, he affirms the *timeless* emphasis of the ninth commandment and also demonstrates the clarity of the New Testament, as disclosed by Jesus Christ (Matt. 5:44-45) and Paul (Eph. 4:15-25; Col. 3:8).

Eighthly, as Allen began to unpack the focus of the tenth commandment, which warns against the sin of covetousness, he reminded these congregations how the prophets Jeremiah and Micah addressed this sin.

In the O.T. Prophets covetousness is commonly connected with acts of violence, oppression and fraud, e.g. Jeremiah 8:10 'everyone . . . is given to covetousness . . . everyone dealeth falsely. Jeremiah 22:17 . . . Micah 2:2 . . . The spirit which will not bring every thought into captivity to the obedience of Xt. [Christ] (2 Cor. 10:5) [is a] wayward desire for anything which a man holds [as] his good. 'I want' regardless of what God designs and wishes. . . . Nothing but the spirit of Xt. [Christ] as revealed in this Passion week can suffice for amendment. Nothing but the spirit of Xt. [Christ] as revealed in this Passion week can suffice for atonement.[2]

Allen's insistence that the 'spirit of Christ', as revealed through Holy Week's Passion, energized the Christian's ability to walk in the Spirit and not fulfill the flesh's desire to covet. At the heart of his argument (within this 10-page sermon) he again reinforced the abiding validity of God's law by saying: 'As I said it is not possible to escape the letter by repressing the Spirit. The law stands. The spirit is the only fulfillment of it. But the Spirit fulfills it. . . . '[3] Integrated within his theology is this pre-eminence of disclosing the purpose of God's law – to not only reveal sin but to reveal the holy character of God – and, to recognize the

---

1. Ibid., no. 231.
2. Ibid., nos. 233-34.
3. Ibid., no. 238.

usefulness of God's law as a standard for sanctification (not justification). This is Pauline theology! The function of God's law, according to Paul, was to reveal that this law stemmed from a holy, just and good God, who, places His law within the hearts of Christians (Romans 7:12; 8:1-4; Hebrews 8:10; 10:16). Allen understood this and was able to teach the Decalogue from a New Covenant perspective. Also, his ordered life as an Anglican reinforced a clear belief and practice of rehearsing the Ten Commandments during the Holy Communion Service.[4] That said, he concluded this sermon series with the parable of the shrewd and unjust steward (Luke 16:10-12) by clarifying any misapplications of its meaning. Basically, he showed how the Christian can properly deal with 'mammon' by saying: 'Christ calls it unrighteous, yet He bids us [to] use it. You can ponder it; you need not just let it go idly from you. . . . Serve God and cease to serve mammon. *Mammon must be your slave not yr* (your) *master*'[5] (original emphasis).

Within the context of this series of messages we discover Allen's method of biblical exegesis as he unpacked the Decalogue by letting Scripture interpret Scripture. This *whole Bible* preacher demonstrated a commitment to the authority of Scripture and taught how the Holy Spirit empowers these laws – divinely implanted – within the hearts of God's covenant people.

To summarize Allen's theology of God's law, as articulated through other sermons he preached elsewhere, he maintained:

1) that in order to understand 'The Decalogue & Xt. [Christ]' that it would be necessary to see it through Jesus' Sermon on the Mount (Matt. 5-7) where there was a 'hearty recog. [recognition] of its divine authority (Matt. 5:17)'[6];

2) that Christ explained God's law as constructive: 'Pos. [Positive] for neg. [negative], universal for partial, local, Love to God and man, Matt. 22:36-40. THE DECALOGUE AC. [according] TO XT. [Christ] . . . Thou shalt love the Lord w. [with] all thy heart, Matt. 22:37 . . . '[7];

3) that the Beatitudes (Matt. 5:1-12) – particularly verse 7, 'Blessed are the merciful for they shall obtain mercy' – is

---

4. The liturgy within the Book of Common Prayer places The Decalogue (and the congregational responses to each commandment) after the first Collect within the Holy Communion service.

5. Sermon no. 241.

6. Sermon 'The Decalogue & Xt. [Christ]', no.187.

7. Ibid.

Jesus' way of explaining its meaning because, Allen believed,
'The law [of] God deals w [with] us as we deal w [with] our
fellowmen: to the merciful thou wilt show thyself merciful (Ps.
18:24); the unmerciful servant (Matthew 18:23f.); in as much
as ye did it to one of these least; Forgive us as we forgive'[1];
and,

4) that Jesus' sermon reinforced the Decalogue's internal purpose
by explaining, for example, that 'Murder includes anger, Matt.
5:22 . . . Adultery includes lust, Matt. 5:28'.[2]

After analysis of these sermons and teachings, my research concluded
that Roland Allen's theology of the Old Testament was shaped by a firm
commitment to the enduring authority of the Ten Commandments. Not
only did he understand that these commandments were valid for the
Christian's faith and practice, but he also, in particular, believed that the
Sabbath, as practised within Christendom, was also good for society-at-
large when he proclaimed that to 'break up Sunday . . . [it] is a social
crime'[3] (original emphasis).

Covenant Blessing

The biblical characters – Noah, Abraham, Sarah, Isaac, Jacob, Joseph,
Ephraim, Manasseh – as disclosed in the Book of Genesis, Allen argued,
were the ones who received covenantal blessings and this he proclaimed
was 'more than well-wishing [and] more than declaration of favour,
prayer or promise or assurance of good to come'.[4] His sermon notes
show how he understood *the blessing* from the Genesis account and
contrasted this with the misuse of blessing and cursing as illustrated
by Balaam (Numbers 23). Allen's understanding of covenantal blessing
was rooted in and stems from the Old Testament context. Once that
background was established for the parishioners, he returned to the
Gospel lesson appointed for that day, so as to explain how Christ

---

1. Sermon on 'The Beatitudes V: The Merciful' Matthew 5:7, preached at
   Chailey, East Sussex (probably St Peter's Church or St George's Chapel) on
   26 July 1908, no. 182.
2. Sermon on 'The Decalogue & Xt. [Christ]', no. 187.
3. Ibid., no. 216.
4. Sermon no. 358 on St. Luke 24:50 'What is Blessing?' (Sunday after Ascension)
   St. John's Harpenden, Hertfordshire (Matins, 16 May 1915); Harpenden,
   Wheathampstead Deanery (1917); Penn Street Church, Buckinghamshire
   (Matins 1920).

gave the 'blessing' to His followers: 'Then he led them out as far as Bethany, and lifting up his hands he blessed them. While he blessed them he parted from them and was carried up into heaven' (Luke 24:50-51). Allen believed that Jesus' blessing upon his disciples – before His ascension – was in *covenantal continuity* with the patriarchal blessings as disclosed in Genesis.

The Prophets

A thought-provoking sermon of Roland's entitled 'On Prophecy and the Prophetic Word' (11 pages in length) engaged with definitions for the prophetic word, as disclosed within the Old Testament. He said:

> When I was a child I learnt about prophets in the O.T. how they foretold coming events, & [and] above all the coming of the Messiah who in the N.T. was revealed as Jesus Christ the Saviour of the world. So far as it went that was good. I saw that they did that, but how or why, I did not know at all.[5]

As a young boy, he began to think critically and question that 'even if he [a prophet] does very clever & [and] wonderful things, we must not believe him' if the words that he proclaimed were 'contrary to the commandment of God'.[6] The sermon continued with comments on Deuteronomy 13:1-3, and also Deuteronomy 18:21-22, successively, in determining the difference between true and false prophets. Consider comments on the latter passage:

> . . . a true prophet cannot teach us to act against our conscience or what is contrary to known truth. But suppose that a prophet speaks in the name, not of another god, but of our own God, how are we to know whether he is really sent by God to speak to us. Here I got into a difficulty. In Deut. xviii 21-22 the question is asked "If thou say in thine heart, how shall we know the word which the Lord hath not spoken?" and the answer given is, "when a prophet speaketh in the name of the Lord, if the thing follow not, nor come to pass, that is the thing which the Lord hath not spoken." But I said what was the good of telling the people of Israel that. If a prophet came to speak to them, they wanted to

---

5. Sermon nos. 333-343 'On Prophecy and the Prophetic Word', St Matthew 11:25, St Luke 10:21.

6. Ibid., no. 333.

know at once whether what he said was God's word to them. If they waited to see whether the prophet's words came to pass, it might be too late to do what he told them to do. The opportunity would be lost.[1]

After considerable reflection (as a young person) on how the prophetic ministry functioned within the context of the Old Testament he still continued to process explanations of the way in which prophets spoke. Various explanations were presented, such as:

1) that the prophet was more of 'a foreteller of events in the future as a forthteller of God's Truth', whereby, the prophet's calling was primarily that of 'a preacher of righteousness that . . . told people beforehand what was going to happen' and was therefore more of 'a preacher than what we call a prophet' who generally proclaimed a message, such as: 'Repent, turn from your evil ways, love righteousness, God will not accept the sacrifices of the wicked . . . '[2];

2) that the prophet was more like 'all clerics' today who begin their sermons with 'In the Name [of the Father, and of the Son and of the Holy Spirit]. Amen.' With this second point, Allen explained the similarity between both the biblical prophets and modern day ministers who speak 'in the Name of God'[3]; and,

3) that the prophetic ministry, he believed, was best understood as follows:

You have, I hope, agreed with me that the essential part of the prophetic word is the expression of an apprehension of the divine truth, that is the nature of God in relation to [the] prophets' own world, that the expression carries with it both a blessing & a curse, & that the end of it is eternal, present in the world, fulfilled for men when its spiritual reality appears to men. . . . We must approach them as the true prophetic words, eternally true in their nature & attempt not to explain them but to accept them. That's the only way in which any prophetic word was ever known by men. The simple minded says simply 'That is True' then hold fast to that, & [and] let no wise man shake you with his worldly wisdom. For you will see soon that his worldly wisdom does not illuminate

---

1. Ibid., no. 334.
2. Ibid.
3. Ibid., no. 335.

his path for him; whilst that one <u>That is True</u> will if you hold to it illuminate your path. The answer to the prophetic word is <u>That is True</u> (original emphasis).[4]

In summary, these select sermons reveal Allen's respect for the Old Testament canon and its application to one's faith and practice. These sermons characterize the unquestionable influence of the Old Testament on his theology, especially with the advancement of his understanding of *truth* – divine truth – as delineated within the context of the prophetic word. This is important in order to understand how the Old Testament's prophetic emphasis provided the central planks for the apostolic principles that became the basis for his missiology. It is this missiology that incorporates a *prophetic proclamation* (similar to what is observed within the Old Testament) and is clearly present throughout his writings. Allen believed that he was compelled to speak *prophetically* to the problems that he observed in various practices of missionary societies. This he did for decades. It is this prophetic focus and the apostolic principles that provided the central planks of his missiology. This will be systematically unpacked in *Roland Allen: A Theology of Mission*, along with another example of Allen's theology of the Old Testament later in his life, when he argued for the significance of planting 'fully equipped' house churches, based on his interpretation of 'the Family Rite' of Passover, as set out in Exodus 12.

Conclusion

Within this work, I have analyzed the context and development of Roland Allen's missiology, thus providing, overall, an *intellectual biography* of his work, and in particular, the beginning stages for a focus on his theology of indigenization. An examination of his developing missionary ecclesiology disclosed that he integrated pneumatology and ecclesiology – Spirit and order – within the framework of a missionary theology of Church growth. This was enhanced, not by strategic methodologies, but through the application of 'apostolic principles'. This study has begun to unpack his conviction that Pauline missiology is *timeless* and capable of producing indigenous self-governing, self-supporting and self-extending churches without foreign control. While such debates and discussions are now relatively commonplace within Christian missiology, a century ago this was not the case. Indeed, in many respects this study has begun to demonstrate that Allen can be considered a pioneer in missiology.

---

4. Ibid., no. 344.

Conclusion

A Summary of *Roland Allen: A Missionary Life*

This research exemplifies that Allen's argument for an apostolic missionary ecclesiology originated from his belief that Pauline missionary methods provided the best prototype for 'missional Christianity'. Examination of the patristic scholars who influenced his thought and writings, makes it possible, for the first time, to understand the significant role that *apostolic mission* played in his missiology (especially within his unpublished works in which he references the early 'missional' document called the *Didachē*, discussed within *Roland Allen: A Theology of Mission*). The research so far shows how Allen wrestled with aspects of western missions' institutional and task-oriented methodologies, in contrast to his understanding of Pauline pneumatology, which he believed was the major stimulus for the empowerment and expansion of the Church's witness. Although Allen conventionally maintained his belief in High Church episcopacy for the planting of indigenous churches, it has become evident that his pneumatological focus actually proposed the prioritization of 'Spirit *before* order'.[1] The result is, firstly, the inevitability for the existence of independent churches and, secondly, in his attempt to preserve, what he believed, were, principles that undergirded apostolic order, a commitment to the ordination of indigenous leaders.

The main part of the historical analysis presented here reveals how the thought of Allen's family, fellow churchmen and theologians and the missionary circumstances, in which he found himself, impacted the germination of his missiology and world view. This work examines the ecclesiological and missiological *milieu* that pervaded his earlier theological development. Firstly, the interviews with Hubert Allen not only shed light on how his grandfather's evangelical faith was influenced by Roland's mother, while his Oxford education shaped his high churchmanship, but also provided an invaluable, personal and earnest portrait, which allows us a warm, vivid and unique image of Roland Allen.[2] Secondly, the archival research exposes the ways in which his

---

1. To be unpacked in *Roland Allen: A Theology of Mission.*
2. As discussed in Chapter 1.

missionary experience in China occasioned his methodological critique of the 'mission station system' and various paternalistic missionary practices. The initial evidence in this chapter, which has been unpacked in subsequent chapters, has paved the way in identifying Allen's emerging missiology of indigenization, which slowly developed while he was serving in China due to the direct influence by Charles Scott and that of John Nevius. This research suggests that Allen's incipient formation for indigenous church-planting stems from the direct influence that the Presbyterian missionary, John Nevius, had on his friend, Charles Scott, and how this filtered down to Allen from Scott during his missionary service in North China.

This research also assesses the ways in which Allen's missionary experience in China motivated him to evaluate the missiological situation of his day and documented how his contribution to the study of indigenous church-planting provided continuing relevance for theories of Church growth in the Majority World during the early stages of dismantling colonialism. My analysis of his *magnum opus, Missionary Methods: St Paul's or Ours?* (1912) reveals Allen's desire to articulate carefully a missionary ecclesiology founded upon a philosophy of ministry, which acquired its impetus from theological and missiological reflection within the problematic environment of a 'missiology from above'. The initial chapters explore Allen's missiology within a colonial context and how he was motivated to articulate and practice an initial 'missiology from below' (i.e., led by indigenous, local leaders) which empowered Chinese Christians to manage their own churches.

The core historical analysis within this book discusses how Allen's thinking about Paul's missionary methods was enhanced through his engagement with the works of William Ramsay and Adolf von Harnack. It was Harnack's insistence on an ecclesiology governed by a charismatic faith that empowers Church expansion, rather than a highly organized system, that informed Allen's charismatic missiology. We can see that the evidence reveals that his opposition to foreign hegemony exercised through mission stations did not develop into a personal disassociation from colonial institutions. This was largely as a result of his acceptance of Ramsay and Harnack's theses regarding early Christianity's success under Roman authority. However, Allen also recognized that while British colonial infrastructure constituted an imposition upon certain indigenous people, nevertheless, it provided a *necessary orderliness* and quite often promoted *peace* within multi-ethnic cultures. Hence, as is now widely recognized, one cannot simply disengage from embedded colonial structures without significant violence being inflicted upon indigenous societies. The engagement with this hegemonic tension and his critique of the 'imperialistic spirit' is not dissimilar to concerns articulated by modern postcolonial theorists such as Robert Young (2001) who have argued that the globalization of powers from above have led to the imposition of injustices upon the people they colonized. While Allen was not a direct influence on Young, it is clear that his work is prescient in this respect, sharing a commonality with certain ideas that have emerged from modern postcolonial analysis. Allen's concern that the misplaced effort put into the desacralization of certain indigenous customs amongst the colonized, provides a critique that is not dissimilar from Young's arguments against western imperialism. Having said that, to claim that Allen's cross-cultural missiology sought to dismantle colonialism would be an *inaccurate* portrayal of the facts of the historical and archival evidence. (Indeed, while Allen's thinking was prescient, before his time; to claim much more than this would be anachronistic.) His contribution to postcolonial studies rests with the principles of indigenization, which helped to found churches led by local leaders who were 'fully equipped' to manage their own affairs without foreign control. The facts reveal that Allen's missionary ecclesiology is designed *to empower* and *not to control*.

The chapter entitled 'The World Dominion Movement and its Evangelical Mission' discloses how the editors of the World Dominion Press depended on the significant contributions of Allen's writings as a missionary theologian. These 'evangelical' publications were missional in nature and spurred their commitment to global evangelism, a consistent focus on planting indigenous churches, encouraged empirical survey work on unreached fields, discouraged against any imposition of hegemonic institutions, and published articles encouraging the value of non-professional missionaries.

This analysis of Allen's missionary journeys to India (1910; 1927-28), Canada (1924), South Africa (1926) and Southern Rhodesia (Zimbabwe; 1926) discloses his unique blend of speaking into the missionary situation through his writings and previous missionary work in China, which gave him a first-hand understanding of world mission. This research highlights that, in 1924, the Survey Application Trust authorized him to perform survey analysis of the work done by missionaries who had been sent to Canada. The Archbishops of both Canterbury and York, we see, promoted this project – 'The Archbishop's Western Canada Fund' – and Allen's visit there allowed Allen to formalize his observations of the developments as a missionary methods-analyst. In terms of mission to India, the archives reveal his ongoing correspondence with three significant bishops – Azariah (Dornakal), Whitehead (Madras), Hubback (Assam). – This ongoing communication (which continued for approximately two decades) kept Allen informed of the developing nature of Church growth within these regions. By the time Allen went to South Africa in 1926, it was clear that his writings on voluntary clergy and non-professional missionaries had already created an atmosphere of debate; he then advanced the 'timeless principles', which, he believed, truly promote the establishment of the Church.

This book imparts that Roland's early years were shaped within an Anglican *ethos*; he was the sixth of seven children born to the Rev. Charles and Priscilla Allen. His father, being a priest and missionary within the Church of England, died when Roland was young. It was his mother's *evangelical faith* that provided the main formative influence and this shaped his spirituality. Two of his brothers – Reginald and Willoughby – also became priests within the Church of England'.[1] This childrearing accounts for how these three brothers continued to have a high view of Scripture as Anglican churchmen. This study furthermore explores the names of those who influenced Roland Allen's life, such as, W.H. Hutton, his mentor and benefactor at St John's College; Gilbert Murray, his professor; F.E. Brightman, his 'dear father in God'; Philip Napier Waggett, Cowley Father and friend for many years; Winfred Burrows, his principal at Leeds Clergy School; Charles Scott, his bishop in China; Sidney J.W. Clark, his friend and benefactor for publication and mission work, Thomas Cochrane, his co-author; H.H. Kelly, missionary priest; Cosmo Gordon Lang, Archbishop of York; W.H. Temple Gairdner, missionary in Cairo; V.S. Azariah, bishop in Dornakal and friend; Charles Gore, Bishop; Henry Whitehead, Bishop in Madras; and many more. This chapter also unveiled that the Allen family – Roland, his wife Beatrice, daughter Priscilla, and son (John) Iohn (with his wife Winifred and their children) – lived in East Africa. When Roland and Beatrice visited in 1931, it became apparent that they were to make Kenya their permanent residence. Hubert Allen's explanation concerning his grandparents' move to Africa was essentially to live closer to their children and grandchildren, to enjoy a healthier climate, and to make

---

1. To digress, Reginald served 'the Gloucestershire parish of Blakeney . . . [later] was chaplain of a school for European boys at Bournabat, near Smyrna in Turkey . . . [and] a few years after the war [was] chaplain to the British community at Dinan, near St Malo in Brittany' (Hubert Allen, *Roland Allen*, 15-16). Willoughby later was 'both Archdeacon of Manchester and Principal of the Egerton Hall theological college . . . [and later] became simultaneously Rector of Chorley, Archdeacon of Blackburn, and an army chaplain,' Hubert Allen, *Roland Allen*, 16.

the transition into an 'inexpensive environment of Nairobi'.[1] Other illustrations of Roland Allen, as can be found in the evidence of the ways in which he spent most of his retirement years, primarily, in Bible study and the contextualization of Gospel ministry into East African culture. This research has advanced exposure and a better understanding of the deposited archives (Bodleian Libraries, Oxford) which contain numerous articles that he wrote (relentlessly) concerning various issues within African culture. Secondarily, he attempted to understand Islamic thought by learning and translating books from Swahili into English, such as:

(1) 'The Story of Mbega' by Abdullah bin Hemedi 'IAjjemy;
(2) 'Utenzi wa Kiyama (Siku ya Hukuma)';
(3) 'Inkishafi';
(4) 'Utenzi wa Kutawafu Naby' (re-edited as 'Utendi wa Kutawafu Nabii', Edward Mellen Press, 1991); and
(5) 'Utenzi wa Abdirrahmani na Sufiyani' by Hemed Abdalla el Buhry. The Roland Allen family exemplified a uniquely Christian witness in 'word and deed' that was cross-cultural and that sought to engage with other religions and cultures through service and interpersonal dialogue.

The final chapter of this book explores the unexamined sermon collection within Roland Allen's archives. Although his most popular books originated from his understanding of the New Testament, it is appropriate for the reader to have clarity here, lest some conclude that he was uninterested in the Old Testament. My analysis of his sermon collection tells us that the opposite is the case. The archival collection reveals how his sermons argued for the significance of the Old Testament text to reveal the holiness and sovereignty of God, particularly, his belief that the Ten Commandments convey this relevance for Christians today. Real scholarly work remains to be done on these sermons, especially to identify fully the theology of covenantal continuity, which he believed existed between the Old and New Testaments. With that in view, this chapter assesses his engagement with the law of God as the prophetic proclamation, which speaks directly to Church and society today.

---

1. Hubert Allen, *Roland Allen*, 154.

Bibliography

Primary Sources

Roland Allen's Books and Pamphlets

Allen, Roland and Alexander McLeish, *Devolution and its Real Significance* (London: World Dominion Press, 1927)

Allen, Roland, *Discussion on Mission Education* (London: World Dominion Press, 1931)

Allen, Roland, *Education in the Native Church* (London: World Dominion Press, 1926. Repr. 1928)

Allen, Roland, *Educational Principles and Missionary Methods: The Application of Educational Principles to Missionary Evangelism* (London: Robert Scott, 1919)

Allen, Roland, *Foundation Principles of Foreign Missions* (May 1910) USPG X622, Box 2, File J, Oxford, Bodleian Library. (Repr. *Essential Missionary Principles*, Cambridge: The Lutterworth Press, 1913. Repr. *Missionary Principles – and Practice*, Grand Rapids: Eerdmans, 1964; *Missionary Principles – and Practice*, London: World Dominion Press, 1964); *Missionary Principles – and Practice* (Cambridge: The Lutterworth Press, 2006)

Allen, Roland, *Gerbert, Pope Silvester II* (London: Spottiswoode & Co, 1892).

Allen, Roland, *Jerusalem: A Critical Review of 'The World Mission of Christianity'* (London: World Dominion Press, 1928)

Allen, Roland, *Le Zoute: A Critical Review of 'The Christian Mission in Africa'* (London: World Dominion Press, 1927)

Allen, Roland, *Mission Activities: Considered in Relation to the Manifestation of the Spirit* (London: World Dominion Press, 2nd edn, 33-page pamphlet, 1930)

Allen, Roland, *Missionary Methods: St Paul's or Ours? A Study of the Church in the Four Provinces* (London: Robert Scott, February 1912; in the Library of Historic Theology. Repr. October 1913. Revd edn published by World Dominion Press, 2nd edn August 1927. Repr. 1930, 1949, 1956. Reset – with memoir by Alexander McLeish – Grand Rapids: Eerdmans, 1962. Repr. 1993. Repr. Cambridge: The Lutterworth Press, 2006) *New Foreword*: Bishop Michael Nazir-Ali, III-IV

Allen, Roland, *Missionary Principles – and Practice* (1st edition [Roland's handwritten marked copy] entitled *Foundation Principles of Foreign Missions*, Bungay, Suffolk: Richard Clay & Sons, May 1910. Repr. Cambridge: The Lutterworth Press, 1913, entitled *Essential Missionary Principles*; Grand Rapids, Michigan: Wm. B. Eerdmans, 1964; London: World Dominion Press, 1964, Cambridge: The Lutterworth Press, 2006)

Allen, Roland and Thomas Cochrane, *Missionary Survey as an Aid to Intelligent Co-operation in Foreign Missions* (London: Longmans, Green, 1920. Repr. BiblioBazaar, 2008)

Allen, Roland, *Non-Professional Missionaries*, privately printed at Beaconsfield (1929)

Allen, Roland, *Pentecost and the World: The Revelation of the Holy Spirit in 'The Acts of the Apostles'* (London: Oxford University Press, 1917)

Allen, Roland, *Sidney James Wells Clark: A Vision of Foreign Missions* (London: World Dominion Press, 1937)

Allen, Roland, *The Case for Voluntary Clergy* (London: Eyre & Spottiswoode, 1930)

Allen, Roland, *The Establishment of the Church in the Mission Field: A Critical Dialogue* (London: World Dominion Press, 1927)

Allen, Roland, *The 'Nevius Method' in Korea* (London: World Dominion Press, 1930) Box 4

Allen, Roland, *The Place of Faith in Missionary Evangelism* (London: World Dominion Press, 8, 1930) 234-41

Allen, Roland, *The Siege of the Peking Legations* (London: Smith, Elder, 1901)

Allen, Roland, *The Spontaneous Expansion of the Church* (London: World Dominion Press, 1927. Repr. 2nd edn 1960, reissued, Grand Rapids: Wm. B. Eerdmans Publishing Co., 1962. Repr. Cambridge: The Lutterworth Press, 2006)

Allen, Roland, *Voluntary Clergy* (London: SPCK, 1923) Box 2, File J

Allen, Roland, *Voluntary Clergy Overseas: An Answer to the Fifth World Call* (privately printed at Beaconsfield, England, 1928) USPG X622, Box 2, File J, Oxford, Bodleian Library

Allen's Translations from Swahili Writings

'The Story of Mbega' (part 1) by Abdullah bin Hemedi 'lAjjemy, *Tanganyika Notes & Records* (1936-37)

'Utenzi wa Kiyama (Siku ya Hukumu)', an appendage to *Tanganyika Notes & Records* (c. 1946) USPG X622, Box 4, Oxford, Bodleian Library

'Inkishafi – A Translation from the Swahili' *African Studies* (December 1946) USPG X622, Box 4, Oxford, Bodleian Library

'Utenzi wa Kutawafu Naby', anon, an appendage to *Journal of the East African Swahili Committee* (June 1956; re-edited as 'Utendi wa Kutawafu Nabii', Edward Mellen Press, 1991)

'Utenzi wa Abdirrahmani na Sufiyani' by Hemed Abdalla el Buhry, *Johari za Kiswahili*, no.2, (1961)

Articles and Works (USPG X622, Oxford, Bodleian Library, Roland Allen archives)

1900

'Of Some of the Causes Which Led to the Preservation of the Foreign Legations in Peking', *The Cornhill Magazine* (September 27) 754-776, Box 2, File J: 1, the Church of England Mission

'Of Some of the Causes Which Led to the Siege of the Foreign Legations in Peking' (November) *The Cornhill Magazine*, no.53/491, 669-680, Box 2, File J: 1, the Church of England Mission

'Of Some of the Causes which Led to the Preservation of the Foreign Legations in Peking', *The Cornhill Magazine* (December) 754-76, no.54; no.492, Box 2, File J

1901

'The Development of Independent Native Churches and their federation in union with the Church of England', paper for a clerical Society in East London, Box 3: 1

'Of some of the Conclusions which may be drawn from the Siege of the Foreign Legations in Peking', *The Cornhill Magazine* (February) 202-12, no.56 and 494

'Church in Japan', *Church Missionary Intelligencer* (April) Box 2, File J: 2

1902

'A Church Policy for North China – I', LIEN, *The Guardian*, 879, Box 1, File B

'The Churches of the Future', *The Guardian* (18 June)

'The Churches of the Future', *The Guardian* (25 June)

'A Church Policy for North China – II', *The Guardian* (July) Box 1, File B

'The Unceasing Appeal for Men for Foreign Missions', *The Guardian* (23 July)

1903

'The Anglican Mission at Yung Ch'ing, North China' (20 February) Box 2, File J: 3

'The Chinese Character and Missionary Methods', *The East and The West* (July): 317-329, Box 2, File J: 35

'The Work of the Missionary in Preparing the Way for Independent Native Churches', (11-12 November) Box 2, File J: 4

1904

'Independent Native Churches', *The Guardian* (24 August) no.3064/1389, Box 1, File B & File C

1907

'Letter to the Parishioners of Chalfont St Peter' (25 November) reprinted in Hubert Allen's *Roland Allen: Pioneer, Priest, and Prophet* (1995) 183-88

1908

'Canada Immigration', *Times* (4 April) Box 1, File A

'Opium Suppression in China', *The Church Times* (1 May) Box 1, File B

'The Supply and Training of Candidates for Holy Orders', *Times* (11 June) Box 1, File J
'The Progress of Education in China', *Cornhill* (November) 655-65, Box 2, File J: 5A & 5B (1-11)

1909

Paper presented *SPG: Laymen's Missionary Association: The Day of Intercession* (January) 37-40, Box 2: 6
'A Grave Indictment', *Church Times* (August) Box 1, File A
'A Grave Indictment', *Church Times* (17 September) Box 1, File A
'A Grave Indictment', *Church Times* (1 October) Box 1, File A
'Missionary Policy in China', *Church Times* (19 November) Box 1, File B
'Spiritual Means for Spiritual Work', *SPG Laymen's Missionary Association* (January & 30 November) Box 2, File J: 6
'The Message of the Christian Church to Confucianists', *The East and The West* (October): 437-452, Box 2, File J: 7

1910

'Foundation Principles of Foreign Missions' (May) Box 2, File J

1911

'An Indian Church Society: A New Movement among Native Christians', *The Church Times* (21 July) Box 1, File B
'A Native Church in the Making', *The Church Times* (8 September) Box 1, File B
'The "Will to Convert in Mission Schools"', *The East and The West* (October) 408-417, Box 2, File J: 8
'A Native Church in the Making: A Contrast', *The Church Times* (10 November) Box 1, File B

1912

'The Influence of "Mission Stations" upon the Establishment of Indigenous Churches', *English Church Review* (November) 500-08, vol.III, no.35, Box 2, File J: 9

1913

'The Influence of Foreign Missions on the Church at Home', *The Commonwealth*, XVIII (August) 242-246, Box 1, File B
'Educational Principles and Missionary Methods', *The English Review*, vol.IV, no.37 (January) 14-25, Box 2, File J: 10

1915

'The Influence of Western Education upon Religion in Non-Christian Lands – I', *The Challenge* (30 April) Box 1, File B

'The Influence of Western Education upon Religion in Non-Christian Lands –
    II', *The Challenge* (7 May) Box 1, File B
'The Right to Ordination', *Challenge* (30 July) Box 1, File B

1918

'The Christian Education of Native Churches', *Church Missionary Review*
    (December) 398-405, Box 2, File J: 12

1919

Book review, *Church Quarterly Review*, art.1. – 'Concerning some Hindrances to
    the Extension of the Church', no.CLXXVII (October) Box 2, File J: 13a-b
The Church Times (14 November) Box 1, File A

1920

'Islam and Christianity in the Sudan', *The International Review of Missions*
    (October) 531-43, XIX/36, Box 2, File J: 14
'The Whole and the Parts in Foreign Missionary Administration', *Church
    Missionary Review* (December) Box 2, File J: 15
'The Relation Between Medical, Educational and Evangelistic Work in Foreign
    Missions', *Church Missionary Review*, 54-62
'The Whole and the Parts in Foreign Missionary Administration', *Church
    Missionary Review*, 329-37
'Missionary Survey as an Aid to Intelligent Co-operation in Foreign Missions',
    World Dominion Press

1921

'The Mission in Corea: Another Call for Men', *The Church Times* (21 October)
    Box 1, File A
'A Tyrannous Tradition', *The Challenge* (18 November) Box 1, File B

1922

'A Conscience Clause in India', *The Record* (19 January) Box 1, File B
'Colonial and Continental Church Society', *The Record* (4 May) Box 1, File A
'SPG Anniversary', *The Church Times* (5 May) Box 1, File A
'Materialism and Atheism: Dangers of South America', *Guardian* (5 May) Box
    1, File A
'The Future of a Great Work: Colonial and Continental Church Society',
    Guardian (5 May) Box 1, File A
'Mission Colleges and Schools: The Worth-while Line', *The Challenge* (26 May)
    Box 1, File B
'Mission Colleges and Schools: The Meaning of Christian Education', *The
    Challenge* (2 June) Box 1, File B
'Mission Colleges and Schools: A Strategic Position', *The Challenge* (9 June) Box
    1, File B

'Mission Colleges and Schools: The True Strategic Position', *The Challenge* (16 June) Box 1, File B

'Western Education and Village Evangelisation: A Criticism of the Report of the C.M.S. Delegation to India', *The Record* (22 June) Box 1, File C

'The Case for Voluntary Clergy: An Anglican Problem', *The Interpreter* (July) Box 2, File J: 16

'Church People Abroad', *Daily Telegraph* (12 July) Box 1, File A

'Mission Colleges in India', *Record* (9 November) Box 1, File A

'The Serious Dearth of Clergy', *Guardian* (8 December) Box 1, File A

1923

'Supply of Clergy', *Church Times* (5 January) Box 1, File A

'Brotherhood: A Contrast between Moslem Practice and Christian Ideas', London: *World Dominion*, 1, 92-94

'Christian Education in China', *Theology* (March) 129-134, Box 2, File J: 17

'The Algoma Association: Help for the Church in Canada', *Church Times* (23 March) Box 1, File A

'The Church in South Africa: Admission of Sub-Deacons in Johannesburg', *Guardian* (18 April) Box 1, File A

'The Church Overseas: South Africa- Diocese of Johannesburg- Admission of Sub-Deacons', *Church Times* (20 April) Box 1, File A

'Colonial and Continental Church Society: Mr Gladstone's Speech', *The Record* (3 May) Box 1, File A

'Universities' Mission to Central Africa: The Bishop of Zanzibar's Letter', *Church Times* (25 May) Box 1, File A

Archbishop's address, Synod (June) Box 1, File A

Letter to the editor, *Church Times* (7 September) Box 1, File A

'The "Colonial and Continental" Centenary Autumn Meeting: Message From H.R.H. The Prince of Wales', *The Record* (15 November) Box 1, File A

'The Church Overseas: Dr Haynes' Work at Bloemfontein – Basuto Movement for Independent Church. A Trek through Zululand', *The Guardian* (14 December) Box 1, File A

1924

'The Bishop of Mombasa's Appeal', *The Record* (7 February) Box 1, File A

'News and Notes: 230 Miles for a Service', *Guardian* (8 February) Box 1, File A

'Voluntary Clergy', *Record* (6 March) Box 1, File B

'The Church Overseas', *Guardian* (21 March) Box 1, File A

'Voluntary Clergy', *Record* (29 May) Box 1, File A

A response from Allen (23 May) to 'Fr Wilfrid Shelley's letter', *Church Times* (30 May) Box 1, File A

'Church Revenues Report', *The Guardian* (30 May) Box 1, File A

'Catholics and a Missionary Policy', *Church Times* (16 May) Box 1, File A

'Catholics and a Missionary Policy', *Church Times* (23 May) Box 1, File A

'Catholics and a Missionary Policy', Allen's response (23 May) to Fr Wilfrid Shelley's previous article, *Church Times* (30 May) Box 1, File A

Letter to editor, *The Living Church* (1 November) Box 1, File A

'The Church in Western Canada: Need of Voluntary Priests', *Church Times* (5 December) Box 1, File A

1925

'The Church in Western Canada: Need of Voluntary Priests', *The Church Times* (16 January)

'A Constitution for the Indian Church', *World Dominion*, 3, (March) 64-68, Box 2, File J: 18

'Leadership – Train Leaders', an article rejected by the *Church Missionary Review* (July) Box 3: 3

'The Essentials of an Indigenous Church', *Chinese Recorder*, 56: 491-96

'The Essentials of an Indigenous Church', *World Dominion*, 3, 110-117

'The Native Church and Mission Education', *World Dominion*, 3, 153-60

'Education in the Native Church', *World Dominion*, 4, 37-44

1926

'Money: The Foundation of the Church', *The Pilgrim*, 6/4 (July) 417-428, Box 2, File J: 20

'The Maintenance of the Ministry in the Early Ages of the Church', *World Dominion*, 4, 218-24

'The Rectory of Fairstead', *Truth* (22 September) Box 1, File E

Address delivered to the Diocesan Synod of Pretoria (26 October) Box 3, File G: 30

1927

'Diary of a Visit in South India', USPG X622, Box 7, File N (1927-28) 1-85, Oxford, Bodleian Library

'The Establishment of Indigenous Churches', *International Review of Missions*, 17, X Series, Box 3

'Itinerant Clergy and the Church', *The East and The West*, Box 3, File G: 30

'The Use of the Term "Indigenous"', *International Review of Missions*, 16 (April) 262-70, Box 2, File J: 22

'The Church and an Itinerant Ministry', *The East and The West*, 25/9 (April) 123-133, Box 2, File J: 2

'Indigenous Churches: The Way of St Paul', *The Church Missionary Review* (June) 147-159, Box 2, File J: 23

'Voluntary Service in the Mission Field', *World Dominion*, 5, 135-43

'Devolution – The Question of the Hour', *World Dominion*, 5, 274-87

'The Establishment of Indigenous Churches', refused by the *International Review of Missions*, Box 3: 5

1928

'Voluntary Clergy', article refused by *St Martin's Review* (14 May) Box 3: 6

Reviews by Allen of 'Industrialism in Japan' (Walter F. France) and 'Buddhism and Buddhists in Japan' (Robert C. Armstrong) *Church Quarterly Review* (October) Box 2, File J: 24

'The Findings of the Jerusalem Conference', *Theology* (November) 296-301, Box 2, File J: 25

'General Smuts on Missions in Africa', *Times Report* (18 November) Box 3: 7

Review of an article by K.S. Latourette 'What is happening to Missions?' *Yale Review* (December) Box 3: 8

'The Need for Non-Professional Missionaries', *World Dominion*, 6, 195-201

'The Work for Non-Professional Missionaries', *World Dominion*, 6, 298-304

'Business Man and Missionary Statesman: Sidney James Wells Clark: An Appreciation', *World Dominion* (December) 3-9

1929

Letter to the Editor, *The Guardian* (4 January) Box 1, File C

'The Imperialism of Missions', *The Living Church* (26 January) Box 1, File B: 14

Review by Allen of 'Our Church's Youngest Daughter', (Eyre Chatterton, Bishop of Nagpur) *Church Quarterly Review*, Box 2, File J: 26

Reviews by Allen of 'Japan and Christ' by M.S. Murao and 'A Transvaal Jubilee' by J.A.I. Agar Hamilton, *Church Quarterly Review*, Box 2, File J: 27

Review by Allen of 'Essays Catholic and Missionary', *Church Quarterly Review* (April) Box 2, File J: 28

'New Testament Missionary Methods', *The Missionary Review of the World*, 52: 21-24, Box 1, File B

'The Methodists and the Prophet Harris', *World Dominion* (April) Box 2, File J: 29

Review by Allen of 'Indirect Effects of Christian Missions in India' by R.S. Wilson, *Church Quarterly Review* (April) Box 2, File J: 30a-b

'Missionary Methods', *The Congregational Quarterly* (April) 165-169, Box 2, File J: 31

'Businessman and Missionary Statesman: Sidney James Wells Clark: An Appreciation', *World Dominion*, 7, 16-22

'The Provision of Services for Church People Overseas', *Theology*, 19, 23-30

1930

'The Ministry of Expansion: the Priesthood of the Laity' (unpublished) Box 3, File G: 27.

'The Place of 'Faith' in Missionary Evangelism' (London: World Dominion Press)

Review by Allen of 'A History of Christian Missions in China' by K.S. Latourette (January) *Church Quarterly Review*, Box 2, File J: 32

'The Church and the Ministry in the Mission Field', (5 January) Box 3: 9

'The Case for Voluntary Clergy', *St Martin's Review*, no.471 (May) 241, Box 1, File D.

Letter to the editor, *The Guardian* (9 May) Box 1, File D

'The Case for Voluntary Clergy', London: Eyre and Spottiswood (July) 333-340, Box 1, File E.

Letter to the editor, 'Railway Church', *The Record* (August) Box 3, File G: 10

'The Place of Medical Missions, *World Dominion*, 8, 34-42

'Lambeth Conference on Voluntary Clergy', *Witness and Canadian Homestead* (22 October) Box 1, File B

1931

'Voluntary Clergy and the Lambeth Conference', *The Church Overseas: An Anglican Review of Missionary Thought and Work*, vol.IV, no.14 (April): 145-53, Box 2, File J:33

'The Chinese Government and Mission Schools', *World Dominion*, 9, 25-30

'The "Nevius Method" in Korea', *World Dominion*, 9: 252-58

1932

'Is the Church Out of Touch with People?' *The East African Standard* (14 May) Box 8: 3.

'A Cathedral Sermon', *The East African Standard* (21 May) Box 8: 4

Letter to the editor, 'The Church in Kenya', *The East African Standard* (24 June) Box 7: 3, 37

Letter to the editor, 'The Church in Kenya', *The East African Standard* (24 May) Box 8: 7, 8

'A Cathedral Sermon', *The East African Standard* (28 May) Box 8: 4

'A Survey of the Condition of the Anglican Church in Kenya', *The Times of East Africa* (28 May) Box 8: 1, 2

Allen's response to the *Churchman* (three questions) *The East African Standard* (4 June) Box 8: 5

'Auxiliary Clergy for Church in Kenya?', *The East African Standard* (4 June) Box 8: 9

'The Church in Kenya', *The East African Standard* (16 June) Box 8: 10

Letter from Allen 'Voluntary Clergy', *Kenya Church Review* (September) no.14, 4

'Voluntary Clergy', *E.A. Standard* (September) no.14: 4-5

1933

'The Priesthood of the Church', *Church Quarterly Review*, 116 (January) 234-44, Box 2, File J: 34

'The Application of Pauline Principles to Modern Missions', *World Dominion*, 11, 352-57

'Missionary Finance' (28 December) Box 1, File D

'Men for the Ministry' (28 December) Box 1, File E

1934

'The Cathedral', *The East African Standard* (5 February) Box 8: 11

'The Cathedral Appeal', *The East African Standard* (16 February) Box 8: 12

'The Work of the Church in Kenya', *The East African Standard* (11 April) Box
    8: 13
Letter to the editor, 'Church Attendance', *The East African Standard* (7 July) Box
    8: 39
'Kenya Sunday', *The East African Standard* (29 September) Box 8: 14

1935

Letter to the editor, 'Conference on Christian Co-operation', *The East African
    Standard* (23 July) Box 8: 21
Letter to the editor, 'Conference on Christian Co-operation', *The East African
    Standard* (30 July) Box 8: 21
Letter to the editor, 'Conference on Christian Co-operation', *The East African
    Standard* (31 July) Box 8: 22
Letter to the editor, 'Conference on Christian Co-operation', *The East African
    Standard* (2 August) Box 8: 22
Letter to the editor, *The East African Standard* (22 October) Box 8: 15
Letter to the editor, 'Prophecy', *The East African Standard* (29 October) Box 8: 15
Letter to the editor, 'Religious Teaching', *The East African Standard* (11
    November) Box 8: 16
Letter to the editor, 'Prophecy', *The East African Standard* (20 November) Box
    8: 17
Letter to the editor, 'Prophecy', *The East African Standard* (29 November) Box
    8: 17
Letter to the editor, *The East African Standard* (29 November) Box 8: 18

1936

Letter to the editor, 'The British Empire: Nucleus of World Unity', *The East
    African Standard* (20 March) Box 7, File N: 40
Letter to the editor, 'The Church in Kenya', *The East African Standard* (7 April)
    Box 8: 24
Letter to the editor, 'A Vacant Bishopric', *The East African Standard* (17 April)
    Box 7: 41
Letter to the editor, 'The Church in Kenya: A Vacant Bishopric', *The East African
    Standard* (21 April) Box 8: 24
Letter to the editor, 'Kenya Contrasts: The Missions and Polygamy', *The East
    African Standard* (1 May) Box 8: 25
'A Week-end Sermon: Regrets I', *The East African Standard* (1 May) Box 8: 26
'A Week-end Sermon: Regrets II', *The East African Standard* (8 May) Box 8: 27
Letter to the editor, 'Kenyan Contrasts: The Christian Missions', *The East
    African Standard*, (11 May) Box 7: 42
Letter to the editor, 'Christian Missions', *The East African Standard* (13 May)
    Box 8: 28
Letter to the editor, 'The Work of Missions', *The East African Standard* (16 May)
    Box 8: 28

Letter to the editor, 'Kenya Contrasts: Polygamy and Mission Teaching' (27 May) Box 8: 29

'A Week-end Sermon: God and Man', *The East African Standard* (5 June) Box 8: 29

Letter to the editor, 'Voluntary Clergy', *The East African Standard* (23 June) Box 8: 63

Letter to the editor, 'On Being Rude – Bumble in Nairobi', *The East African Standard* (29 June) Box 7: 43

Letter to the editor, 'On Being Rude – Bumble in Nairobi', *The East African Standard* (30 June) Box 8: 63

Letter to the editor, 'African Girlhood: A Mission Problem', *The East African Standard* (24 July) Box 8: 30

Letter to the editor, 'African Girlhood' *The East African Standard* (7 August) Box 8: 66.

Letter to the editor, 'African Girlhood: Mission Problem', *The East African Standard* (11 August) Box 8: 31

Letter to the editor, 'African Girlhood', *The East African Standard* (22 August) Box 8: 32

Letter to the editor, 'A Mission Problem', *The East African Standard* (25 August) Box 8: 33

Letter to the editor, 'A Mission Problem', *The East African Standard* (28 August) Box 8: 33

Letter to the editor, 'Native Customs: The Position of Missions', *The East African Standard* (14 September) Box 7: 44

Letter to the editor, 'Native Customs: The Position of Missions', *The East African Standard* (16 September) Box 8: 34

Letter to the editor, 'African Customs: A Kavirondo Case', *The East African Standard* (2 October) Box 8: 35

Letter to the editor, 'The League of Nations', *The East African Standard* (27 November) Box 8: 36

Letter to the editor, 'Security: The League of Nations', *The East African Standard* (4 December) Box 8: 37

1937 (File E)

Letter to the editor, 'Christianity in Britain', *The East African Standard* (2 April) Box 8: 39

Letter to the editor, *The East African Standard* (16 April) Box 7: 45

Letter to the Editor, 'Christianity in Kenya', *The Spectator* (18 June) Box 1, File E

Letter to the Editor, 'Christianity in Kenya', *The Spectator* (July) Box 1, File E

Letter to the Editor, 'Clergy in Kenya', *The Spectator* (30 July) Box 1, File E

Letter to the editor, 'Clergy in Kenya', *The Spectator* (30 July)

Letter to the editor, 'The Church and Paid Clergy', *East Africa and Rhodesia* (19 August) Box 8: 38

Letter to the editor, 'The Church in East Africa – The Provincial Problem', *The East African Standard* (17 January) Box 8: 40

Letter to the editor, 'The Church in East Africa – The Provincial Problem', *The East African Standard* (21 January) Box 8: 41

'Church Province Plan Checked – Nairobi Conference of Dioceses will not now take Place', *The East African Standard* (21 January) Box 8: 61

'The Church in East Africa – An Invitation and the Sequel', *The East African Standard* (13 January) Box 8: 62

Letter to the editor, 'The Bible and Prophecy', letter to the editor, *The East African Standard* (30 April) Box 7: 46

Letter to the editor, 'Divine Planning', *The East African Standard* (14 June) Box 8: 40

Letter to the editor, 'Divine Planning', *The East African Standard* (17 June) Box 8: 40

Letter to the editor, 'A New Chaplain', *The East African Standard* (16 August) Box 8: 42

Letter to the editor, 'The Work of a Chaplain', *The East African Standard* (6 September) Box 8: 42

1939

Letter to the editor, 'The Church of England in Kenya', *The East African Standard* (22 May) Box 8: 43

Letter to the editor, 'The Church of England in Kenya', *The East African Standard* (26 May) Box 8: 44

Letter to the editor, 'Refugees', *The East African Standard* (2 June) Box 8: 44

Letter to the editor, 'The Church in Kenya', *The East African Standard* (24 July) Box 8: 43

Letter to the editor, 'The Church in Kenya', *The East African Standard* (28 July) Box 8: 44

Letter to the editor, 'To the Communicants at St Mark's Church' (26 November) Box 8: 71, 72

1940

Letter to the editor, 'A Limuru Church', *The East African Standard* (23 January) Box 8: 46

Letter to the editor, 'A Limuru Church (1)', *The East African Standard* (26 January) Box 8: 46

Letter to the editor, 'A Limuru Church', *The East African Standard* (31 January) Box 8: 46

Letter to the editor, 'A Limuru Church (2)', *The East African Standard* (2 February) Box 8: 46

Letter to the editor, 'The Church of England in Kenya', *The Sunday Post* (7 March) Box 8: 47

Letter to the editor, 'An Appeal to Laymen – The Church of England in Kenya', *The Sunday Post* (17 March) Box 8: 48

1941

Letter to the editor, 'War Aims', *The East African Standard* (6 May) Box 8: 49

Letter to the editor, 'Refugees', *The East African Standard* (9 May) Box 8: 49
Letter to the editor, 'Refugees', *The East African Standard* (19 May) Box 8: 50
Letter to the editor, 'Refugees', *The East African Standard* (1 June) Box 8: 50
Letter to the editor, 'Refugees', *The East African Standard* (14 June) Box 8: 73
Letter to the editor, 'Refugees', *The East African Standard* (19 June) Box 8: 74
Letter to the editor, 'Refugees', *The East African Standard* (24 June) Box 8: 74

1942

Letter to the editor, 'The Bible', *The East African Standard* (19 May) Box 7: 47
Letter to the editor, 'The Bible', *The East African Standard* (9 June) Box 7: 47
Letter to the editor, *The East African Standard* (June) Box 7: 48
Letter to the editor, *Hibbert Journal*, 'Theological Colleges' (September) Box 3, File G: 12
Letter to the editor, 'Peace and Goodwill', *The East African Standard* (26 December) Box 7: 50

1943

'The Family Rite v. The Temple Rite' (unpublished) Box 1, USPG Archives, Rhodes House, Oxford
Letter to the editor, 'Peace and Goodwill', *The East African Standard* (5 January) Box 8: 51
Letter to the editor, 'Peace and Goodwill', *The East African Standard* (8 January) Box 8: 52
Letter to the editor, 'Peace and Goodwill', *The East African Standard* (15 January) Box 8: 52
Letter to the editor, 'Church Reform', *The East African Standard* (27 January) Box 8: 53
Letter to the editor, 'Church Reform', *The East African Standard* (3 February) Box 7: 51
Letter to the editor, 'The Price of Maize', *The East African Standard* (26 May) Box 8: 53
Letter to the editor, *Church Times*, 'The Supply of Clergy after the War' (June) Box 3, File G: 11
Letter to the editor, 'East Africa Church Province', *The East African Standard* (24 September) Box 8: 53
Letter to the editor, *The East African Standard* (11 August) Box 8: 54
Letter to the editor, 'African Representation', *The East African Standard* (20 August) Box 8: 54
Letter to the editor, 'The Good Earth', *The East African Standard* (13 December) Box 8: 54
Letter to the editor, 'The Good Earth', *The East African Standard* (27 December) Box 8: 55
Letter to the editor, 'Church Reform', *The East African Standard* (8 February) Box 8: 55

1944

'Religious Toleration' (unpublished, 1944) USPG, Box 7.

Letter to the editor, 'The Clergy', *The East African Standard* (February) Box 8: 57

Letter to the editor, 'A Church Statement', *The East African Standard* (10 April) Box 8: 57

Letter to the editor, 'Swing it, Padre!', *The East African Standard* (29 April) Box 8: 58

Letter to the editor, 'Bestial Doctrine', *The Sunday Post* (7 May) Box 8: 58

Letter to the editor, 'Kenya's Immorality', *Kenya Weekly News* (12 May) Box 8: 59

1946

Letter to the editor, 'The White Man's Burden', *The East African Standard* (8 October) Box 8: 59

1947

Letter to the editor, *The Sunday Post* (4 February) Box 8: 60

Letter to the editor, *The East African Standard* (4 February) Box 8: 60

Undated and Unpublished Manuscripts

'The doctrine of the Holy Spirit: Analysis', Box 3, File G: 13

'Dr Paul Monroe on the Imperialism of Missions in China', Box 3, File G: 14

'A Survey of the Condition of the Church in Kenya', Box 3, File G: 15

'The Place of Voluntary Clergy in the Church', letter to the editor, *Guardian*, Box 3, File G: 16

'The Report of the Archbishop's Committee on the Supply of Candidates for Holy Orders is Now Before Us', Box 3, File G: 17

'Realization', Box 3, File G: 18

'The Transformation of an Indigenous Christian Movement into a Mission', Box 3, File G: 19, 20

'Medical Missions', Box 3, File G: 21

'The Lesson of the Archbishop's Western Canada Fund', Box 3, File G: 22

'The Medical Missionary', Box 3, File G: 23

'The Church and an Itinerant Ministry', Box 3, File G: 24

'Denationalization'; 'The Elements in Holy Communion'; 'Reading a Qualification for Holy Baptism: extracts from a report of a committee on Discipline submitted to the Bishop in 1926', Box 3, File G: 25

'Missionary Dialogues: The Devil', Box 3, File G: 26

'Acts: Analysis', Box 3, File G: 29

'Resume', Box 1, File A

'The Advancing Church – Assembly's Concern: Problems of Vacant Posts Overseas', *Home News*, Box 1, File E

'Priesthood of the Church', Box 7, File N

'The Influence of Western Education upon Religion in Non-Christian lands',
    Box 7, File N
'The Teachers First Consideration', Box 7, File N
'Provision of Services for Church People Overseas', Box 7, File N
'Influence of Foreign Missions on the Church at Home', Box 7, File N
Notebook: Mission Ke Nauker, Box 7, File N

Teaching Notes on the New Testament (Box 3)

'Acts', (1906-1907)
'I Corinthians'
'I Corinthians 3:2-13 'The Dispensation of Grace'
'II Corinthians 1-4, Appeal for Unity'
'Galatians'
'Ephesians'
'Ephesians 1:3-14'
'Philippians'
'Philippians: Final Exhortations'
'Gospel of St Paul to Thessalonians'
'II Thessalonians'
'II Thessalonians: Final Exhortations'
'Hebrews'
'Revelation: The Epistles to the 7 Churches'

Box 4, File H

Preface (Nairobi) MSS 'New Wine: New Patch'
1. The Sower; The Tares
2. The Net; The Seed growing secretly: the mustard seed: the leaven; The
    Hidden Treasure: the Pearls; The Unmerciful servant; The Labourers; The
    Good Samaritan
3. The Importunate Friend; The Rich Fool; The Barren Fig Tree; The Great
    Supper
4. The Lost Sheep; The Lost Piece of Money; The Prodigal Son; The Unjust
    Steward; Dives and Lazarus; The Unjust Judge
5. The Pharisee and the Publican; The Ten Virgins; The Talents; The Two Sons;
    The Wicked Husbandmen
6. The Unjust Steward; The Pharisee and the Publican; The Rich Man
    and Lazarus; The Good Samaritan; The Prodigal Son; The Sower; The
    Unmerciful Servant

Letters

Allen's letter to the Bishop of Central Tanganyika, Box 6, letter 137A (10 June,
    1930); bilateral communication between Bishop V.S. Azariah and Allen, Box
    6, USPG Archives, Rhodes House, Oxford. Deposited papers: Roland Allen

File K

10 Oct. 1921	Draft letter regarding the Bishop of Bloemfontein
25 Jan. 1922	Letter from Bishop of Eastern Oregon
10 Aug. 1922	Letter from Bishop of Bloemfontein
3 Aug. 1923	Letter from Canon Farrel
3 Aug. 1923	Letter from Rev. Van Tassel Sutphen
9 Oct. 1923	Draft letter to Bishop of Kootenay
2 Nov. 1923	Draft letter to W.C. Mayne, Cheshire
2 Nov. 1923	Draft of letter to Bishop of Kampala
30 Nov. 1923	Letter from Bishop of Saskatchewan
11 Dec. 1923	Letter from Bishop of Kootenay
21 Dec. 1923	Draft letter regarding the bishop of Mombasa's appeal
29 Dec. 1923	Letter from the Bishop of Dornakal
3 Jan. 1924	Draft letter to the Bishop of Saskatchewan
3 Jan. 1924	Draft letter to the Bishop of Kootenay
30 Jan. 1924	Draft letter to Bishop Azariah
10 May 1924	Draft letter to Bishop of Lagos
13 May 1924	17.a Draft letter to Mr Clark
13 May 1924	17 b. Draft letter to Mr Clark
22 June 1924	Reply from Bishop of Lagos
24 May 1924	Letter from Bishop of Algoma
17 July 1924	Letter from Leigh T. Tarleton
29 Oct. 1924	Letter from A.B. Varley, Saskatchewan
13 Nov. 1924	Draft of letter to Bishop of Brandon
18 Nov. 1924	Letter from Natural Resources Intelligence Service, Ottawa
23 Nov. 1924	Letter from Davidson, Toronto
26 Nov. 1924	Draft letter, Varley, Regina
5 Dec. 1924	Draft letter, Davidson
9 Dec. 1924	Letter from Archdeacon of Calgary
11 Dec. 1924	Letter from Archdeacon Ingles, Toronto
23 Dec. 1924	Two Letters: Tilsley, Elizabethville, Congo & Allen
3 Feb. 1925	Letter from Varley, Regina
20 Feb 1925	Letter from Luttman-Johnson, Saskatchewan
13 Feb. 1925	F. Junkinson's letter regarding Bishop of Qu'Appelle's criticism of Allen's view of voluntary clergy
30 May 1925	Draft letter to Troth Williams
30 May 1925	Draft letter to H. Tilt, Kornal
12 June 1925	Draft letter to P.N. Waggett
15 June 1925	Reply from Waggett
16 June 1925	Draft letter to Waggett
24 June 1925	Draft letter to Bishop of Melanesia
10 July 1925	Draft letter to Mr McIntyre, Toronto
15 July 1925	Letters from Geoffrey Warwick and Thornton of British Honduras

25 Aug. 1925	Correspondence between Bishop of Saskatchewan and Junkison
25 Aug. 1925	Letter from E.A. McIntyre, Toronto
10 July 1925	Draft letter to the *Record*
21 July 1925	Draft letter to Bishop Motoda, Tokyo
27 July 1925	Letter from Troth Williams
11 Aug. 1925	Draft letter to Lacey
12 Aug. 1925	Letter from Lacey
9 Sept. 1925	Letter to Ralfe Davies
29 Oct. 1925	Draft letter to Lloyd
7 Jan. 1926	Letter from C.W.S. Williams, Oxford University Press
6 March 1926	Letter from Bishop of Gloucester
12 March 1926	Letter from Bishop of Gloucester
20 March 1926	Note from the Bishop of Chichester
22 March 1926	Draft letter to Bishop of Chichester
13 Aug. 1928	Letter from Charles Williams, OUP
28 Aug. 1926	Letter from Waldeth, on behalf Mr Lancaster
9 Sept. 1926	Letter from Bishop of Bloemfontein
2 Sept. 1926	Draft letter to Bishop of Pretoria
2 Sept. 1926	Draft letter to Bishop of Bloemfontein
4-11 Sept. 1926	Letter from Bishop of Johannesburg
17 Sept. 1926	Draft headed '*Aide Memoire*' for Bishop of Pretoria
18 Sept. 1926	Letter from the Bishop of St John's
30 Sept. 1926	Letter from C. E. Baber, Pretoria
29 Oct. 1926	Letter from Theodore Stibson, Kimberley
10 Nov. 1926	Letter from J. Agar Hamilton, Pretoria
7 Oct. 1926	Letter from Troth Williams from Delhi
28 Apr. 1927	Letter from Dr Leys
6 May 1927	Draft letter to Dr Leys
12 May 1927	Draft letter to Cochrane
15 July 1927	Draft letter to Spencer, Kumamoto, Japan
21 July 1927	Copy of letter to the Bishop of Bombay
4 Aug. 1927	Draft letter to the editor, *Church Times*
12 Aug 1927	Draft letter to the Bishop of Chichester
6 Sept. 1927	Letter from Charles Williams, OUP
19 Sept. 1927	Letter from Spencer, Kumamoto, Japan
7 Oct. 1927	Draft letter to Spencer
24 Oct. 1927	Draft letter to Bishop of Kampala
10 May 1928	Letter from Clarke, SPCK
16 May 1928	Letter from Clarke, SPCK
19 May 1928	Drafts of three letters to Cochrane
17 June 1928	Letter from Streeten, Bloemfontein
27 June 1928	Letter from Bishop of Khartoum, Cairo
2 July 1928	Letter from Bishop of Grahamstown
12 July 1928	Letter from Archdeacon Rix, Prince Rupert, B.C.
17 July 1928	Letter from John Popkin, Brandon, Manitoba

9 Aug. 1928	Letter from Bishop of Grahamstown
10 Aug. 1928	Draft letter to Bishop of Grahamstown
27 Aug. 1928	Postcard from the Bishop of Grahamstown
19 July 1928	Letter from Theodore Stibson (Bishop of Kimberley)
? Aug. ? 1928	Letter from Mary Scharlieb
6 Aug. 1928	Letter from Archbishop of York's secretary
7 Aug. 1928	Letter from Davidson, the Archbishop of Canterbury
7 Aug. 1928	Letter from Bishop of Oxford
9 Aug.	Draft letter to Bishop of Oxford
8 Aug. 1928	Letter from Geoffrey Warwick
11 Aug. 1928	Letter from Bishop of Oxford
16 Apr.	Letter from Geoffrey Warwick
17 Oct. 1928	Letter from Streeter, Bloemfontein
13 Aug. 1928	Letter from Bishop of Southampton
13 Aug. 1928	Receipt from British Museum for copy of *Voluntary Clergy Overseas*
15 Aug. 1928	Letter from the Bishop of Lichfield
10 Aug. 1928	Letter from the Bishop of Kilmore, Cavan
18 Aug. 1928	Postcard from the Bishop of Grahamstown
21 Aug. 1928	Letter from Henry Whitehead, Madras
22 Aug. 1928	Letter from Lancelot Cooke, Jerusalem
24 Aug. 1928	Letter from Bishop William White, Toronto
28 Aug. 1928	Letter from Adam, Diocese of Calgary
4 Sept. 1928	Letter from R.L.W. Lennan, Assam, India
5 Sept. 1928	Letter from Geoffrey Parratt, SPCK
3 Sept. 1928	Letter from Bishop F. Norris, Peking, China
5 Sept. 1928	Letter from Revd. J.M. Comyn-Ching, Edmonton, Alberta
11 Sept. 1928	Letter from Bishop Quinlan, Natal
9 Oct. 1928	Draft letter to Quinlan, Natal
16 Sept. 1928	Letter from Gerald Herring, Transvaal
28 Sept., 1928	Letter from Henry L. Morley, Kamloops, B.C.
29 Oct., 1928	Letter from William C. Nelson, Bishop of Nelson, New Zealand
5 Oct. 1928	Copy of notice on the Church Congress by Geoffrey Warwick
8 Oct. 1928	Letter from the Bishop of Bradford
8 Oct. 1928	Letter from the Bishop of Middleton
7 Nov. 1928	Letter from Bishop Edward L. Parsons, San Francisco
21 Oct. 1928	Letter from Bell, Salisbury, South Rhodesia
22 Nov. 1928	Letter from J.C. Davidson, Archdeacon of Toronto
1 Nov. 1928	Letter from the Bishop of Fredericton, New Brunswick
12 Nov. 1928	Draft letter to Bishop of Fredericton, New Brunswick
24 Sept. 1928	Letter from the Bishop of Wellington, New Zealand
30 Nov. 1928	Letter from G. Hibbert-Ware, Durban
17 Aug. 1928	Letter from the Bishop of Ontario
31 Jan. 1929	Letter from R.A. Streeten

8 March 1929	Letter from the Bishop of San Joaquin, California
3 May 1929	Letter from W.K. Lowther Clark, SPCK
20 May 1929	Letter from the Bishop of Nyasaland
1 July 1929	Draft letter in reply to the Bishop of Nyasaland
14 Sept. 1929	Letter from the Bishop of Nyasaland
1 Nov. 1929	Draft letter in reply to the Bishop of Nyasaland
10 June 1930	Draft letter of the Bishop of Central Tanganyika
2 April 1930	Draft letter to Bishop of Central Tanganyika
Not dated	Draft letter to the Bishop of Pretoria
Not dated	Visiting card Walter Anderson, Stovel Company Limited, Winnipeg

Correspondence Regarding Voluntary Clergy, File L

3 Dec. 1924	Draft letter to R.W. Allin
13 June 1925	Letter from George Hubback, Bishop of Assam
15 June 1925	Letter to Bishop of Assam
18 June 1925	Letter from the Bishop of Assam.
22 June 1925	Draft of letter to *The Guardian*
23 June 1925	Letter from the Bishop of Assam
25 June 1925	Letter to the Bishop of Assam
11 Aug. 1925	Draft letter to Bishop of Assam
14 Aug. 1925	Reply from Bishop of Assam
14 Aug. 1925	Draft letter to Bishop of Assam
28 Aug. 1925	Letter from Bishop of Assam
31 Aug. 1925	Letter to the Bishop of Assam
2 Sept. 1925	Letter from Bishop of Assam
4 Sept. 1925	Letter to Bishop of Assam
31 May 1926	Letter from Bishop of Assam
4 Sept. 1926	Letter to Bishop of Assam
13 Oct. 1926	Draft letter to Bishop of Assam
21 Nov. 1926	Letter from Bishop Assam
23 Dec. 1926	Draft letter to Bishop of Assam
24 Jan. 1927	Letter from Bishop of Assam
27 Feb. 1927	Draft letter to Bishop of Assam
24 March 1927	Letter from the Bishop of Barking
17 April 1927	Letter from Bishop of Assam
21 May 1927	Draft letter to *Church Times*
14 June 1927	Letter from R.A. Bennett, *Truth*
16 June 1927	Draft letter to editor of *Truth*
18 July 1927	Letter from Bishop of Assam
10 Aug. 1927	Draft reply to Bishop of Assam
18 Oct. 1927	Letter from R.A. Bennett, *Truth*
4 Dec. 1927	Letter from James Pederson, New York
12 Dec. 1927	Letter from R.A. Bennett, *Truth*

20 Jan. 1928	Letter from R.A. Bennett, *Truth*
26 Jan. 1928	Letter from F. Deaville Walker, *The Foreign Field*
1 March 1928	Letter from Sir John Murray
1 March 1928	Draft letter to Bishop of Assam
7 March 1928	Letter from Bishop of Assam
29 March 1928	Letter from C.E. Turner
31 March 1928	Draft letter to the Bishop of Egypt and Sudan (Llewellyn A. Gwynne)
31 March 1928	Draft letter to C.E. Turner
3 Apr. 1928	Draft letter to C.E. Turner
5 Apr. 1928	Draft letter to the editor, *Record*
9 Apr. 1928	Letter from H.A. Kennedy, Edgbaston
26 Apr. 1928	Letter from Bishop of Egypt and the Sudan
1 May 1928	Letter from C.E. Turner
1 May 1928	Draft letter to Bishop of Assam
1 May 1928	Letter from Sir John Murray
21 May 1928	Letter from the Bishop of Egypt and the Sudan
27 May 1928	Letter from the Bishop of Assam
29 May 1928	Letter from *St Martin's Review*
3 June 1928	Draft letter to the Bishop of Egypt and the Sudan
19 June 1928	Draft of letter to the editor, *The Times*
19 June 1928	Draft letter to Bishop of Assam
11 July 1928	Letter from H. Maynard Smith
12 July 1928	Letter from Bishop of Assam
13 July 1928	Letter marked from Cecil Bunbury
9 Aug. 1928	Draft of letter to Bishop of Assam
20 Sept. 1928	Letter from Bishop of Assam
27 Sept. 1928	Letter from the Coadjutor Bishop of Cape Town, South Africa
15 Oct. 1928	Draft reply to Bishop, Cape Town
2 Nov. 1928	Draft of letter to the editor, *N.C.C. Review*
29 Nov. 1928	Letter from Bishop of Assam
20 Apr. 1929	Letter from the Bishop of Southampton
22 Apr. 1929	Draft reply to Bishop of Southampton
25 Apr. 1929	Reply from Bishop of Southampton
26 Apr. 1929	Letter from Bishop of Southampton
26 Apr. 1929	Draft of letter to Maynard Smith
27 Apr. 1929	Draft letter to Bishop of Southampton
4 May 1929	Letter from the Bishop of Southampton
6 May 1929	Draft letter from the Bishop of Southampton
17 May 1929	Note from Bishop of Southampton
11 June 1929	Draft of letter to Cochrane
24 June 1929	Letter from Douglas Jerrold, Eyre & Spottiswoode regarding *The Case for Voluntary Clergy*
2 July 1929	Copy of letter to Douglas Jerrold
26 Aug. 1929	Letter from R.M., Eyre & Spottiswoode

1 Nov. 1929	Draft of letter to Bishop of Nyasaland.
21 Mar. 1930	Letter from Ruth Rouse, Wimbledon
24 March 1930	Letter from Ruth Rouse, C.A. Missionary Council, enclosing alterations to Memorandum on *Voluntary Clergy*
24 Mar. 1930	Draft of letter to Ruth Rouse
11 Apr. 1930	Letter from Douglas Jerrold, Eyre & Spottiswoode
12 Apr. 1930	Draft of reply from Douglas Jerrold
14 Apr. 1930	Letter from Douglas Jerrold
11 June 1930	Letter from Bishop of Assam
25 Aug. 1930	Letter from Bishop Sanford
26 Aug. 1930	Draft of reply to Bishop Sanford
28 Aug. 1930	Letter from the Bishop of Grahamstown
29 Aug. 1930	Draft of reply to Bishop of Grahamstown
2 Sept. 1930	Letter from Bishop of Grahamstown
3 Sept. 1930	Draft of reply to Bishop of Grahamstown
8 Sept. 1930	Letter from Bishop of Grahamstown
10 Sept. 1930	Letter from Bishop of Buckingham
12 Sept. 1930	Letter from the Bishop of Manchester
13 Sept. 1930	Draft reply to Bishop of Manchester
15 Sept. 1930	Draft letter to the editor, *The Times*
17 Sept. 1930	Draft of letter to Bishop of Grahamstown
22 Sept. 1930	Letter from the Bishop of Manchester
25 Sept. 1930	Draft of reply to Bishop of Manchester
18 Feb. 1931	Letter from the Bishop of Cape Town
10 Mar. 1931	Draft reply to Bishop of Cape Town

File M: Reviews of Voluntary Clergy (1922-23)
(These letters are itemized by number)

100. Roland Allen (handwritten)
101. The Bishop of Pretoria
102. L. Ingham Baker
103. Canon J.M. Wilson
104. The Bishop of Southampton
105. The Bishop of Gibraltar
106. The Bishop of Gibraltar
107. Translation of a letter from V.d. Goltz in *Theologische Literaturzeitung*
108. P.O. Smith
109. Eugene Stock
110. Bishop Henry Whitehead (Madras)
111. Typed review from the *Yorkshire Post*, 25 July 1923
112. C. Hopton
113. Eugene Stock
114. The Rev. H.O.S. Whittingstall

Secondary Sources

Act of Uniformity, The (1662), 'The Case for Uniformity', Church of England

Allchin, A.M., *The Spirit and the Word* (Faith Publications, 1963)

Aikman, D., *The Beijing Factor: How Christianity is Transforming China and Changing the Global Balance of Power* (Oxford/Grand Rapids, 2003)

Allen, Hubert J.B., *Roland Allen: Pioneer, Priest, and Prophet* (Cincinnati: Forward Movement Publications and Grand Rapids: Eerdmans, 1995)

Allen, Hubert J.B., 'The Parables of Christ are Timeless: An example of Roland Allen's originality introduced by his grandson', in *Transformation: An International Journal of Holistic Mission Studies*, vol.vol.29, no.3 (July 2012; London: SAGE Publications)

Allen, Hubert J.B., 'Would Roland Allen Still Have Anything to Say to Us Today?', *Transformation*, 29(3) (July 2012) 179-85

Allen, J.W.T., *Tendi: Six Examples of a Swahili Classical Verse Form with Translations & Notes*, (Nairobi: Heinemann, 1971. Repr. Bungay, Suffolk: Richard Clay; The Chaucer Press, 1971), Rhodes House, University of Oxford, Special Collections & Western MSS, Bodleian Library of Commonwealth and African Studies, Rhodes House, Oxford University Library Service

Allen, Priscilla, 'Roland Allen – a Prophet for this Age', *The Living Church*, 192/16 (20 April 1986)

Antonio, Edward P. (ed.) *Inculturation and Postcolonial Discourse in African Theology* (New York: Peter Lang Publishing, 2006)

Bate, H.N., 'Frank Edward Brightman 1856-1932', Proceedings of the British Academy, vol. 19 (London: Humphrey Milford, Oxford University Press, 1933)

Beckwith, Roger, *Elders in Every City: The Origin and Role of the Ordained Ministry* (Carlisle: Paternoster Press, 2003)

Bediako, Kwame, *Theology & Identity: The Impact of Culture upon Christian Thought in the Second Century and in Modern Africa*, Regnum Studies in Mission (Oxford: Regnum Books, 1992)

Blyden, Edward Wilmot, 'The Call of Providence to the Descendants of Africa in America' (New York, 1862)

Boer, Harry R., *Pentecost and Missions* (Grand Rapids: Eerdmans and London: The Lutterworth Press, 1961)

Boer, Harry R., 'Roland Allen – Voice in the Wilderness', *World Dominion Press*, vol.xxxii, no.4 (July/August 1954) Box 8: 1, Rhodes House, Oxford. Deposited papers: Roland Allen

Book of Common Prayer, The, 1662, Cambridge: Cambridge University Press, 2002

Bosch, David J., *Transforming Mission: Paradigm Shifts in Theology of Mission* (Maryknoll: Orbis Books, 2002)

Branner, John K., *Roland Allen, Donald McGavran and Church Growth*, Master of Arts in Missiology Thesis for Fuller Theological Seminary, 1975

Bray, Gerald L., *Sacraments & Ministry in Ecumenical Perspective*, Latimer Studies 18 (1984)

Brown, Peter, *The Rise of Western Christendom*, second edn (Oxford: Blackwell Publishing, 2003)

Cable, Mildred and Francesca French, *Through Jade Gate and Central Asia: An Account of Journeys in Kansu, Turkestan and the Gobi Desert* (London: Constable & Co. Ltd., 1927).

Carson, D.A., *Collected Writings on Scripture* (Nottingham: Apollos [IVP], 2010)

Chamberlain, M.E., *The Scramble for Africa* (London and New York: Longman, 1999). An account of David Livingstone's missionary exploration in Africa is concisely recorded in Part Four: Documents, 'The Victorian Image of Africa', Document 1: David Livingstone: Humanitarian

Cheng, Andrew Chih-yi, *Hsuntzu's Theory of Human Nature and its Influence on Chinese Thought* (Peking: Yenching University, 1928)

Chicago-Lambeth Quadrilateral, The, Article III, Part IV, The Reformed Episcopal Church (2002).

Church, R.W., *The Oxford Movement: Twelve Years, 1833-1845* (ed.) Geoffrey Best (Chicago: University of Chicago Press, 1970)

Clark, Charles Allen, *The Korean Church and the Nevius Method* (Fleming H. Revell, 1930)

Clark, Sidney J.W., *The First Stage in the Christian Occupation of Rural China* (London: World Dominion Press, 1923)

Cochrane, Thomas, *Roland Allen* (London: World Dominion, 1948)

Cook, Matthew, Rob Haskell, Ruth Julian and Natee Tanchanpongs, *Local Theology for the Global Church: Principles for An Evangelical Approach to Contextualization*, Globalization of Mission Series (Pasadena: William Carey Library, 2010)

Cross, F.L. and Livingstone, E.A., (eds.) *Dictionary of the Christian Church*, Peabody: Hendrickson Publishers and Oxford: Oxford University Press, 1997)

Dann, Robert Bernard, *Father of Faith Missions: The Life and Times of Anthony Norris Groves* (Milton Keynes: Authentic Media, 2004)

Dann, Robert Bernard, *The Primitivist Missiology of Anthony Norris Groves: a radical influence on nineteenth-century Protestant mission* (Chester: Tamarisk Books/Oxford: Trafford Publishing, 2007)

Davis, Gerald Charles, Eric Chong and H. Boone Porter, *Setting Free the Ministry of the People of God* (Cincinnati: Forward Movement, 1984)

de Groot, J.J.M., *The Religious System of China: Its Ancient Forms, Evolution, History and Present Aspect, Manners, Customs and Social Institutions Connected Therewith*, six volumes (Taipei: Ch'eng Wen Publishing, 1892. Repr. 1976)

Donovan, Vincent J., *Christianity Rediscovered* (London: Canterbury Press, 2009)

Ekstrom, Ragnar, *The Theology of Charles Gore* (Lund, 1994)

Elliot, Elisabeth (ed.) *The Journals of Jim Elliot* (Grand Rapids: Fleming H. Revell, 1978. Repr. 2008)

Elliott-Binns, L.E., *Religion in the Victorian Era* (Cambridge: James Clarke & Co., 1936)

Etherington, Norman (ed.) *Missions and Empire*, The Oxford History of the British Empire (Oxford: Oxford University Press, 2005)

Evans, G.R. and J.R. Wright, *The Anglican Tradition: A Handbook of Sources* (London: SPCK, 1991; Gregory the Great, Bishop of Rome, 590-604, *Letter to Abbot Mellitus*, Doctrinal Documents, 1102)

Ferguson, Niall, *Empire: The Rise and Demise of the British World Order and the Lessons for Global Power* (New York: Basic Books, 2004)

Ferguson, Niall, *Civilization: The Six Killer Apps of Western Power* (London: Penguin Books, 2011)

Finch, Sarah (ed.) *The Way, the Truth and the Life: Theological Resources for a Pilgrimage to a Global Anglican Future*, Theological Resource Team of GAFCON (Vancouver: Regent College Publishing and London: The Latimer Trust, 2008)

French, Francesca, *Thomas Cochrane: Pioneer & Missionary Statesman* (London: Hodder & Stoughton, 1956)

Giles, Herbert A., *Religions of Ancient China* (London: Archibald Constable, 1905)

Goheen, Michael W., *"As the Father Has Sent Me, I Am Sending You": J.E. Lesslie Newbigin's Missionary Ecclesiology* (Utrecht: Uitgeverij Boekencentrum, 2000)

Gonzalez, Justo L., *The Story of Christianity* (Peabody: Prince Press, 2004)

Gore, Charles, *Dissertations: On Subjects Connected with the Incarnation* (London: John Murray, 1895)

Gore, Charles, *Lux Mundi: A Series of Studies in the Religion of the Incarnation* (London: John Murray, 1890)

Gore, Charles, *Orders and Unity* (London: John Murray, 1909)

Gore, Charles, *The Ministry of the Christian Church* (London: Rivingtons, 1889. Repr. 1919) Preface v. by C.H. Turner

Guelzo, Allen C., *For the Union of Evangelical Christendom: The Irony of the Reformed Episcopalians* (University Park: The Pennsylvania State University Press, 1994)

Haddan, Arthur W., *Apostolical Succession in the Church of England* (London, Oxford and Cambridge: Rivingtons, 1879)

Harnack, Adolf von, *The Mission and Expansion of Christianity in the First Three Centuries* (Gloucester: Peter Smith, [1902, German translation], 1972)

Harper, Susan Billington, *In the Shadow of the Mahatma: Bishop V.S. Azariah and the Travails of Christianity in British India*, Studies in the History of Christian Missions (Grand Rapids: Eerdmans, 2000)

Harper, Susan, 'The Dornakal Church on the Cultural Frontier', (Chapter 9) in *Christians, Cultural Interactions, and India's Religious Traditions*, J.M. Brown and R.E. Frykenberg (eds) (Grand Rapids: Eerdmans, 2002) 183-211

Hastings, Adrian, *A History of African Christianity, 1950-1975* (Cambridge: Cambridge University Press, 1979)

Hick, John, *God Has Many Names: Britain's New Religious Pluralism* (London/Basingstoke: The MacMillan Press, 1980)

Hocking, William Ernest, *Re-Thinking Missions: A Laymen's Inquiry After One Hundred Years* (New York and London: Harper & Brothers Publishers, 1932)

Hodge, Mark, *Non-Stipendiary Ministry in the Church of England* (London: The

Central Board of Finance of the Church of England, 1983. Repr. London: The General Synod of the Church of England by CIO Publishing, 1984)

Hoekendijk, Johann C., *Kirche und Volk in der Deutschen Missionswissenschaft* (Munich: Chr. Kaiser Verlag, 1967)

Hoekendijk, Johannes Christiaan, *The Church Inside Out* (Philadelphia: Westminster, 1966).

Howse, Ernest Marshall, *Saints in Politics: The 'Clapham Sect' and the Growth of Freedom* (London: George Allen & Unwin, 1973)

Hutton, William Holden, *S. John Baptist College*, Oxford University College Histories (London: F.E. Robinson, 1898)

Jenkins, Philip, *The Next Christendom: The Coming of Global Christianity* (New York: Oxford University Press, 2002)

Kelly, Herbert, *An Idea in the Working* (London-Oxford, 1908)

Kindopp, Jason and Carol Lee Hamrin (eds) *God and Caesar in China: Policy Implications of Church-State Tensions* (Washington, DC: 2004)

Kraemer, Hendrik, *A Theology of the Laity* (London: The Lutterworth Press, 1958)

Kraemer, Hendrik, *The Christian Message in a Non-Christian World* (London: The Edinburgh House Press, 1969)

Legge, James, *The Four Books* (Hong Kong: Wei Tung Book Co., 1885)

Legge, James, *The Sacred Books of China: The Texts of Confucianism*, (first edition, 1879. Repr. Delhi: Shri Jainendra Press, 1966)

Leithart, Peter J., *Between Babel and Beast: America and Empires in Biblical Perspective*, Theopolitical Visions, 14 (Eugene: Cascade Books, 2012)

Lockhart, J.G., *Cosmo Gordon Lang* (London: Hodder and Stoughton, 1949)

Mason, Alistair, *History of the Society of the Sacred Mission* (Bury St Edmunds: St Edmundsbury Press Limited, 1994)

Maurice, Frederick Denison, *The Kingdom of Christ: Or Hints to a Quaker Respecting the Principles, Constitution, & Ordinances of the Catholic Church*, Volumes 1 and 2 (London: 1838. Repr. London: SCM, 1958)

Metz, Johann-Baptist, *Theology of the World* (New York: Herder & Herder, 1969)

Metzner, Hans Wolfgang, *Roland Allen: Sein Leben und Werk: Kritischer Beitrag zum Verstandnis von Mission und Kirche* (Gutersloh, Gerd Mohn, Gutersloher Verlagshaus, 1970)

Moberly, Robert Campbell, *Ministerial Priesthood* (London: J. Murray, 1897)

Montgomery, H. H., the Rt. Rev., *Charles Perry Scott: First Bishop in North China* (Westminster: The Society for the Propagation of the Gospel in Foreign Parts, 1928)

Moorman, J.R.H., *A History of the Church in England* (London, 1986)

Muller, James Arthur, *Apostle of China: Samuel Isaac Joseph Schereschewsky 1831-1906* (New York: Morehouse Publishing Co., 1937)

Murray, Iain, *The Puritan Hope: Revival and the Interpretation of Prophecy* (Edinburgh: The Banner of Truth Trust, 1971)

Murray, Stuart, *Church After Christendom* (Milton Keynes: Paternoster Press, 2008)

Murray, Stuart, *Planting Churches: In the 21st century* (Waterloo: Herald Press, 2010)

Nazir-Ali, Michael, *From Everywhere to Everywhere: A World View of Christian Mission* (London: Collins Flame, 1991)

Nazir-Ali, Michael, *Frontiers in Muslim-Christian Encounter* (Oxford: Regnum Books, 1987)

Nee, Watchman, *Concerning Our Missions* (1939. Repr. *The Normal Christian Church Life* (Anaheim: Living Stream Ministry, 1980)

Neill, Stephen, *A History of Christian Missions* (London: Penguin Books, 1964. Reprint, Harmondsworth: Penguin Books, 1986)

Neill, Stephen, *Colonialism and Christian Missions* (London: The Lutterworth Press, 1966)

Neill, Stephen, *The Unfinished Task* (London: The Lutterworth Press, 1957)

Nevius, John L., *The Planting and Development of Missionary Churches* (Shanghai: Presbyterian Press, 1886. Repr. Hancock: Monadnock Press, 2003)

Newbigin, Lesslie, 'Bringing Our Missionary Methods under the Word of God', *Occasional Bulletin from the Missionary Research Library*, 13 (1962) 1-9

Newbigin, Lesslie, 'Religious Pluralism and the Uniqueness of Jesus Christ', *International Bulletin of Missionary Research*, repr. in *The Best in Theology*, vol. vol.4, J.I. Packer (gen. ed.) (Carol Stream: Christianity Today, 1990)

Newbigin, Lesslie, *The Gospel in a Pluralist Society* (London: SPCK, 1989)

Newman, John Henry, 'Tract One: Thoughts on the Ministerial Commission' in *Tracts for the Times* (London: J.G. & F. Rivington, 1838)

Nias, John, *Flame From an Oxford Cloister: The Life and Writings of Philip Napier Waggett S.S.J.E. Scientist, Religious, Theologian, Missionary Philosopher, Diplomat, Author, Orator, Poet* (London: The Faith Press, 1961)

O'Connor, Daniel and others, *Three Centuries of Mission: The United Society for the Propagation of the Gospel 1701-2000* (London: Continuum, 2000)

Okoh, Nicholas, Vinay Samuel and Chris Sugden, *Being Faithful: The Shape of Historic Anglicanism Today: A Commentary on the Jerusalem Declaration* (London: The Latimer Trust, 2009)

Oldham, J.H., *The World and the Gospel* (London: United Council for Missionary Education [UCME], 1917 [1916])

O'Loughlin, Thomas, *The Didachē: A Window on the Earliest Christians* (London: SPCK and Grand Rapids: Baker Academic, 2010)

Partridge, Christopher and Helen Reid (eds) *Finding and Losing Faith: Studies in Conversion* (Milton Keynes, UK: Paternoster Press, 2006)

Paton, David M., *Christian Missions and the Judgment of God* (London: SCM Press, first edn 1953, second edn 1996)

Paton, David M. (ed.) *The Ministry of the Spirit: Selected Writings of Roland Allen* (Grand Rapids: Eerdmans, 1960. Repr. London: World Dominion Press, 1965)

Paton, David, *New Forms of Ministry* (London: Edinburgh House Press, 1965)

Paton, David, *Reform of the Ministry: A Study of the Work of Roland Allen* (London: The Lutterworth Press, 1968)

Payne, J.D., *Roland Allen: Pioneer of Spontaneous Expansion* (self-published, 2012)

Porter, Andrew, *Religion versus Empire? British Protestant Missionaries and Overseas Expansion, 1700-1914* (Manchester/New York: Manchester University Press, 2004)

Rack, Henry D., *Reasonable Enthusiast: John Wesley and the Rise of Methodism* (London: Epworth Press, 1989)

Ramsay, William Mitchell, *St Paul the Traveller and the Roman Citizen* (London: Hodder and Stoughton, 1895/96. Repr. 1902)

Rutt, Steven R., 'An Analysis of Roland Allen's Missionary Ecclesiology', *Transformation*, 29(3) (Oxford: SAGE Publications, July 2012) 200-213

Rutt, Steven R., 'Roland Allen's Apostolic Principles: An Analysis of his "The Ministry of Expansion"', *Transformation*, 29(3) (Oxford: SAGE Publications, July 2012) 225-243

Sanneh, Lamin, *Disciples of All Nations: Pillars of World Christianity* (Oxford: Oxford University Press, 2008)

Schnabel, Eckhard J., *Paul the Missionary: Realities, Strategies and Methods* (Downers Grove: InterVarsity Press, 2008)

Seth-Smith, David, *The Zoo Man Talks about the Wild Animals of Our Country* (Worcester: Littlebury & Company, 1900. Repr. 1945)

Shenk, Wilbert R., *Henry Venn – Missionary Statesman* (Maryknoll: Orbis Books, 1983)

Smith, Adam, *Wealth of the Nations* (London: Dent [1776], 1910) 2 Vols

Stanley, Brian, *The Bible and the Flag: Protestant Missions and British Imperialism in the Nineteenth and Twentieth Centuries* (Leicester: Apollos [IVP], 1990)

Stanley, Brian, *The World Missionary Conference, Edinburgh 1910*, Studies in the History of Christian Missions (SHCM) (Grand Rapids/Cambridge: Eerdmans, 2009)

Stott, John R.W., *Christian Mission: In the Modern World* (Downers Grove: InterVarsity, 1975)

Tan, Jin Huat, *Planting an Indigenous Church: The Case of the Borneo Evangelical Mission* (Oxford: Regnum, 2011)

Talltorp, Ake, *Sacrament & Growth: A Study in the Sacramental Dimension of Expansion in the Life of the Local Church, as reflected in the Theology of Roland Allen* (Uppsala: Swedish Institute for Missionary Research, 1989)

Talltorp, Ake, 'Sacraments for Growth in Mission: Eucharistic Faith and Practice in the Theology of Roland Allen', *Transformation: An International Journal of Holistic Mission Studies*, 29(3) 214-224, (July 2012) note 10 (222)

Taylor, Dr and Mrs Howard, *Biography of James Hudson Taylor* (London: Overseas Missionary Fellowship, 1965)

Taylor, John V., *The Primal Vision: Christian Presence Amid African Religion* (London: SCM Press, 1963)

Temple Gairdner, W.H., *Brotherhood – Islam's and Christ's* (Edinburgh: Edinburgh House Press, 1923)

Temple Gairdner, W.H., *Edinburgh 1910: An Account and Interpretation of the World Missionary Conference* (Edinburgh and London: Oliphant, Anderson & Ferrier, 1910)

Temple Gairdner, W.H., *W.H.T.G. to His Friends* (London: Society for Promoting Christian Knowledge, 1930).

Thompson, H.P., *Into All Lands: The History of the Society for the Propagation of the Gospel in Foreign Parts 1701-1950* (London: SPCK, 1951)

Waggett, Philip Napier (SSJE) *Religion and Science*, Handbooks for the Clergy, A.W. Robinson, (Longmans, 1904)

Walls, Andrew F., *The Missionary Movement in Christian History: Studies in the Transmission of Faith* (Maryknoll: Orbis Books, 2009 [1996])

Ward, Kevin, and Brian Stanley (eds) *The Church Mission Society and World Christianity 1799-1999*, Studies in the History of Christian Missions (Grand Rapids: Eerdmans, 2000)

Warren, M.A.C., *Caesar the Beloved Enemy: Three Studies in the Relation of Church and State*, Reinecker Lectures at the Virginia Theological Seminary, Alexandria, Virginia, February 1955 (London: SCM Press, 1955)

Warren, Max A.C., *Problems and Promises in Africa Today* (Hodder, 1964)

Warren, Max, *The Christian Mission* (London: SCM Press, 1951)

Warren, Max A.C., *The Missionary Movement from Britain in Modern History* (London: SCM, 1965)

Warren, Max A.C., *The Triumph of God* (Longmans, 1948)

Warren, Max A.C., *The Truth of Vision* (Canterbury Press, 1948)

Warren, Max (ed.) *To Apply the Gospel: Selections from the Writings of Henry Venn* (Grand Rapids: Eerdmans, 1971)

Williams, W.R., *Ohio Friends in the Land of Sinim* (Mount Gilead: 1925)

Woodhead, Linda, *An Introduction to Christianity* (Cambridge: Cambridge University Press, 2011)

Woodhead, Linda, Hiroko Kawanami and Christopher Partridge (eds) *Religions in the Modern World: Traditions and Transformations* (London and New York: Routledge, second edn, 2009)

Yates, Timothy, *Christian Mission in the Twentieth Century* (Cambridge: Cambridge University Press, 1996)

Yang, H., and Daniel H.N. Yeung (eds) *Sino-Christian Studies in China* (Newcastle, 2006)

Young, Robert, *Postcolonialism: An Historical Introduction* (Oxford and Malden: Blackwell Publishers, 2001)

Young, Robert, *Postcolonialism: A Very Short Introduction* (Oxford: Oxford University Press, 2003)

Periodicals / Journals

Aagaard, Johannes, 'The Soft Age Has Gone', *Missiology*, 10, 263-77 in Bosch, *Believing in the Future* (1982) 27-28

Allen, Roland, 'Indigenous Churches: The Way of St Paul', *Church Missionary Review* (paper read by Roland Allen at the *Church Missionary Society Conference of Missionaries*, June 1927) 147-159, High Leigh, Box 2, Number 23, Rhodes House, Oxford

——, 'The Priesthood of the Church', *Church Quarterly Review*, art.IV (January 1933) 234-44, Rhodes House, Oxford

Cerney, Pavel 'The Relationship between Theology and Missiology: The Missiological Hermeneutics', *European Journal of Theology*, XIX (2010; Nottingham: Paternoster Periodicals, 104-109).

Multiple contributors, *East and the West, The* (April 1909)

Multiple contributors, *English Historical Review, The*, vol.7, London (October 1892) Pusey House Library, Oxford, S:59.00.c2, Miscellania: Hagiology

Multiple contributors, *Interpreter, The*, 'The Case for Voluntary Clergy: an Anglican Problem' (July 1922): 314ff

Kraft, Charles H., 'Dynamic Equivalence Churches: An Ethnotheological Approach to Indigeneity', *Missiology*, vol. 1, no. 1 (January 1973) 39-57

Latourette, Kenneth Scott, Review of *A History of Christian Missions in China* by Roland Allen, *Church Quarterly Review* (January 1930) 317

Multiple contributors, *North China Mission Quarterly, The*, 'First Impressions' (October 1896) 53-56.

Multiple contributors, *Quarterly Paper of the Mission of the Church of England in North China*, vol.III, pp.17, 27, 48

Shenk, Wilbert R., 'Missionary Encounter with Culture', *International Bulletin of Missionary Research*, 15, 104-9

Smith, Bardwell L., 'Liberal Catholicism: An Anglican Perspective', *Anglican Theological Review*, (3/1972) vol.54, 175-193

Stanley, Brian, 'From the "poor heathen" to "the glory and honour of all nations": Vocabularies of Race and Custom in Protestant Missions, 1844-1928', *International Bulletin of Missionary Research*, vol.34, no.1, January 2010 (New Haven, Connecticut: Overseas Ministries Study Center, 2010) 3-10

Werbner, Richard, 'The Charismatic Dividual and the Sacred Self', *Journal of Religion in Africa*, vol. 41.2 (2011) 180-205 (Leiden: Brill)

Internet and DVD Sources

http://www.youtube.com/watch?v=7di4zMGIZY8 Professor Richard J Evans FBA, Gresham Professor of Rhetoric, 'Formal and Informal Empire in the nineteenth Century', Gresham College lecture (Sponsored by The City of London Corporation and the Mercers' Company) [Accessed: 2/11/2017, 3:23 PM]

Recorded Minutes

Members of the St John's College Debating Society, UGS V.1, Lent Term 1890 – Lent Term (13 March) 1892, St John's College archives; interview with Michael Riordan, archivist (St John's College, Oxford)

St John's College Essay Society, UGS VI.1, 20 January 1889 – Lent Term (13 March) 1892, St John's College archives; interview with Michael Riordan, archivist (St John's College, Oxford)

PHD Dissertations

Cheruvil, Joseph, *Roland Allen's Missionary Insights: Their Relavance to a North Indian Context*, 296 pages, Belgium: Katholieke Universiteit Leuven, 1993, Publication Number AAT C348052

Payne, Jervis David, *An Evaluation of the Systems Approach to North American Church Multiplication Movements of Robert E. Logan in Light of the Missiology of Roland Allen*, 334 pages, Kentucky: The Southern Baptist Theological Seminary, 2001, Publication Number: AAT 3042375

Thompson, Michael Don, *The Holy Spirit and Human Instrumentality in the Training of New Converts: An Evaluation of the Missiological Thought of Roland Allen*, California: Golden Gate Baptist Theological Seminary, 1989, Publication Number: AAT 8923304

Index of Names

Index of Scripture

Old Testament

New Testament